Teaching Children Self-Control

Preventing Emotional and Learning Problems in the Elementary School

Teaching Children Self-Control

Preventing Emotional and Learning Problems in the Elementary School

Stanley A. Fagen
Supervisor of Professional Development
Montgomery County Public Schools

Nicholas J. Long
Professor of Special Education
The American University

Donald J. Stevens

Charles E. Merrill Publishing Co.
A Bell & Howell Co.
Columbus, Ohio

Published by
Charles E. Merrill Publishing Co.
A Bell & Howell Co.
Columbus, Ohio 43216

International Standard Book Number: 0–675–08783–X

Library of Congress Catalog Card Number: 74–80933

2 3 4 5 6 7 8 9 10—78 77 76

Printed in the United States of America

Preface

This book is about freedom and responsibility. We believe that the increasing incidence of disruptive behavior in the classroom reflects an educational neglect of skills needed for prevention of serious learning and emotional problems. Since our own experience in special educational and consultative programs has required us to deal with the problem of disruptive behavior more frequently than any other aspect of teacher-learner transaction, we have been spurred by the serious drain on teacher resources and pupil potential which accompanies disruptions in the classroom into a continuing search for more effective intervention strategies.

From an earlier emphasis on intervention at the level of reaction, crisis, and psychotherapy, we have moved to the position that disruptive behavior signifies a limitation in skills—on the part of either the child or the educational system. Our thinking has changed as a result of careful analysis of children's disruptive behavior. Through a process of classroom observation, literature review, and shared reflection, we have identified a core set of eight skills that seem to determine an individual's capacity to maintain free control over his own behavior.

As a society, we have assumed that our commitment to the principle of individual freedom was enough to foster responsible freedom of action. Most of us have been filled with idealized thoughts about American democracy, yet we are woefully lacking in satisfying experiences of the democratic process. Schools have always affirmed an obligation to prepare young people for constructive citizenship. Unfortunately, little has been done to promote the requisite skills for responsible participation in the democratic process. We are convinced that the capacity for self-control is a necessary precondition for the responsible exercise of freedom.

Teaching Children Self-Control: Preventing Emotional and Learning Problems in the Elementary School enters this educational void and offers a structured, integrated curriculum for the development of self-control (*i.e., one's capacity to direct and regulate personal action or behavior flexibly and realistically in a given situation*).

The book is organized into three main parts. Part One presents the theoretical and conceptual structure upon which the self-control curriculum is based. Part Two describes the eight curriculum areas and their subsidiary units and tasks. Part Three describes important issues pertaining to the self-control curriculum and provides closing remarks.

This book is intended primarily for future teachers as well as for those established teachers who are concerned about preventing the development of emotional and learning problems in schools. We expect that the curriculum portion alone will be of major interest to future teachers and to in-service elementary school and special education teachers.

The more theoretical sections should provoke discussion among counselors, pupil personnel workers, and curriculum specialists and be of interest to mental health professionals, particularly clinical and school psychologists. We hope that educational researchers will view the self-control curriculum as an invitation to develop creative methods for assessing and evaluating psychoeducational curricula.

The development of the self-control curriculum would not have been possible without the dedication and aid of many teachers and administrators in the District of Columbia Public School System and at Hillcrest Children's Mental Health Center, Washington, D.C. In particular, we wish to express our appreciation to Lozelle DeLuz, principal of Meyer Elementary School; Fred Couzzens, principal of Harrison Elementary School; John Harps, principal of Lechie

Elementary School; and Gilbert Diggs, assistant superintendent of the Model Schools Division in the District of Columbia.

James Kounin, executive director of the Eugene and Agnes Meyer Foundation has provided continuing support and encouragement throughout the self-control project. Special thanks are due to Burwell Vaden for maintaining his easy competence and warm disposition through many long hours and unexpected meetings. Michael Deem has contributed a great deal to this book with his sensitive and rich observations. We would also like to acknowledge Steve Checkon, Geraldine Meltz, Phyllis McDonald, Judy Tarr, and Jeff Robertshaw of the Mark Twain School in Montgomery County, Maryland, for their helpful critiques of the final draft. We are grateful to Lisa Ritzenberg for the caring manner in which she prepared the complete manuscript.

To our wives, Val and Jody, we offer our heartfelt thanks. Without their patience and understanding during times of stress, this book could never have been written.

Finally, we honor and cherish the memory of our beloved friend and partner, Don Stevens, whose untimely passing inspires us to carry on with even greater commitment.

S.A.F.
N.J.L.

Silver Spring, Maryland
July, 1974

Contents

PART ONE

Foundations for the Self-Control Curriculum

1

In studying the growths of civilizations we found that they could be analyzed into successions of performances of the drama of challenge—and—response . . .

Arnold Toynbee, *A Study of History*, 1946

Countering Disruptive Behavior in the School

THE PROBLEM OF DISRUPTIVE BEHAVIOR

Most teachers have experienced the frustration of having a promising class period sabotaged by an abrupt insult, a shove, or appearance of any one of a hundred other disturbances that children employ to burst teacher's bubbles about classroom success. It may not even be the occurrence of an outward interference that disrupts the class; it can be a child's quiet rocking back and forth or staring off into space. When a student's behavior violates the rights of others or obstructs the fulfillment of his own positive goals, it may be considered disruptive. More specifically, *disruptive behavior in the school can be defined as behavior which is incompatible with volitional, socially acceptable efforts to master the required or assigned task.*

We are painfully aware of the great waste of human potential that accompanies disruptive behavior in school (Bower, 1966; Glidewell and Swallow, 1968; Joint Commission on Mental Health of Children, 1970). The results are evidenced by disillusionment and antagonism toward education, negative self-concepts, and general underdevelopment of resources for coping with life's problems. Further evidence is the extent of public concern about high delinquency and drop-out rates, excessive misbehavior and disorder, gross limitations in basic learning skills, and the struggle of the educational system to insure constructive socialization (Clark, 1965; Elliot, 1966; Graubard, 1969; Miller, 1970; Morse, 1967).

Disruptive school behavior is a vital point for concentration of study for several significant reasons: (1) it raises a far-reaching question as to the adequacy of prior teaching leading toward the development of self-control (whether in family, school, or community efforts); (2) it interferes with on-going group attention and usually detracts from the learning atmosphere; (3) it often reveals an insufficiency of self-resources for coping with school expectations; (4) it may indicate the mobilization of negative and maladaptive reactions to stress; (5) it can signal resistance and dissatisfaction with the class content or process; and (6) it can provide clues to specific weaknesses in self-control.

With increasing recognition by educators that sizeable numbers of school children evidence faulty emotional and behavioral controls, major efforts to provide special programs and resources have developed (Bateman, 1966; Cruickshank, 1967; Morse, Finger, and Gilmore, 1968). These efforts have been spurred by the realization that referral to an outside-school facility has only limited application and impact. Some of these special educational programs follow from the assumption that constitutional or neurological deficits underlie most classroom disruption, while other programs hinge on improving adverse socio-cultural conditions. With regard to the former approach, we agree that there is little question that much behavior characterized as impulse-ridden, hyperactive, and distractive is associated with dysfunctions in visual perception, perceptual-movement integration, and fine motor coordination. Furthermore, significant gains have been reported from visual-motor training programs (Barsch, 1967; Frostig and Horne, 1964; Kephart, 1971; Rappaport, 1968).

There is also evidence that many children, particularly those from poor, lower-class homes, have learned to adapt to harsh or unstable circumstances by means of impulsive, unstable, and often explosive actions (Chilman, 1966; Deutsch, 1967; Herzog, 1967; McKinley, 1964). These children place little value on self-control, probably because they derive scarce material or social satisfaction from delaying immediate actions. Unfortunately for these youngsters, the majority element of society, which largely controls pathways to economic, social, political, and personal success, demands higher levels of self-control and forethought—levels which cannot be satisfied readily by those who find the action-impulse mode appropriate for their every-day subcultural existence. In contrast to the ever-increasing number of effective visual-motor training programs, there are few programs which attempt directly to teach self-control in a school setting.

Fantini and Weinstein (1968) have suggested that urban school children are contending with greater levels of frustration and impulsivity than they ever have because of their increased awareness of psychosocial inequities. In our judgment the school must begin to teach the learner constructive ways of behaving or face the possibility of having unwittingly contributed to dangerous alternatives. "The learners' frustration, anger, hostility at the realization that they have been victims of a negative environment trigger emotional energies which are not being dealt with constructively either outside or inside the urban school" (p. 18).

In particular, we are impressed and concerned by research indicating that widespread underachievement occurs among minority-group children, in spite of their high desire and aspiration for educational accomplishment (Bell, 1965; Coleman, 1966). For example, Katz (1967) has presented convincing evidence that the socialization of academic motivation is extremely detrimental for most black youngsters. He maintains that effective scholastic motivation depends on self-control, in other words, ". . . an outcome of a socialization process involving the internalization of standards of excellence and of affect-mediating evaluative responses to one's own performance" (p. 140). Based on several studies with urban elementary school children, Katz found that black children consistently evaluated their own efforts negatively, even when they were working under conditions of privacy and following successful completion of a task. "What they seem to have internalized was a most effective mechanism for self-discouragement. The child, in a sense, had been socialized to impose failure upon himself" (p. 164).

This "socialization to impose failure" appears to have two primary sources: lack of adult modeling or teaching of the behavioral skills necessary to satisfy academic expectations (Deutsch, 1967; Radin, 1968; Riessman, 1962); and critical and blaming attitudes reflected by teachers and parents (Gottlieb, 1966; Guskin and Guskin, 1970; Howard, 1968). Rather than experiencing a "deprivation of culture," children of the ghetto suffer from "a deprivation of approval." Many youngsters feel helpless and frustrated when subjected to elevated expectations of parents and teachers aspiring to help them for they lack the specific instruction needed to fulfill school tasks. It is not surprising, given these conditions, that truancy and disruptiveness are serious problems.

Most educators are keenly aware that school curricula *must* have relevance and meaning to and in terms of real-life experience. Otherwise, the learner is left on his own to handle as best he can complex social realities. While it has been difficult to develop and implement more humanistic curricula, there is now a broad base of support for school programs which extend learning beyond cognitive skills and knowledge and into facets of self-understanding and relations with others (Biber, 1967; Brown, 1970; Glasser, 1969; Jones, 1968; Lyon, 1971; Rogers, 1969; Rosenberg, 1972). Enduring value from school learning experiences would seem to be enhanced by integrating objectives of subject knowledge, cultivating personal talent, and preparing for positive social action. This "three-tiered" model for school responsibility encourages a blend of cognitive and affective involvement which is indispensable for complete learning (Joyce, 1966).

An imaginative educational program which concentrates on weaknesses in self-control and coping with every-day frustrations and which can be incorporated realistically within public school systems is needed. Although such a program must integrate emotional, intellectual, and interpersonal learning components to be effective, if these multi-linkages can be established within the framework of a systemized, conceptually sound curriculum, then real potential for a powerful impact on both the learner and his teaching environment exists.

The challenge is clear. A child must come to believe himself capable of controlling his own behavior—even in the face of anticipated frustration. He must discover that through self-directed efforts he can effectively cope with difficulty rather than be victimized by exposure to excessive demands. In essence, the process of learning needs to become a humanizing sequence of challenges and responses through which children find satisfaction in the progressive development of life skills.

RATIONALE AND PURPOSES OF THE SELF-CONTROL CURRICULUM

Any child or group of children with lags or weaknesses in self-control can be helped substantially by a curriculum tailored to develop skills and confidence in this area. Our position is that a specialized curriculum, presented within a context of positive relationship and sensitive teaching, offers the most direct and enduring means of overcoming disturbances associated with problems in self-control.

Children who are behaviorally disruptive are likely to experience many other social and emotional difficulties as well. This is because the child's inappropriate behavior triggers negative responses from others, which, in turn, contribute to the child's feelings of inadequacy, badness, deficiency, and social rejection (Branden, 1969; Coopersmith, 1967; Lorber, 1966). While different roots for impulsive behavior do exist, our principal belief is that major problems for impulsive children derive from poor interpersonal teaching rather than from inherent causes. Thus, we maintain that impulsive behavior creates profound difficulties for social and emotional adjustment and that these difficulties can be reduced by strengthening capacities for self-control. *The emphasis here is on building adaptive controls, interrupting self-defeating behavior cycles, and preventing serious behavior and learning problems.*

While other modes of intervention, such as counseling, parent casework, or individual tutoring, are not discounted, a specialized teaching curriculum has the best potential for getting to the core deficits. In other words, a child who struggles unsuccessfully to reduce anxiety and fear connected with felt weaknesses may be helped best by purposeful training to overcome those weaknesses.

Much present educational and mental health effort has been directed toward managing, understanding, or treating the maladaptive behaviors of children with identifiable limitations. It is time to pay at least equal attention to remediating or correcting the basic weaknesses which may very well be the driving force behind these maladaptive behaviors. Only through development, testing out, and evaluation of new programs can we hope to acquire more effective methods of intervention.

Given the various ramifications of disruptive behavior, it is logical that a curriculum aimed at improving self-control would have several purposes. These purposes may be enumerated as follows:

1. To reduce disruptiveness, improve school adjustment, and prevent behavior and learning disorders.
2. To strengthen the emotional and cognitive capacities which children need in order to cope with school requirements.
3. To build control skills which allow for an effective and socially acceptable choice of action.

4. To enhance value for the teacher-learner and educational process.
5. To promote a more desirable educational balance between cognitive and affective development than that which currently exists.

The present approach to self-control is not predicated, however, on the belief that inhibition of action is necessary. There is no denying that quickness to react and direct release of feeling in action can be extremely valuable—for personal fulfillment as well as for effecting change in others. Our intention is not to sap this potential source of strength from those who have it but, rather, to enhance their satisfaction by introducing means for self-control. By adding the necessary resources for modulation and discrimination, the teacher can help a child's response to be guided by flexible choice as opposed to intense repression and control.

SUMMARY

We have defined disruptive behavior in the classroom as behavior which is incompatible with volitional, socially acceptable efforts to master the classroom task. The widespread occurrence of such behavior in schools represents a serious challenge for contemporary education, since the consequences of disruptive behavior for the individual and the group are far-reaching and usually indicative of dysfunction in the teaching-learning process. For the individual, disruptive behavior may reflect an insufficiency of personal resources for coping with school expectations and the mobilization of negative, maladaptive reactions to stress. For the group, disruptive behavior carries a violation of personal rights and the threat of unhealthy disorder.

Children may be predisposed to behavior disruption as a result of sensory-neurological or social learning influences. In either case, these youngsters appear motivated to succeed but lack the requisite skills for exercising self-control. While understanding and sound management of disruptive behavior is important, the most effective educational intervention is at the preventive and remedial levels. We maintain that there is a critical need for curriculum approaches to building competency for self-control. Several purposes of the self-control curriculum have been stated, including the prevention of behavior and learning disorders, promotion of the emotional and cognitive capacities needed to cope with school requirements, and development of control skillls which allow for an effective and responsible choice of action.

REFERENCES

Barsch, R. *Achieving Perceptual-Motor Efficiency.* Seattle, Washington: Special Child Publications, 1967.

Bateman, B. "Learning Disorders." *Review of Educational Research* 26 (1966): 93–119.

Bell, R. R. "Lower-Class Negro Mothers' Aspirations for Their Children." *Social Forces* 43 (1965): 493–500.

Biber, B. "A Learning-Teaching Paradigm Integrating Intellectual and Affective Processes." In *Behavioral Science Frontiers in Education,* edited by E. Bower and W. G. Hollister, pp. 112–55. New York: Wiley, 1967.

Bower, E. "Personality and Individual Social Maladjustment." In *Social Deviancy among Youth, Sixty-fifth Yearbook of the National Society for Study of Education,* edited by W. Wattenberg, pp. 103–34. Chicago: University of Chicago Press, 1966.

Branden, N. *The Psychology of Self-Esteem.* Los Angeles: Nash, 1969.

Brown, G. I. *Human Teaching for Human Learning.* New York: McGraw-Hill, 1970.

Chilman, C. *Growing up Poor.* Washington, D.C.: U.S. Department of Health, Education & Welfare, Welfare Administration Publication Number 13, 1966.

Clark, K. *Dark Ghetto.* New York: Harper & Row, 1965.

Coleman, J. S., et al. *Equality of Educational Opportunity.* Washington, D.C.: U.S. Department of Health, Education & Welfare, 1966.

Coopersmith, S. *The Antecedents of Self-Esteem.* San Francisco: Freeman, 1967.

Cruickshank, W. "The Exceptional Child in the Elementary and Secondary Schools." In *Education of Exceptional Children and Youth,* 2d ed., edited by W. Cruickshank and G. Johnson, pp. 99–139. Englewood Cliffs, New Jersey: Prentice-Hall, 1967.

Deutsch, M. "The Disadvantaged Child and the Learning Process." In *The Disadvantaged Child,* edited by M. Deutsch, pp. 39–57. New York: Basic Books, 1967.

Elliot, D. "Delinquency, School Attendance, and Dropout." *Social Problems* 13 (1966): 307–14.

Fantini, M., and Weinstein, G. *Making Urban Schools Work: Social Realities and the Urban School.* New York: Holt, Rinehart & Winston, 1968.

Frostig, M., and Horne, D. *The Frostig Program for the Development of Visual Perception.* Chicago: Follett, 1964.

Glasser, W. *Schools without Failure.* New York: Harper & Row, 1969.

Glidewell, J., and Swallow, C. "The Prevalance of Maladjustment in Elementary Schools." Report prepared for the Joint Commission on the Mental Health of Children. Chicago: University of Chicago, 1968. Mimeographed.

Gottlieb, D. "Teaching and Students: The Views of Negro and White Teachers." In *The Disadvantaged Learner*, edited by S.W. Webster, pp. 437–46. San Francisco: Chandler, 1966.

Graubard, P. *Children against Schools: Education of Disturbed and Delinquent Children.* Chicago: Follett, 1969.

Guskin, A., and Guskin, S. *A Social Psychology of Education.* Reading, Massachusetts: Addison-Wesley, 1970.

Herzog, E. *About the Poor: Some Facts and Some Fictions.* Washington, D.C.: U.S. Department of Health, Education & Welfare, Children's Bureau Publication Number 451, 1967.

Howard, D. P. "The Needs and Problems of Socially Disadvantaged Children as Perceived by Students and Teachers." *Exceptional Children* 34 (1968): 327–35.

Joint Commission on Mental Health of Children. *Crisis in Child Mental Health: Challenge for the 1970s.* New York: Harper & Row, 1970.

Jones, R., *Fantasy and Feeling in Education.* New York: New York University Press, 1968.

Joyce, B. *Restructuring Elementary Education: A Multiple Learning Systems Approach.* New York: Teachers College, Columbia University, 1966.

Katz, I. "The Socialization of Academic Motivation in Minority-Group Children." *Nebraska Symposium on Motivation* 15 (1967): 133–91.

Kephart, N. *The Slow Learner in the Classroom,* 2d ed. Columbus, Ohio: Charles E. Merrill Publishing Co., 1971.

Lorber, N. "Inadequate Social Acceptance and Disruptive Classroom Behavior." *Journal of Educational Research* 59 (1966): 360–62.

Lyon, H. *Learning to Feel—Feeling to Learn: Humanistic Education for the Whole Man.* Columbus, Ohio: Charles E. Merrill Publishing Co., 1971.

McKinley, D. G. *Social Class and Family Life.* New York: The Free Press, 1964.

Miller, J. "Disadvantaged Families: Despair to Hope." In *Psychology and the Problems of Society,* edited by F. Korten, S. Cook, and J. Lacey, pp. 179–97. Washington, D.C.: American Psychological Association, 1970.

Morse, W. C. "The Education of Socially Maladjusted and Emotionally Disturbed Children." In *Education of Exceptional Children and Youth,* 2d ed., edited by W. Cruickshank and G. Johnson, pp. 569–629. Englewood Cliffs, New Jersey: Prentice-Hall, 1967.

Morse, W.; Finger, D.; and Gilmore, G. "Innovations in School Mental Health Programs." *Journal of Educational Research* 38 (1968): 461–77.

Radin, N. "Some Impediments to the Education of Disadvantaged Children." *Children* 15 (1968): 171–76.

Rappaport, S. *Public Education for Children with Brain Dysfunction.* Syracuse, New York: Syracuse University Press, 1968.

Riessman, F. *The Culturally Deprived Child.* New York: Harper & Row, 1962.

Rogers, C. *Freedom to Learn: A View of What Education Might Become.* Columbus, Ohio: Charles E. Merrill Publishing Co., 1969.

Rosenberg, M. *Mutual Education.* Seattle, Washington: Special Child Publications, 1972.

2

But then at a certain point in time and place there occurred the most momentous revolution yet achieved by mankind . . . the discovery that the state exists for man, not man for the state, and that the individual human personality, spirit, soul—call it what you will—contains within itself the meaning and measure of existence and carries as a result the full range of responsibility and choice.

Adlai E. Stevenson, from an address to the graduation class of Smith College, June 6, 1955

The Struggle for Self-Control

SELF-CONTROL AND DEMOCRACY

A basic tenet of our free, democratic society is that each and every citizen has a right to responsible participation in those daily events which shape his life and the lives of others around him. Thus, we recognize that the strength of our democratic system depends upon the degree to which all people experience personal satisfaction in their life pursuits. Civil rights and liberties are cherished as insurance against external control, and we presumably are willing to go to war to preserve our right against tyranny and dictatorship. In short, the idea of personal or self-control over our lives is woven into the fabric of our value system.

This natural relationship between self-control and the democratic process provides a basic reason for our commitment to teaching self-control. *We believe that while the value for self-control is profound and enduring, insufficient attention has been given to developing the personal skills or educational opportunities which foster the responsible and fulfilling expression of self-control.*

The Paradox of American Education

American education has been charged with the responsibility of helping to socialize and prepare young people for effective participation in the democratic system, for it is through education that individuals are supposed to develop the knowledge and capacity to participate fully and responsibly in the decision-making events relating to their lives. However, an obvious paradox exists when we note the continuing criticism of the educational system for not fostering the creativity, self-participation, and human consideration for which it was mandated (Glasser, 1969; Holt, 1966, 1967; Illich, 1971; McClellan, 1968; Reimer, 1971; Silberman, 1970).

As Schwilck and Meade (1970) wrote in their foreword to a conference report on the school and the democratic environment sponsored by the Danforth and Ford Foundation: "Students hear about libertarian precepts, but they see and experience authoritarian treatment. Such differences between theory and reality only feed student unrest" (pp. v-vi).

Many educators have attributed student unrest and militancy to a basic frustration of the need for power. Thus, Weisbord (1970) stated: "Above all . . . they want some control and influence over their environment" (p. 10). Commenting upon the widespread estrangement of American students during the late 1960s, Tannenbaum (1969) said: "Their common goals seem to be the loosening of social controls that would permit much wider latitude for self-determination and even the freedom to dishonor time-honored traditions" (p. 1). Miller (1972) considered the magnitude of recent youth protest in America to reflect a revolution against suppression and control of man's "subjective functioning."

In 1970, Marker and Mehlinger affirmed that students were seeking to reduce the discrepancies they perceived between democratic ideals and the realities of the everyday school environment:

> Students participate directly in two political worlds: the authority structure of the school and the authority structure of their own peer culture. Some students are participating directly in a third political world: local and national politics. From his civics teacher a student learns about an American political system in which all men are born with inalienable rights; yet some of these rights and privileges are unavailable to him at school . . . The irony is that the schools have long urged students to be concerned with social issues and accept the value that they should participate. Now students want to participate, to help make the rules under which they live,

> and the schools are unprepared to cope with the political energy of their clients (pp. 52, 54).

Heist (1970), after reviewing the research on student activism and campus disorders during the previous ten years, made a similar but stronger indictment:

> . . . like the ethnic minorities of darker hues who were never understood or accepted, eventually granted legal but never human citizenry, and usually dealt a separate form of justice, so the mass of students, with few exceptions, have been treated as lesser creatures, with few of the rights and privileges of educational citizenship, only infrequently accepted and seldom understood. The latter has become increasingly true, for as in our relationships with certain ethnic peoples, we have dealt with students chiefly as a mass and rarely as individuals (p. 397).

Internal versus External Control of Reinforcement

Rotter (1966) has proposed that the concept of internal-external control of reinforcement can account for a wide range of personality characteristics and overt behavior. Internal control refers to the belief that events are contingent upon one's own behavior or that one has power to influence situational outcomes. In contrast, an orientation to external control of reinforcement means that what happens is viewed as a matter of fate or luck or in the hands of some powerful outside force.

Indications are that promotion of internal control is associated with self-assertiveness, activism, hopefulness, and positive coping, whereas an ideology of external control accompanies defeatism, helplessness, passivity, and depression (McGhee and Crandall, 1968; Rotter, 1966; Rotter, Seeman, and Liverant, 1962). These findings support Singer's (1965) notion that belief in personal control is a principle goal of all educational efforts to promote self-change, as exemplified in the therapeutic process: ". . . [this] single proposition . . . underlies all forms of psychotherapy: the proposition that man is capable of change and of bringing this change about himself . . . ." Moreover, evidence exists to show that clients who improve in psychotherapy sustain an increased belief in internal control and that such a change can be brought about in a relatively brief period of time—i.e., nine to eleven sessions (Felton and Biggs, 1972; Gillis and Jessor, 1970).

Forward and Williams (1970) conducted a fascinating investigation of internal-external control and black militancy. Their results suggest that persons who are high in internal control but lacking opportunities to effect change in their environment may resort to violence. Following the factor analysis of the Rotter IE Scale suggested by Gurin, Gurin, Lao, and Beattie (1969), Forward and Williams found that blacks who evaluated the Detroit riot of 1967 as "good" scored higher on personal control (belief in own capacity to effect change) than blacks who judged the riot to be "bad." Since the groups were not different in their ideologies regarding control, the investigators concluded that "those at the vanguard of ghetto militancy are those who are highly motivated and extremely confident of their own ability to shape their future, but aware that the socioeconomic system is working against them to prevent them from achieving their goals" (p. 91).

The point to be made here is that militancy and revolt cannot be attributed to a state of helplessness and despair. Rather, it appears that such action may reflect the hostile assertion of personal power in a situation where other alternatives seem to be unavailable. We agree with Hook (1970) that violence is not justifiable but we also suggest that it can become a deliberate behavioral choice when other options appear to be closed. Clearly, there is a great need for the individual to exercise influence on oppressive external events, or he may well erupt into violent actions.

Toward a Facilitating Role for Authority

The struggle to obtain or maintain self-control against perceived tyranny in a system seems to be expressed in three patterns of youth behavior: militant revolution, nonviolent withdrawal, and delinquency. Friedenberg (1969), for example, drew a clear distinction between the nonviolent "hippie" types and those who riot. He pointed out, as did Keniston (1965), that hippies were striving to get out of (not into) a modern world which they perceived as threatening to choke individuality. In addition, Gold (1969) reminds us that delinquency can serve as a means of overcoming concerns about powerlessness. He reports that alienation from self is not typical for delinquents but, rather, that the negative identity inherent in delinquency is a means of developing a sense of self.

We are impressed that so many sources converge at the common conclusion that *motivation for self-control has been an extremely powerful factor in the disruptive or deviant behavior of large num-*

bers of young people. Furthermore, we are deeply concerned by the educational system's apparent reluctance to provide for the development and exercise of self-control. Somehow, in our reverence and respect for the importance of knowledge and education, we have tended to promote a distorted atmosphere in which fact-disseminating authoritarian figures also have sought to create open-minded, free-thinking, participation-oriented young adults. It would be hard to imagine a more inconsistent arrangement of models and behavior to be performed.

A few educational revolutionaries argue that all formal schooling is inherently oppressive, in that educators are responsible for shoveling whatever is presently accepted as necessary by those in authority into passive "learners" (Freire, 1971; Illich, 1971). These writers see the educational bureaucracy as cold, controlling, and unyielding—as creating conditions which foster "a cultural schizophrenia in which the student is forced to choose between his own relation to reality or the one demanded by the institution" (Marin, 1969, p. 65). The anguish behind these beliefs cannot help being appreciated when we pause to reflect on the fact that only recently has the U.S. Supreme Court affirmed for the first time that school children have the same rights of free speech under the First Amendment to the Constitution as do adults.

But we do not agree that schools are inherently oppressive. We do not accept only two alternatives—rigid control or total anarchy. We believe that authority can be applied toward the creation of "freedom from threat and freedom of choice" (Rogers, 1961, p. 180). Illich (1972) has faulted schools for imposing a "hidden curriculum" upon children, one in which "it does not matter if the teacher is authoritarian so long as it is the teacher's authority that counts" (p. 6). We maintain that authority can encourage self-expression and responsible choice, just as it can demand obedience and conformity.

Among the definitions for authority in *Webster's New Collegiate Dictionary* are: "an individual cited or appealed to as an expert," and "power to influence or command thought, opinion, or behavior" (p. 59). Certainly the concept of authority itself provides sufficient latitude for a role of responsibility in assuring freedom of thought and feeling. Scribner (1972) has suggested replacing the word "teacher" with that of "enabler," and Rogers (1969) has emphasized "facilitation of learning." We assert that the right to be heard does not require the need to be "right."

Perhaps it is our own discomfort with the thought that we, as adults, are not absolute sources of truth that prevents us from truly respecting the smaller or younger beings in our classrooms. Authority can be sanctioned to create and maintain a "looser structure" (Weisbord, 1970) which guarantees the exercise of self-control. Our democratic goal of responsible participation in decision making requires the ability to develop alternative proposals and to appreciate one's own as well as others' viewpoints. It is time for schools to serve as models and to facilitate practice in these functions rather than just promulgating facts about man and his environment. In a very real sense, *we believe that a self-control curriculum of the sort presented in this book is needed to effect change in school system priorities as much as it is to enhance student skills.*

SELF-CONTROL AND MASTERY OF INNER IMPULSES

We have said that one aspect of the concept of self-control is active participation and expression rather than mere passive reception, conformity, or indifference (i.e., that self-control is an alternative to external control). Another basic dimension of the self-control concept is mastery of one's own impulses in the process of active self-assertion. Teachers everywhere are frustrated when confronted with youngsters who act upon their every whim and inclination, for such youngsters not only are free of external control, but also frequently act as if they were unguided by inner controls. Thus, *self-control connotes more than freedom from external control; it signifies a capacity to direct and regulate one's own behavior.*

Child development researchers have noted added difficulties in socialization for youngsters with unusually intense levels of internal drive (Anderson, 1963; Bergman and Escalona, 1963; Chess, Thomas, and Birch, 1965; Escalona, 1968; Rutter, Birch, Thomas, and Chess, 1964). Standards for acceptable behavior demand considerable control of self-impulses. In order to enter into positive relationships, children must present a compromising capacity as an admission ticket; uncompromising or rigid behavior provides limited possibilities for positive relationships. It is evident from the literature that children who lack ability to regulate impulses are highly vulnerable to social rejection and to associated emotional and learning disorders (Bullock and Brown, 1972; Cruickshank, 1967; Eisenberg, 1966; Laufer and Denhoff, 1957; Lyons and Powers, 1963; Marwit and Stenner, 1972; Schrager, Lindy, Harrison, McDermott, and Wilson, 1966).

Anxiety Related to Losing Behavior Control

Anxiety about losing behavior control is a common concern of most human beings, in varying degrees and patterns. This anxiety or fear revolves around two main expressive modes—overt behavior and predisposition to behave (including fantasy, thoughts, feelings).

Overt behavior: Excessively primitive or impulsive behavior creates social conflict and retaliation in most instances. In addition, when impulsive behavior occurs with high frequency, fear of adult punishment becomes a strong concern. Major influences generating this pattern of behavior can stem from three different sources, among which are *psychoneurological inadequacies*, *constitutional inadequacies*, and *socialization failures*.

Children who cannot control their behavior because of *psychoneurological inadequacies* seem to have concomitant difficulties in learning and mastering cognitive skills. They tend to deprecate themselves, be reluctant about the world, and possess a sense of deficiency and inadequacy.

Children who cannot control their behavior because of *constitutional inadequacies* tend to focus their concern into hurt and power struggles. Anxiety seems to revolve around inflicting hurt and fear of retaliation for aggressive deeds. In these children, learning may be disrupted by inattentiveness, but cognitive skills are often intact. Medication often reduces the frequency of inappropriate behavior sufficiently to promote achievement.

Children who cannot control their behavior because of *socialization failures* tend to justify their behavior as necessary and essential in their environment (i.e., as they experience severe and unjust retaliation from others following impulsive actions, they begin to reject any curbs on behavior and feel entitled to acting out). As research has shown, when dependency needs are not met, internalization of controls fails (Bandura and Walters, 1963; Sears, Maccoby, and Levin, 1957). Massive rejection and retaliation leads to fear of punishment, but not to self-control. Instead, impulse release is strengthened by the conviction that social agents only inflict pain and that pleasure must be self-attained.

Predisposition to behave: Children often develop anxiety in anticipation of behavior. This anxiety is mobilized around thoughts and feelings rather than overt actions; for example, when a child comes to feel anxious about hurting his mother, he seeks to reduce the discomfort created by this thought, perhaps by giving her a present, by staying close to her, or by trying a number of other protective behaviors.

Anxiety relating to behavior dispositions seems to have three sources in social learning:

1. *Counter-reactions to earlier excesses of overt behavior.* In terms of this source of anxiety, we can think of the many people who invest exhausting amounts of energy in suppressing behavior to assure acceptance and security. In these people, earlier incidents of discharge propel great efforts at control in order to insure that frightening events do not recur.
2. *Vicarious learning.* In this case, youngsters learn to avert social outbursts which they perceive as resulting in great harm and suffering. For example, children who witness acute marital turmoil and violence frequently learn to avoid controversy or negative expression.
3. *Inadequate experience.* If a child only sees nonassertive, nonaggressive behavior; nonsexual, nonaffectionate behavior; or nonhelpful, noncooperative behavior, he will often conclude that assertive, sexual, and helpful behaviors are wrong. Rewards come from emulating practiced behaviors and as these responses increase in strength, the prospects for development of the nonexperienced behaviors shrink drastically. Inadequate experience also leads to awkward and exaggerated responses when the unpracticed behavior is expressed. For example, the child who has not been exposed to children his own age may enthusiastically rush to his first party only to scare off the other children by his desperate efforts to befriend everybody, or the boy who has never used a hammer may swing it so hard that he breaks something.

In review, we are saying that impulsive behavior is inevitably accompanied by social disapproval which promotes a sense of wrongdoing and associated discomfort about lack of control. Two fundamental reaction patterns exist for handling social rejection, namely, continued uncontrolled outbursts and inhibitory efforts. In the former case, unchecked inner impulses continue to flow into unacceptable behavior. In the latter instance, overt behavior is restrained, but an affective component may stimulate thought or fantasy suggestive of gross behavior. Common to both reaction patterns, however, is a residue of anxiety about losing behavior control which may interfere with interpersonal relations and successful task achievement. As applied here, the concept of self-control embraces *both* the capacity to restrain or inhibit behavior and the capacity to accept and express impulses through socially acceptable modes.

SELF-CONTROL AND THE RESPONSIBLE EXERCISE OF FREEDOM

The notion of forced, external control is inherently repugnant to a liberal, freedom-seeking society. The spirit of democracy calls for an atmosphere conducive to nurturing the free expression of feelings and behavior. At the same time, however, we are concerned that this freedom not become a license to infringe upon or injure the rights of others. It is an implicit rule that the exercise of personal freedom requires modulation of behavior in conjunction with concern for the needs of others. No one can simply do or act as he pleases, unless such behavior is totally irrelevant to the lives of others. Behind the closed doors of a privately owned apartment, the exercise of freedom can be unmitigated, for here the rights of others need not necessarily be involved. In strolling the streets, however, the expression of freedom takes on different form and is subject to the rights of car owners, store keepers, bus passengers, neighborhood dwellers, and even dogs. In other words, freedom of behavior carries a situational yardstick—behavioral freedom is not an absolute to be interpreted independent of fellow beings.

However, a deeper freedom exists in the realm of ideas and feelings. Every human being has the fullest right to feel and think as he sees fit, so long as the expression of such inner experience is not publicly damaging. There are no other limits to that right. To our way of thinking, *the responsible exercise of freedom must set definite limits on behavior but also should allow free rein for personal feelings and beliefs*. This distinction between behavioral action and thought or feeling is of critical importance to the concept of self-control as well as to understanding the theory and practice of teaching children self-control.

We regard the responsible exercise of freedom as a dynamic yet orderly process of transaction between an individual and his social surroundings. This process involves: exposing the self to needs and reactions of others, expressing one's own thoughts and feelings, accepting the frustration inherent in not having all needs met, negotiating differences to produce compromise or mutual exchange, accepting consequences of an uncompromising stance (e.g., going to jail, getting fired). Successful attainment of the responsible exercise of freedom clearly requires a high degree of self-control, the development of which can be facilitated by appreciating the following points:

1. Impulses towards action must be frustrated during the process of socialization—even in a democratic, "free" society. Such frustration is necessary in order to protect the rights of other people, whether parents, siblings, teachers, or strangers.
2. Frustration generates further impulses to action, and frustration-instigated reactions are usually loaded with negative affect.
3. In the absence of awareness that feelings and thoughts can be freely expressed, anxiety-based efforts at control emerge. Anxiety-based efforts at control require protective behavior which, in turn, results in increasing distance from genuine parts of one's personal experience.
4. The maintenance of such avoidance produces a constriction of reactive potential and behavior choice and results in increased rigidity and inflexibility. Such inflexibility of reaction interferes with the development of self-control as well as corrupting one's feeling of freedom.
5. Communication of these frustration-instigated reactions as honest and responsible personal expressions forms a real basis for renewed hope and satisfaction. The realization of one's freedom to express personal thoughts and feelings in response to frustration creates real acceptance and a truly free sphere of human experience.

An irony in our national life is that while we treasure the ideal of freedom, we lack the strength to absorb the free expression of negative affect from others. It is as if we preferred a myth of freedom to the reality of experience. We act as if democracy should bring pleasure to all, even though we know this is impossible. We are afraid to profit from others' experiences of frustration, as if this knowledge might destroy each of us and the total system. Instead of using reactions to frustration for self-evaluation, understanding, and positive change, we wait until frustration-instigated reactions culminate in massive discharges of anger and hostility.

To face squarely the realities of responsible freedom it is necessary to establish norms for interpersonal behavior which are as equitable and reasonable as possible and courageously address the reactions to frustration which such standards must create. Furthermore, the management of freedom requires a willingness on our part to learn from frustration-instigated expressions of thought and feeling. Our greatest hope for improvement in the quality of life is interwoven with our greatest fears for disorder. It is in the experience of pain and disappointment that either growth or destruction is forged. Is our response to criticism to be attack or reappraisal? Is our response to alienation and distrust to be rejection or a reaching out? Is our response to hate to be vengeance or reconciliation?

SUMMARY

This chapter has dealt with the individual's struggle for self-control in terms of two very different but equally profound life issues: the assertion of self to create or maintain freedom from external control (*between the individual and society*) and the assertion of one's own conscious resources to direct and regulate inner drives and impulses (*within the individual himself*).

Our American heritage is rooted in the protection of the right of individual citizens to have a voice in the events which shape their lives. As a nation, we have placed a precious and enduring value on individual liberty and free participation in decision-making processes. Yet despite these ideals, we have given insufficient attention to the development of the personal skills or educational opportunities which foster a responsible and fulfilling expression of self-control.

American education is faced with a glaring paradox—the discrepancy between its charge to prepare youth for effective participation in the democratic system and its apparent difficulty providing for acceptable displays of student power. Although considerable research indicates that personal adaptation and integrity is associated with internal control of reinforcement, there is also strong evidence that motivation for internal or self-control has been an extremely powerful factor in the disruptive or deviant behavior of large numbers of young people. Clearly, the educational establishment must find ways to convert abuses of authority into more facilitating roles. We maintain that authority can be sanctioned to create a "looser structure," one which guarantees the exercise of self-control. *In fact, we believe that this self-control curriculum is needed to affect change in school system priorities as much as it is to enhance student skills.*

Aside from the individual's efforts to exert influence on the external world, there is a continuing developmental struggle to gain mastery over inner drives and impulses. Children with excessive impulsivity are at a serious disadvantage and commonly develop learning and emotional disorders. It also appears that most people experience anxiety about losing behavior control, whether this happens as a result of imagined or overt behavior. Anxiety associated with regular behavioral outbursts is often characteristic of children with psychoneurological, constitutional, or socialization inadequacies. On the other hand, when anxiety is associated with the predisposition to behave, three sources of social learning seem influential—counter-reactions to earlier excesses, vicarious learning, and inadequate experience.

Regardless of the particular *source* of anxiety about losing control or the *pattern* of response to this anxiety (i.e., release or inhibition), such anxiety tends to interfere with interpersonal relations and successful task achievement. Thus, *an important objective of the self-control curriculum is to reduce anxiety over loss of control by increasing skill and confidence in regulating inner impulses.*

A key element in reaching this objective revolves around the distinction between freedom of action and freedom of thought and feeling. We postulate that while the responsible exercise of freedom requires mutual acceptance and sharing of thoughts, these feelings *must occur* within a context of appropriate limits on behavioral action. However, socialization efforts have generally opposed acceptance of the negative feelings which accompany inevitable frustrations.

As a consequence of social failure to respect the human right to think and feel "undesirable" things, unhelpful restrictions have been placed on creative possibilities for communication and problem solving. Socializing agents have tended to reinforce needless feelings of anxiety and unhealthy behaviors of avoidance. The responsible exercise of freedom must include self-governed expressions of negative reactions to frustration. Because of irrational fears that negative feelings or thoughts will culminate in destructive action, the struggle for self-control has been made far more painful than it need be. Fortunately, however, the struggle continues.

REFERENCES

Anderson, W. W. "The Hyperkinetic Child: A Neurological Appraisal." *Neurology* 13 (1963): 968–73.

Bandura, A., and Walters, R. H. *Social Learning and Personality Development.* New York: Holt, Rinehart & Winston, 1963.

Bergman, D., and Escalona, S. K. "Unusual Sensitivities in Very Young Children." In *The Psychoanalytic Study of the Child,* Vol, V. edited by Ruth S. Eissler, et al., pp. 121–53. New York: International University Press, 1963.

Bullock, L., and Brown, R. "Behavioral Dimensions of Emotionally Disturbed Children." *Exceptional Children* 38 (1972): 740–41.

Chess, S.; Thomas, A. T.: and Birch, H. G. *Your Child Is a Person.* New York: Viking Press, 1965.

Cruickshank, W. "Hyperactive Children: Their Needs and Curriculum." In *The Teaching-Learning Process in Educating Emotionally Disturbed Children,* edited by P. Knoblock and J. Johnson, pp. 47–63. Syracuse, New York: Syracuse University Press, 1967.

Eisenberg, L. "The Management of the Hyperkinetic Child." *Developmental Medicine and Child Neurology* 8 (1966): 593–98.

Escalona, S. K. *The Roots of Individuality: Normal Patterns of Development in Infancy.* Chicago: Aldine, 1968.

Felton, G., and Biggs, B. "Teaching Internalization Behavior to Collegiate Low Achievers in Group Psychotherapy." *Psychotherapy* 9 (1972): 281–83.

Forward, J., and Williams, J. "Internal-External Control and Black Militancy." *Journal of Social Issues* 26 (1970): 75–92.

Freire, P. *Pedagogy of the Oppressed.* New York: Herder & Herder, 1971.

Friedenberg, E. Z. "Current Patterns of a Generational Conflict." *Journal of Social Issues* 25 (1969): 21–38.

Gillis, J., and Jessor, R. "Effects of Brief Psychotherapy on Belief in Internal Control: An Exploratory Study." *Psychotherapy* 7 (1970): 135–37.

Glasser, W. *Schools without Failure.* New York: Harper & Row, 1969.

Gold, M. "Juvenile Delinquency as a Symptom of Alienation." *Journal of Social Issues* 25 (1969): 121–35.

Gurin, P.; Gurin G.; Lao, R.; and Beattie, M. "Internal-External Control in the Motivational Dynamics of Negro Youth." *Journal of Social Issues* 25 (1969): 29–54.

Heist, P. "Activist Students Challenging the Social Scientists." In *Psychology and the Problems of Society,* edited by F. Lorten, S. Cook, and

J. Lacey, pp. 395–405. Washington, D.C.: American Psychological Association, 1970.

Holt, J. *How Children Fail.* New York: Delta, 1966.

———. *How Children Learn.* New York: Delta, 1967.

Hook, S. *Academic Freedom and Academic Anarchy.* New York: Cowles, 1970.

Illich, I. "The Breakdown of Schools: A Problem or a Symptom?" *Journal of Research and Development in Education* 5 (1972): 3–17.

———. *Deschooling Society.* New York: Harper & Row, 1971.

Keniston, K. *The Uncommitted: Alienated Youth in American Society.* New York: Dell, 1965.

Laufer, M., and Denhoff, E. "Hyperkinetic Behavior Syndrome in Children." *Journal of Pediatrics* 50 (1957): 463–73.

Lyons, D., and Powers, V. "Study of Children Exempted from Los Angeles Schools." In *Conflict in the Classroom,* edited by N.J. Long, W.M. Morse, and R. Newman, pp. 138–44. Belmont, California: Wadsworth, 1965.

Marin, P. "The Open Truth and Fiery Vehemence of Youth." *The Center Magazine* 2 (1969): 61–74.

Marker, G., and Mehlinger, H. "Schools, Politics, Rebellions, and Other Youthful Interests." In *The School and the Democratic Environment,* edited by The Danforth Foundation, pp. 38–54. New York: Columbia University Press, 1970.

Marwit, S., and Stenner, A. J. "Hyperkinesis: Delineation of Two Patterns." *Exceptional Children* 38 (1972): 401–6.

McClennan, J. *Toward an Effective Critique of American Education.* Philadelphia: J. B. Lippincott, 1968.

McGhee, P., and Crandall, V. "Beliefs in Internal-External Control of Reinforcements and Academic Performance." *Child Development* 39 (1968): 91–102.

Miller, W. "Roots of the Revolution: A New Image of Man." *Educational Leadership* 30 (1972): 13–15.

Reimer, E. *School Is Dead: An Essay on Alternatives in Education.* Garden City, New York: Doubleday, 1971.

Rogers, C. *On Becoming a Person.* Boston: Houghton Mifflin, 1961.

———. "Self-Directed Change for Educators: Experiments and Implications." In *Preparing Educators to Meet Emerging Needs,* edited by E. L. Morphet and D. L. Jesser, pp. 57–74. New York: Citation, 1969.

Rotter, J. B. "Generalized Expectancies for Internal versus External Control of Reinforcement," *Psychological Monographs* 80 (1966): 1–28.

Rotter, J. B.; Seeman, M.; and Liverant, S. "Internal versus External Control of Reinforcements: A Major Variable in Behavior Theory." In *Decisions, Values, and Groups*, Volume 1, edited by N. F. Washburn, pp. 473–516. London: Pergamon, 1962.

Rutter, M.; Birch, H.; Thomas, A.; and Chess, S. "Temperamental Characteristics in Infancy and the Later Development of Behavior Disorders." *British Journal of Psychiatry* 110 (1964): 651.

Schrager, J.; Lindy, J.; Harrison, S.; McDermott, J.; and Wilson, P. "The Hyperkinetic Syndrome: Some Consensually Validated Behavioral Correlates." *Exceptional Children* 32 (1966): 635–37.

Schwilck, G., and Meade, E. "Foreword." In *The School and the Democratic Environment*, edited by The Danforth Foundation, pp. iv-ix. New York: Columbia University Press, 1970.

Scribner, H. B. "Leadership for Change: My First Year in New York City as Chancellor of the Public Schools." *Journal of Research and Development in Education* 5 (1972): 18–28.

Sears, R. R.; Maccoby, E. E.; and Levin, H. *Patterns of Child Rearing*. Evanston, Illinois: Row, Peterson, 1957.

Silberman, C. *Crisis in the Classroom*. New York: Random House, 1970.

Singer, E. *Key Concepts in Psychotherapy*. New York: Random House, 1965.

Tannenbaum, A.J. "Introduction: Alienated Youth." *Journal of Social Issues* 25 (1969): 1–5.

Weisbord, M. R. "What Do We Want from Our Schools?" In *The School and the Democratic Environment*, edited by The Danforth Foundation, pp. 1–16. New York: Columbia University Press, 1970.

3

We are further finding that curricula which help a child deal with his feelings and emotions, which teach principles of self-control, and which help the child cope with the pressures and frustrations of an industrial society are desperately needed yet almost totally lacking . . . .

Report to the President of the White House Commission on Children, 1970, p. 125

Self-Control as an Educational Objective

FILLING AN EDUCATIONAL VOID

The basic mission of public education is to prepare youth to engage intelligently and responsibly in the business of life and society (National Education Association, 1961). However, while schooling has equipped many young people to advance in science, business, and agriculture through application of hard work and intellectual understanding, the graduates of our educational systems have been less competent in their capacity to willingly seek and freely choose among available alternatives.

In 1959, President Eisenhower appointed a special commission to "set up a series of goals in various areas of national activity" and to develop an outline of policies and programs for the attainment of these goals. The first goal identified in the ensuing Report of the President's Commission on National Goals (1960) concerned the responsibility of government to the individual.

> The status of the individual must remain our primary concern. All our institutions—political, social, and economic—must further enhance the dignity of the citizen, promote the maximum develop-

> ment of his capabilities, stimulate their responsible exercise, and widen the range and effectiveness of opportunities for individual choice (p. 3).

In further enunciating this primary goal, the Commission Report stated:

> The great ideas that have moved the world have sprung from unfettered minds. The spirit of liberty, in which they thrive, makes one man hesitate to impose his will on another. It relies on the conviction that the truth will emerge from free inquiry and exchange of views . . . . Schools and institutions of higher education . . . have a particular responsibility to ensure freedom of expression by students, faculty, and administrators alike . . . . There are subtle and powerful pressures toward conformity in the economic, social, and political world. They must be resisted so that difference of taste and opinion will remain a constructive force in improving our society (p. 3).

This fundamental commitment to truth and the belief that truth emerges from free and open inquiry holds tremendous promise—as well as challenge. For it means in the marketplace of ideas and feelings, no man is a master. The pursuit of truth essentially becomes a dedication to listening, respecting, evaluating, and sharing perceptions of life with other human beings, and such a pursuit requires high levels of self-control. It requires an ability to comprehend and select alternatives, to delay or modify one's own needs in order to appreciate the needs of others, and to respect one's own thoughts and feelings as worthy of exerting influence on important decisions. In more specific terms, we regard effective and responsible freedom of choice to be contingent upon the following four factors: *awareness of existing alternatives; awareness and respect for others' reactions to these alternatives; awareness and respect for one's own reactions to these alternatives; and a reflective, rational basis for decision.*

Some Basic Educational Distortions

Unfortunately, preparation for effective and responsible freedom of choice has been seriously impeded by three major educational distortions: overemphasis on externally controlled academic tasks, restrictive competition for grades and recognition, and focus on narrow academic products. In other words, schools have developed several powerful attitudes and tendencies which are in conflict with skill development for effective choice making.

These distortions have promoted feelings of doubt and inadequacy, as well as a sense of emptiness and defensiveness about exercising personal choice in too many students. The self-control curriculum is intended to compensate for these distortions while, at the same time, teaching skills for effectively exercising choice directly.

Externally controlled academic tasks: This particular distortion is evident when the teacher defines the nature of the task without giving sufficient consideration to the learner's needs, interests, and abilities. In effect, the teacher decides what is to be done, when, and by whom without significant input from the student.

Such a condition results in excessive demands upon and frustration to the learner, an irrelevant curriculum, communication gaps, feelings of powerlessness in the learner, and abuses of power by the teacher. Adaptation to this kind of educational distortion usually results in passivity and conformity, passive-resistiveness, and indirect or displaced expressions of resentment (e.g., vandalism, scapegoating).

Restrictive competition for grades and recognition: This distortion exists when the number of students receiving positive reinforcement is restricted substantially. That is, praise, acclaim, encouragement or affection are offered on a *space available* basis. The competition distortion stimulates feelings of superiority and inferiority, envy, rivalry, distrust, and selfishness among students. Cheating and exploitation are commonly rewarded by such a system. An intellectual caste system is created in which a gross sense of defeatism occurs for the large number of students who are not included in the "top fifth percentile" (or tenth, or twentieth, etc.). Development of personal pride in one's sincere efforts and striving for individual improvement is severely hampered for most students when this distortion becomes significant because their work never seems good enough—either to them or to their teachers.[1]

---

[1]See A. Kirschenbaum, S. Simon, and R. Napier, *WAD JA GET? The Grading Game in American Education* (New York: Value Associates, 1971), for an intriguing account of the value basis for our longstanding preoccupation with grades and grading, and the forces to be confronted in exploring practical alternatives.

Focus on narrow academic products: American education historically has concentrated on tangible signs of productivity. Thus, the classroom focus has been on the correct answer—the pertinent fact—the material outcome. These outcomes have been evaluated, rated, and judged to the point where they have even been seriously considered as a criterion for teacher pay.

However, when classroom rewards are either withheld or not offered at all until a completed product meets some predetermined standard of performance, an unhealthy distortion results. In such a situation, there is a disturbing neglect of the social-emotional and conceptual processes which are necessary to mediate progress. For example, although reading aloud or writing a creative story may be important outcomes in themselves, they become sterile when a child's fear of expressing ideas is overlooked.

It is our belief that these distortions have tended to create a needlessly impersonal and restrictive educational culture—one which creates much inferiority and frustration but relatively little self-pride. Schools have tended to foster a narrow definition of right and wrong which centers on intellectual hoarding and regurgitation of specific facts. Up until recent times, education has been all but devoid of appreciation for individual differences and shared understanding. This is especially important, for to appreciate differences, one has to accept unique expressions and reactions—to welcome their disclosure.

Shifting the Criteria for Educational Success

Self-control already has been described as including a belief in one's effectiveness to influence or act upon the environment; however, when effectiveness is defined in terms of agreement with authority, few students can gain a real sense of personal control. Rather than submit to authority-based criteria for success, many such students decide to withhold or evade educational tasks. These "nonperformers" include students who lack the skills needed to complete assigned tasks as well as those who rebel against the impersonality and materialism they find around them. Unfortunately, in the past, the choice to not perform has also been a choice to fail. That is, the learner is left with the feeling that he has not attained the desirable ("worthwhile," "valuable," "acceptable") outcomes, and feelings of inadequacy and ineffectiveness are antithetical to the development of self-control which, in contrast, generates positive esteem and self-regard.

If, as Horn (1964) points out, the ends for which we educate are to include "helping the child to acquire attitudes of accepting change as normal and inevitable . . .; developing a sense of independence . . .; building a desire and enthusiasm for learning . . ." (p. 142), then other criteria for success besides "correct answers" have to become real. New criteria are needed which promote a sense of skillfulness in actively managing and mastering self-life problems—criteria which *all* children can attain.

In her book *New Priorities in the Curriculum*, Louise Berman (1968) advocates a different set of criteria for appraising student progress, based upon a goal of developing "process-oriented persons." Such persons are seen as "ongoing, growing, developing beings . . . who are able to handle themselves and the situations of which they are a part with adequacy and ease" (pp. 9–10). Berman describes eight process skills which should be emphasized in school programs: perceiving, communicating, loving, decision making, knowing, organizing, creating, and valuing. It is important to note that these skills are evidenced by the way in which children perform important functions rather than by what they produce as end results. As Berman notes, for a school to highlight process criteria of this type, it must view culture as moving with the emerging trends rather than holding to the already accomplished procedures and regard the individual as contributing to what is in the process of being created rather than simply consuming what has already been created.

In essence, *the educational void of which we are speaking is created by ignoring the genuine worth of each individual as he engages in the process of attempting and reacting to externally assigned tasks.* Regardless of the outcome of one's task efforts, there are seeds for rich satisfaction in the very act of applying personal resources toward a particular task. These personal resources may or may not be focused on completing the assigned task; in fact, it is sometimes a major accomplishment to realize that an assigned task is inappropriate or irrelevant.

Meaningful expression of personal resources may occur through cognitive activity, such as attending, comprehending, remembering, and organizing, or affective activity, such as clarifying, sharing, and valuing feelings. The point is that all teaching-learning transactions *must* allow for variations of involvement with the task. The process of learning is related more closely to the personalized application of learner resources than to *any* external criterion of accomplishment. Consider, for example, the number of students who master exams while hating the subject matter and, probably, the teacher as well.

In contrast are the learners who become engrossed with the content of a discipline and stretch their interest and curiosity by validly questioning the seemingly obvious or expected. In our terms, self-control assures the possibility of exercising personal choice about one's own manner or degree of involvement in a given situation.

A WORKING DEFINITION OF SELF-CONTROL

We already have stated our conviction that self-control must become an educational objective if young people are to be adequately equipped to face the stresses of daily living. Movement toward this objective is spurred by definition in operational terms of the nature, structure, and process of self-control. While aspects of self-control have been considered by many authors in a wide variety of contexts, we know of no case of the construct's having been viewed as a centralizing function comprised of discrete, teachable skills.

Self-control is here defined as *one's capacity to direct and regulate personal action* [*behavior*] *flexibly and realistically in a given situation*. This definition contains the following key ingredients:

1. Self-control is viewed as a *capacity* in the sense that more or less of it may be displayed depending on the amount of skill needed at a particular moment in time.
2. Behavior must be *willfully directed* so that focused, discriminating actions can be taken. Narrowly fixed or widely diffused responses are evidence of weaknesses in self-control.
3. Behavior must be *self-regulated* in the sense that levels or intensities of expression are subject to voluntary modification. Such regulation pertains to adjustment of response to a personally desired level of display. Persistently intense or lethargic responses suggest serious deficiencies in self-control.
4. The *locus of action is the person himself* rather than the situation or the behavior of others in that situation. To identify self-control, we need to know if a child is acting within his own desires. Some children are ingenious at getting others to do their bidding (e.g., to express their hostility, to satisfy their need for property) but are unable to present personal needs directly. Other youngsters may innocently

submit to the activities led by others even while experiencing overwhelming impulses to do something else. In the latter case, self-control is tenuous despite the appearance of calm.

5. Self-control implies *flexibility in response* so that behavior may or may not be expressed. It ought to be clear that we are talking not about inhibition of behavior but about freedom to choose between alternatives—including that of action versus inaction.
6. Self-control involves *realism* in that predispositions to action are aroused by stimuli which have observable substance and influence. We have witnessed some very well-regulated behavior involving anger, sympathy, or love which has been an outgrowth of private fantasy activity. A child speaking intently and sensitively to an imaginary playmate may fulfill the requirements of self-direction, regulation, and flexibility, but the unreality of his act belies self-control. The emphasis here is on the mastery of personal behavior under *real observable* conditions of impulse arousal.
7. Self-control should be considered in relation to a given situation since impulses and skills aroused in one context may be strikingly different in another. For example, many children function beautifully when the classroom is highly structured, but become wild when faced with ambiguity or unclarity.

In approaching the teaching of self-control as an educational objective, we have sought to meet five criteria for valid educational objectives, as developed by Smith, Stanley, and Shores (1957). According to these authors, objectives must: be conceived in terms of the demands of the social circumstances, lead toward the fulfillment of basic human needs, be consistent with democratic ideals, be either consistent or noncontradictory in their relationship with one another, and be capable of reduction to behavioristic terms.

SELF-CONTROL IN RELATION TO MEETING TASK REQUIREMENTS

We have claimed that the development of self-control leads to the responsible exercise of freedom which includes personal competence in relation to the environment and mastery of inner experience. In a very basic way, we regard self-control as a prerequisite for satisfaction with oneself and one's efforts, to the extent that pride in self is built upon attainment of personal goals. Performance in a vacuum tells us nothing about self-satisfaction, but performance in relation to one's hopes or aspirations forms the essence of self-esteem (Diggory, 1966). Capacity for self-control is seen then as an organizing construct which determines success in performing according to one's own goals.

It is important to recognize, however, that individual goals are heavily influenced by agents of social approval. A parent who wants his son to hit a ball sets a goal which the son invariably internalizes. It is almost absurd to contemplate the son's saying to himself, "Dad's goal for me is too hard; I'll be happy if I can just swing the bat." Were children able to set appropriate goals for themselves, they would be spared countless hurts and humiliations. As teachers, we are continuously setting goals for children. Write this theme; read that page; add these figures; turn in that homework, etc. Each time we assign a task or give an instruction, we have presented a goal for children to attain. And, it is in the nature of children's need for love and attention that they will seek to carry out our wishes or, at least, to attach value to the request.

In the course of shaping an independent, viable identity, children resist, defy, rebel, and reject our tasks. We must realize that such a response is necessary if they are to become more than mere carbon copies. However, the importance of the task assigned by and for the adult is not lost to the child. When a child *chooses* not to fulfill a task in the service of his own pride in self-assertion, his esteem may not suffer; in fact, it may grow. But when a child does not fulfill a task because he *cannot*, the consequence for personality development is much different. In both cases, the child senses the importance of task achievement to the adult. With the former instance, lack of task completion is not perceived as failure. In the latter case, however, feelings of failure and inadequacy abound. The pain of such feelings gradually generates protective behaviors like denial, disinterest, and dropping out, and the child's self-esteem is dealt a heavy, often lasting, blow.

When children are unable to channel responses towards normal classroom assignments, they are seriously handicapped indeed. While it is true that recently developed educational emphases on learning centers and individualized instructional programs are reducing the stress created by global task assignment, there is always a core set of behavior expectations to be followed. Inability to perform according to these expectations can become a basic source of disturbance for the child and of dissatisfaction for him, his classmates, and his teacher (Hobbs, 1967; Rosenberg, 1968; Werry, 1968). Frequent experiences of behaving in ways that one finds personally undesirable breed shame and self-hate (Quay, Morse, and Cutler, 1966). In other words, absence of self-control leads to lowered self-evaluation.

A purpose of this book is to focus attention on the concept and importance of self-control. Far more importantly, however, by identifying skills which we think underlie the capacity for self-control and by offering suggestions for improving these skills, we hope to increase the chances that every child can smile when looking in a mirror.

THE STRUCTURE OF SELF-CONTROL

We view the capacity for self-control as deriving from the integration of eight skill-clusters which have been identified on the basis of systematic observation and analysis of disruptive behavior in the classroom. Using the "Stress-Threat Analysis" method suggested by Fagen and McDonald (1969), children were observed in both regular public schools and a special therapeutic school for emotionally handicapped youngsters. Since the "Stress-Threat Analysis" procedure calls for analyzing the consistency of relationship between antecedent task requirements and the occurrence of behavior disruption, disruptive behavior was considered under four major categories: inappropriate verbalizations, physical aggression, random motor activity, and general avoidance behaviors. To be considered disruptive, pupil behavior had to be incompatible with purposeful work efforts and, therefore, disruptive to the learning *process,* although not necessarily to the classroom *atmosphere.*

Fagen and McDonald found support for their hypotheses that: "consistency in relationship between antecedent task requirement factors and behavior disruption is likely to reflect stress and threat reactions to real limitations in skills required to complete the task, and inconsistency or variability in this relationship is more suggestive of disturbances arising from other than skill limitations, i.e., emotional and social factors" (p. 220).

Whereas this initial research referred to cognitive task requirements as skill factors and emotional and social factors as "other than skill limitations," subsequent study showed that social factors could be conceptualized and identified as skill-clusters, just as could the more clearly cognitive factors. For example, by noting that some children regularly had temper tantrums whenever an obstacle was placed in their path to a desired goal (be it academic, recreational, or material), it was possible to regard their behavior as reflecting gross lack of skill in accepting and managing frustration.

As a result of repeated observation and categorization, capacity for self-control in the classroom came to be seen as deriving from eight skill-clusters. Four of these skill-clusters seem to depend heavily on intellectual or cognitive development, while the other four seem more related to emotional or affective development. These eight skill-clusters are summarized as follows:

1. *Selection*—Ability to perceive incoming information accurately
2. *Storage*—Ability to retain the information received
3. *Sequencing and ordering*—Ability to organize actions on the basis of a planned order
4. *Anticipating consequences*—Ability to relate actions to expected outcomes
5. *Appreciating feelings*—Ability to identify and constructively use affective experience
6. *Managing frustration*—Ability to cope with external obstacles that produce stress
7. *Inhibition and delay*—Ability to postpone or restrain action tendencies
8. *Relaxation*—Ability to reduce internal tension

Each of the above skill-clusters is viewed as representing a basic parameter of self-control, with each subsuming several interrelated functions. Skills 1 through 4 are regarded as being more cognitive, while skills 5 through 8 are the more affective skills. Part Two, The Self-Control Curriculum, presents teaching tasks designed to develop skill in each of the above eight areas. In addition, statements of rationale and teaching goals are offered in support of each curriculum area, with goals relating to specific sub-skills and their teaching units. Taken as a whole, the eight curriculum areas or clusters of skills form the bases for self-control.

As has been indicated, the parameters of self-control are an admixture of abilities from both the cognitive and affective domains. The achievement of self-control demands effective grappling with both intellectual and emotional problems. And while it appears that parameters load differentially on intellectual or emotional processes, affect and intellect may interact across all areas. For example, "Storage" pertains to memory processes which are traditionally regarded as a cognitive ability; nevertheless, it is common knowledge that memory may be disrupted by anxiety or emotional stress—even to the point of amnesia. "Appreciating feelings," on the other hand, clearly aims at affective experience but, at the same time, it requires retention of verbal concepts (e.g., sadness, joy, resentment) if feeling states are to be correctly identified. Our contention is that the mastery of affective experience undoubtedly enhances cognitive performance and is likely to be enhanced by intellectual mastery.

Figure 1 depicts the integration of the eight skill-clusters into a total capacity for self-control in the classroom.

AN APPROACH TO SKILL DEVELOPMENT

The strategy incorporated into the self-control curriculum is based on a pragmatic, behavioral point of view regarding skill development. We are not concerned that some of our skill-clusters sound unfamiliar. Instead, legitimacy in identifying an area of skill is evaluated here in terms of whether behavioral processes can be stated, separated from other skill functions, and modified by learning experience.

Our operational definition of a skill or ability is any response pattern (cognitive or affective) which can be improved through teaching and can be voluntarily expressed. Clearly, some response patterns will generate more interest than others and will be taken more seriously. For example, skill in saying "thank you" will not particularly impress anybody, but ability to read rapidly draws effusive accolades. The labeling of a skill is, however, irrelevant to the process of teaching or improving skillful performance. It is of no matter that saying "thank you" or speed reading is labeled as a skill unless performance in either can be improved through teaching and practice.

In determining the meaningfulness of a particular skill-focus, however, criteria other than volitional control and teachability

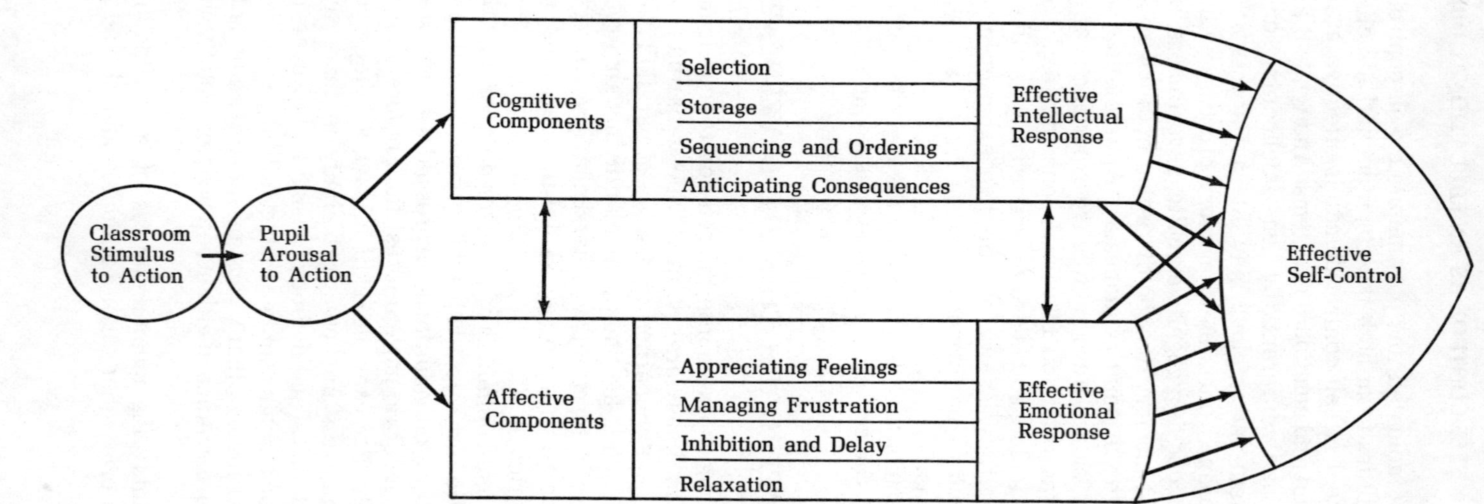

Figure 1: *Capacity for Self-Control as an Integration of Skill-Clusters*

become important; these criteria are specifically *adaptability* and *process-orientation*. Adaptability refers to the range of situations in which the skill can be applied. For example, discrimination of foreground from background is a skill which has adaptive value in a wide range of contexts, while the ability to lay bricks has limited application. Adaptability is determined by the degree to which a skill involves processes that are appropriate to many situations rather than just a few.

Process-orientation, although closely related to adaptability, differs in its reference to the internal functions of a skill. Here, the emphasis is on the cognitive and affective processes that occur within the learner prior to final action. For example, parallel parking a car in tight places may be viewed as an external skill requiring practice in using forward and reverse gears or wheel turning. On the other hand, skill in parking may be more meaningfully developed by focusing on the process of relaxing under tension or coordinating eye-hand movements. With a process-orientation, the educational focus is on those cognitive and affective operations which pave the way for overt, response outcomes.

Any situation where skill is required involves two major dimensions, response outcomes and internal processes mediating these outcomes. Since teaching responsibility implies promoting skill development in the learner, the question is how to best facilitate such skill development. Much depends on how the teacher-learner transaction is conceptualized in terms of skill focus. Figure 2 illustrates the primary alternatives available for focusing on skill development in the teacher-learner transaction.

An example of skill development is in order at this point. A teacher may define the task of a geography lesson as "learning capitals of states," with the focus of skill development placed on producing the names of capitals from memory. Or the teacher may define the task as remembering environmental relationships, with the skill focus on the processes of combining, relating, and storing items of information.

The present self-control curriculum adopts a process-oriented focus, as advocated by Berman (1968). To implement a process focus, we ask what internal skills are necessary to produce some external behavior. In so doing, we are not deferring to mysticism, Freudian homunculi, or inexplicable powers within people. Instead, we believe that internal processes can be described and operationalized. Naturally, inference and abstraction are required. For example, we regard ability to appreciate feelings as a process skill,

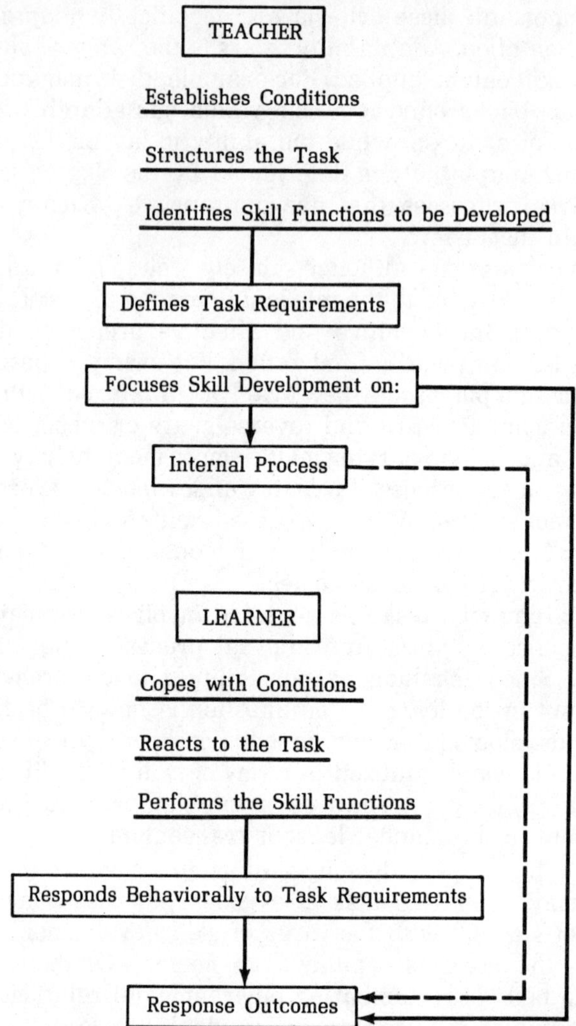

Figure 2: *Alternatives for Focusing Skill in the Teacher-Learner Transaction*

for operationally it is described as involving accurate identification of feelings, effective management of feelings by use of words and socially acceptable reactions, reinterpretations of feeling events, and initiation of positive feelings. Each of these subskills can be developed through purposeful teacher activity, and each can be evaluated in terms of overt behavior. Thus, if a child feels sad we cannot x-ray his sadness, but we can help him communicate the inner feeling through words or gestures.

We do not concede that the private experiences of human beings are unreachable and unteachable. For us, cognitive and affective dimensions of experience are equally legitimate targets for education. This point also is emphasized by Fagen and Checkon (1972):

> Affective education involves teaching and learning about own and others' feelings and, like other subjects, is enhanced by the integration of ideas, feelings, and actions . . . . In our view, the major deterrent to measurement of competency in affective education derives from aversive attitudes, rather than methodological or conceptual problems. Because affective education involves more personal, often uncomfortable phenomena, it has been perceived as less accessible to measurement. It is this perception of inaccessibility that has stalled advances in measurement rather than technical obstacles. Technical issues are essentially the same for affective education as in any other educational field (p. 1).

SUMMARY

The cornerstone of our national identity and purpose is the creation and protection of individual freedom of choice. Freedom of choice, however, demands a high degree of mutual respect and self-discipline. While family and church can and do play an important role in preparing youth for future citizenship, American society has entrusted public education with the responsibility of nurturing enlightened, open-minded people.

Preparation for effective and responsible freedom of choice depends upon attainment of four conditions: awareness of existing alternatives; awareness and respect for others' reactions to these alternatives; awareness and respect for one's own reactions to these alternatives; and a reflective, rational basis for decision-making.

Our educational system has placed a higher priority and been more successful in fostering technical and career competence than it has in developing competence for making personal and interpersonal decisions. Three major educational distortions have hampered growth in the ability to choose flexibly among behavior alternatives—the crux of self-control. These distortions are externally controlled academic tasks, restrictive competition for grades and recognition, and focus on narrow academic products.

We question the assumption that enlightenment through knowledge and scholastic achievement can or will provide the means for effectively exercising freedom of choice.

We have defined self-control as one's capacity to direct and regulate personal action (behavior) flexibly and realistically in a given situation. Up to the present time, there have been no systematic educational programs focusing on the development of self-control. Such a focus requires adoption of a process-oriented approach to skill building.

Capacity for self-control is seen as a composite set of eight different skill-clusters which are identified as: Selection, Storage, Sequencing and ordering, Anticipating consequences, Appreciating feelings, Managing frustration, Inhibition and delay, and Relaxation. Each of these eight skills can be taught in the classroom, through the application of specific curriculum tasks and activities.

Taken together, the eight skills represent an integration of cognitive and affective factors which mediate possibilities for regulating action. The presence of these skills enables a learner to make personally and socially acceptable choices regarding task requirements—choices which preclude the feelings of inadequacy which so often accompany task performance or nonperformance. Through mastery of these self-control skills, the learner incorporates the necessary self-pride and respect for open-minded reflection on available alternatives.

The self-control curriculum focuses on the internal or mediating processes for skill achievement. Thus, tasks are predominantly process-oriented, with few activities requiring correct answers or narrow outputs. We affirm that inner experiences (affects or thoughts) can be treated operationally so that significant improvement can occur in process skills which mediate response outcomes.

REFERENCES

The American Assembly, Columbia University. *Goals for Americans: The Report of the President's Commission on National Goals.* Englewood Cliffs, N.J.: Prentice-Hall, 1960.

Berman, L. *New Priorities in the Curriculum.* Columbus, Ohio: Charles E. Merrill Publishing Co., 1968.

Diggory, J. *Self-Evaluation: Concepts and Studies.* New York: Wiley, 1966.

Fagen, S., and Checkon, S. "Issues in Measuring Teacher Competence for Affective Education." Paper presented at the American Educational Research Association meeting, 1972, in Chicago, Illinois.

Fagen, S., and McDonald, P. "Behavior Disruption in the Classroom: Potential of Observation for Differential Evaluation and Program Planning." *Clinical Proceedings of Children's Hospital* 25 (1969): 215–26.

Hobbs, N. "The Re-education of Emotionally Disturbed Children." In *Behavioral Science Frontiers in Education*, edited by E. Bower and W. Hollister, pp. 339–54. New York: Wiley, 1967.

Horn, F. "The Ends for Which We Educate." *Educational Forum* 28 (1964): 142–43.

Kirschenbaum, A.; Simon, S.; and Napier, R. *WAD JA GET? The Grading Game in American Education*. New York: Values Associates, 1971.

National Education Association. *The Central Purpose of American Education*. Washington, D.C.: National Education Association, 1961.

Quay, H.C.; Morse, W.C.; and Cutler, R. L. "Personality Patterns of Pupils in Special Classes for the Emotionally Disturbed." *Exceptional Children* 32 (1966): 297–301.

Rosenberg, M. *Diagnostic Teaching*. Seattle, Washington: Special Child Publications, 1968.

Smith, B. O.; Stanley, W.; and Shores, J. H. *Fundamentals of Curriculum Development*. New York: Harcourt Brace Jovanovich, 1957.

Werry, J. "The Diagnosis, Etiology, and Treatment of Hyperactivity in Children." In *Learning Disorders*, Vol. 3, edited by J. Hellmuth, Chapter 7. Seattle, Washington: Special Child Publications, 1968.

4

So then Sir Launcelot lift up the tomb, and there came out an horrible and fiendly dragon, spitting fire out of his mouth. Then Sir Launcelot drew his sword and fought with the dragon, and at the last and with great pain Sir Launcelot slew that dragon . . .

Sir Thomas Mallory, *Le More D'Arthur,* circa 1470

The Psychoeducational Curriculum Approach to Humanizing Teaching

BREAKING THE FEELING BARRIER

Much of our educational philosophy is based on the assumption that socialization means the gradual, steady process of bringing emotions under intellectual control. As simple as this notion appears, though, it has been polluted by fear and misunderstanding. One consequence of this view has been to seek to extinguish excessive emotionalism through ever-increasing intellectualization (e.g., instead of allowing affective experience to develop, we learn to start talking it away; adults idealize their mental control and feel shame at their moments of emotional release through crying, yelling, or attacking). Social rituals are developed to provide isolated opportunities for affective release (e.g., movies, plays, funerals, weddings), but these emotional moments are carefully separated off from everyday relationships and experiences. We come to overvalue being smart, using one's head, and talking about life; and we deprecate being "immature," "losing one's head," and openly displaying reactions to life.

A fundamental law of learning theory is that extinction of response is facilitated by the strengthening of an incompatible response. As mental processes are employed to evade and replace emotionality, the latter become incompatible with intellectual achievement. Disconcerted by the potential primitiveness of emotion and in love with man's intellectual greatness, we proceed to squeeze affect from us as unwanted and unnecessary. Emotional exploration is relegated to the practice of psychiatry or psychology as if they were occult disciplines, and the result is that the mental health professionals are viewed with suspicion. Today we are intellectually aware that feelings influence performance—that emotion cannot be extinguished. But, for many, emotional experience is synonymous with loss of control.

The world of education has largely been identified with the world of intellect. Scholars are viewed as being wise, knowing, intellectually precise, and exacting. Universities, colleges, and schools have been constructed as towers of thought, and they have been filled with "great minds." No wonder youths have so often felt untouched, cold, and uninvolved in educational endeavors!

In recent years, however, there has been an outcry—an appeal for humanism in educational institutions. Contrary to the view that emotional experience should be extinguished by intellectual development, proponents of humanistic education maintain that civilized behavior emerges, not from suppression of emotions, but from a functional use of those emotions in negotiating life problems. There is an exciting realization that man's intellectual superiority over animal not only permits him an expanded world of cognition but also promises him an opportunity for enlightened, enriched utilization of his emotions.

Many writers have noted man's failure to reach the fulfillment of his human potential (Maslow, 1962; Otto, 1967; Rogers, 1969; Shostrom, 1969; Torrance, 1971). One argument is that the higher, more rewarding interpersonal experiences, like love, compassion, support, and cooperation, cannot be attained until more basic biological, intrapersonal needs have been satisfied. The implication is that thwarting need impairs positive interpersonal capacities and hampers constructive emotional functioning. Psychoanalytic and social learning accounts of child development converge in agreement that extreme early deprivation experiences sharply limit successful social relationships (Bowlby, 1952; Gewirtz, 1961; Provence and Lipton, 1962).

There is a considerable body of research to indicate that serious mental and emotional handicaps may follow severe privations in physical and social need-gratification (Goldfarb, 1945; Menlove, 1965; Spitz, 1946; Spitz and Wolf, 1946). Treatment of individuals with such distressing early histories has been proven to require intense, long-term, positive relationships and massive corrective experiences to overcome past hurts. While these studies explain the problems of select cases, the widespread lack of enriched interpersonal relations among people cannot be blamed entirely on such extreme conditions. Most of us thrive in a relatively caring environment, are exposed to differences in emphasis, style, and value, and receive a fair amount of nourishment, rest, protection, stimulation, and affection. Nonetheless, all of us have been exposed to repeated frustration of our wishes, and this frustration has created a fundamental challenge to our emotional development.

Personal frustration is a natural consequence of the reality of others. Human beings would be unable to live with one another with respect for each others' rights unless individual desires were frustrated and modified to some extent. In the animal kingdom, the seeking of desired objects is often equated with life and death. In the human kingdom, the seeking of that which is wanted is associated with both joy and frustration. If we share anything as people, we share our need to dream. However, reality subjects us all to less than we would wish, and we experience this reality as painful affect.

Unfortunately, we have not learned to manage the pain of frustration very well. Our children react to frustration with outbursts of anger or tears, with withdrawal or rejection. It is commonplace to see adults counterattack such childish reactions with criticism and punishment. Emotional responses to frustration are unpleasant—this is the nature of frustration. But so vulnerable are we all to witnessing unpleasantness that we strive to curb such honest responses almost before they erupt. *What we have learned to fear in emotional reactivity is the discomfort and dissatisfaction within ourselves. If we were to become comfortable with self-experiences of frustration, we also would become more accepting of others' need to show distress.*

Without conscious efforts to learn and teach management of frustration, we are left with our natural inclination to take flight from unpleasant feelings; such flight only draws us farther away from each other. Until we are able to face ourselves and our inner discomforts, we will be unable to share deeply, to engage or trust in others. This tenet of human behavior appears to be a major factor in the widespread appeal of sensitivity and encounter groups in this country (Burton, 1969; Lakin, 1972; Rogers, 1969; Solomon and Berzon, 1972).

To advance beyond the present barriers against emotional development, we need to appreciate the following points:

1. Humanization and self-growth require the mutual use and awareness of intellect and emotion.
2. Failures in human relations often derive from reluctance to deal with pain and unpleasantness.
3. Experiences of frustration are necessary for personal development.
4. Enrichment of human relations depends upon a willingness to accept, share, and appreciate the emotional states of oneself and others.

THE PSYCHOEDUCATIONAL CURRICULUM: CONCEPT, NEED, AND FUNCTION

In the past, educational efforts have focused on impersonal subject matter and feelings have been viewed as irrelevant or interfering with learning. The movement toward affective education has turned matters upside down, however, and educating people about emotions is now regarded as a legitimate—indeed a necessary—school activity. From our point of view, affective education simply refers to "teaching and learning about self and others' feelings (emotions, values, beliefs)" (Fagen and Checkon, 1972). It is teaching that has human feelings, emotions, and interpersonal behavior as a primary subject. In other words, with or without a formal subject designation (e.g., science, home economics, mathematics), affective education is happening whenever there is a planned focus on teaching about feelings.

As was described in Chapter 3, the self-control curriculum includes four components which are regarded as being primarily cognitive and four which are considered affective. This differentiation among components derives from the definition of affective education as teaching and learning about one's own and others' feelings. Thus, Appreciating feelings, Managing frustration, Inhibition and delay, and Relaxation are all considered skills for coping with inner feelings. On the other hand, Selection, Storage, Sequencing and ordering, and Anticipating consequences are regarded as cognitively loaded skills for coping with external stimulus events.

Because we believe that teaching must follow a twin path of feelings and ideas for optimal learning to occur, we prefer to use the term "psychoeducational" to define our curriculum, even though our usage differs somewhat from meanings previously assigned to this term by others. The term appeals to us in that it is not pathology-oriented (in contrast with "clinical education") or exclusively affective (in contrast with "affective education"). At the same time, the term accents the close connection between education and psychology—the teaching of human beings and the study of human behavior.

The remaining sections of this chapter will focus on several aspects of a psychoeducational curriculum. First, we shall consider the concept itself; then, the need for such a curriculum. Finally, the functions of a psychoeducational curriculum will be discussed in relation to its rationale and guidelines.

Conceptual Attributes of a Psychoeducational Approach[1]

The concept "psychoeducational" takes an amorphous shape as it appears sporadically in the literature. Morse, Cutler, and Fink (1964) discuss the concept as a balance between educational and clinical emphases, with educational decisions made after consideration of the underlying motivation of children. Glavin (1970) characterizes the concept as focusing on the role of unconscious processes and states that ventilation and acting out of conflict should be encouraged so that new learning can occur in the presence of a "crisis teacher." Knoblock and Reinig (1971) point to the coordination of clinical and educational data to understand the child's present functioning level adequately; they place equal emphasis in the learning climate on affective and cognitive development; they recognize that group processes and dynamics are factors

[1]The material presented in this section is based upon S.A. Fagen, "A Psychoeducational Approach to Specifying and Measuring Competencies of Personnel Working with Disturbance in Schools." Paper presented at the Council for Exceptional Children meeting, 1971, in Miami Beach, Florida.

needing attention; and they advocate the premise that all learning takes place within the context of a relationship with teachers. Morse (1966) has discussed the psychoeducational team as a mechanism for collecting and interpreting information about a child and for providing consultation and support to the teaching efforts.

Perhaps the most complete statement regarding the psychoeducational model is contained in the revised edition of Long, Morse, and Newman's book (1971). These authors perceive the psychoeducational model as embracing several major assumptions:

1. An educational milieu must be developed in which attention is given to everything that affects pupil interaction with school, staff, peers, and curriculum.
2. It is important to understand the teacher-pupil relationship.
3. Learning must be invested with feelings to give it interest, meaning, and purpose.
4. Conflict can be used productively to teach new ways of understanding and coping with stress.
5. Collaborative skills are essential for teachers using the curriculum.
6. Creative arts are vital forms for learning and for the program.
7. Each pupil is different in style and functional level.
8. The same behavior can have many causes, while the same cause can be expressed through many behaviors.

Given the varied ways in which the concept has been used as well as the fact that "psychoeducational" has been interpreted as theory, methodology, and viewpoint, it is necessary to state those attributes which *we* apply to the concept. In identifying these attributes, we have sought to reflect common usage, while extending the concept for more flexible application. For example, we believe that the tendency to interpret the psychoeducational perspective as implying an exclusive cause-effect relation from emotional dysfunction to learning dysfunction severely limits appreciation for the concept's value.

The position taken here is that the *psychoeducational approach postulates a circular, interacting relationship between thoughts and feelings such that cognitive experience affects emotional experience affects cognitive experience, etc.* Thus, the child who cannot learn to read might develop intensely adverse emotional reactions to failure, while the child with severe anxiety over performance might experience great difficulty learning to read.

In essence, the following conceptual attributes identify a psychoeducational approach:

1. Cognitive and affective processes are in continuous interaction at all times.
2. Behavior comprises verbal and nonverbal expressions of a total functioning person, and it is that person, not the expression, that is most important.
3. Behavior is a source of concern when it promotes or perpetuates personal unhappiness, conflict, and self-depreciation; *or* when it creates serious disturbance with existing social norms, thereby resulting in feelings of rejection and alienation.
4. Understanding behavior means understanding phenomenally relevant aspects of a child's life space. For the teacher, this means appreciating transactions between the child and the teacher, the curriculum, the peer group, and the educational system.
5. Understanding behavior requires an awareness of cognitive, affective, and motivational processes in self and others.
6. Understanding behavior is achieved through assessment of and communication with and about the learner and significant others in his life space.
7. Changing or modifying self-defeating behavior involves a process of establishing identifiable objectives which are set in relation to total personal functioning.
8. Understanding behavior facilitates creating conditions for optimal behavior change.
9. The ultimate criterion for personal growth is the extent to which positive behavior derives from *self-control* rather than external control.
10. Emotions are critical personal events that must become understood, accepted, and valued.

11. The scope of learning involves increasing understanding and satisfactions in relationship to things, symbols, the self, and others.

The Need for Psychoeducational Curricula

Traditionally, psychologists have placed relatively greater weight on motivational-emotional factors than on education; education, on the other hand, has been concerned primarily with the development of intellect. In more recent years, a campaign has been mounted within educational circles to embrace the value of personal motives and to release the headlock on academic content. Movements to individualize instruction, humanize education, and promote affective learning all share in being part of the backlash against impersonal, noncontact teaching.

In their pamphlet "Toward a Contact Curriculum," Fantini and Weinstein (1969) convincingly advocate moving from an "emphasis solely on cognitive, extrinsic content" to "an equal emphasis on affective, inner content" (p. 54). Fantini and Weinstein make a clear commitment to precluding a psychologically sterile educational approach:

> It is our general hypothesis that what makes the most contact is that which is the most "relevant" . . . and which makes a connection between the affective or feeling aspects and the cognitive or conceptualizing aspects of the learner. (p. 55)

Combs (1967) expresses a similar sentiment when he says:

> The goal of education must be self-actualization, the production of persons willing and able to interact with the world in intelligent ways. To achieve that end, educators must concern themselves with both halves of the equation: the person and the world, the learner and the subject. Unbalanced concern with either half can destroy the very ends we seek (p. vi).

It at last appears that the interaction of affect and cognition has been recognized. The community of feelings and emotions has been accorded first-class citizenship. Certainly this was the intent of Krathwohl, Bloom, and Masia's monumental effort (1964) in proposing a taxonomy of educational objectives for the affective domain to match the respect paid earlier to objectives in the cognitive domain (Bloom, 1956). In discussing the simultaneous achievement of cognitive and affective goals, these authors graphically depict a closely interactive relationship.

> Perhaps it is analogous to a man scaling a wall using two step ladders side by side, each with rungs too wide apart to be conveniently reached in a single step. One ladder represents the cognitive behaviors and objectives, the other the affective. The ladders are so constructed that the rungs of one ladder fall between the rungs of the other. The attainment of some complex goal is made possible by alternately climbing a rung on one ladder, which brings the next rung of the other ladder within reach (p. 60).*

Kelly (1965) adopts a similar position in an editorial for *Educational Leadership* (1965):

> Subject matter and feeling are so closely intertwined that they can no longer be considered a duality. Everyone who learns something has some feeling about it, and so, as in so many other areas, they are inseparable. No matter what we do, affective learning goes on anyway. When this affective learning is positive, the learner becomes constructive in his behavior (p. 455).

George Brown (1971) makes the same point in his book *Human Teaching for Human Learning*. He introduces the term "confluent education" to explain "the integration or flowing together of the affective and cognitive elements in individual and group learning" (p. 3). For Brown, the term "affective" refers to the feeling or emotional aspect of experience and learning and to the learning of attitudes or values. "Cognitive" refers to intellectual functioning, including subject content learned and the intellectual process required for learning. Brown notes that ". . . there is no intellectual learning without some sort of feeling, and there are no feelings without the mind's being somehow involved" (p. 4).

We have been motivated in the present effort to develop a psychoeducational curriculum for teaching self-control by our strong conviction that learning experiences which integrate cognitive and affective processes are desperately needed for children to develop into beautiful human beings.

---

*Used with permission of the publisher.

The Function of a Psychoeducational Curricula

The basic function of a psychoeducational curriculum is to provide for planned learning situations which stimulate two major personal developments: constructive expression of affective experience and integration of facts and feelings. Such a curriculum must include clear statements of teacher goals (which can be translated into learner objectives), specific learning activities, and a variety of teaching strategies for building interest and self-esteem. Furthermore, each of these curriculum parameters must be consistent with, and facilitating of, the major dimensions (i.e., constructive expression of affective experience and integration of facts and feelings).

The next two sections of this chapter will provide background, meaning, and purpose for building these two dimensions into curriculum.

THE CONSTRUCTIVE EXPRESSION OF AFFECTIVE EXPERIENCE

As we have already noted, the landmark volume *Taxonomy of Educational Objectives, Handbook II: Affective Domain* makes a compelling case for viewing learning as a process to be facilitated by the interaction of cognitive and affective domains. For example, in order for affective objectives to proceed from "responding" to "valuing" to "organization" to "characterization," there must be an exploration and crystallization of feelings.[2] This fact is particularly evident at the "organization" point in the affective hierarchy since at this level, "there is an attempt to provide the child a conscious base for making choices. Thus he will be able to defend his choices if

---

[2]The Affective Domain of the *Taxonomy of Educational Objectives* sets forth five levels of objectives. The five objectives represent a theoretical continuum describing the "process by which a given phenomena or value passes from a level of bare awareness to a *position of some power to guide* or control the behavior of a person" (p. 27). The authors regard this process as one of "internalization" (Krathwohl, Bloom, and Masia, 1964).

Level 1 on the continuum is the category of "receiving" (attending), which consists of awareness, willingness to receive, and controlled or selected attention. Level 2 is "responding," which involves acquiescence in responding, willingness to respond, and satisfaction in response. The Level 3 objective is "valuing" and comprises acceptance of a value, preference for a value, and commitment. Level 4 is "organization" and can be subdivided into two categories, conceptualization of a value and organization of a value system. The highest level of internalization is considered to be "characterization by a value or value complex."

challenged and will know the basis of his attitude regarding what is good" (p. 155). Implicit in this objective is the notion that one should be able to expose personal feelings and convictions to others without fear of defeat or wrongdoing.

Unfortunately, the affective objectives presented by Krathwohl, Bloom, and Masia are quite limited since they are focused exclusively on personal investment in belief or ideology. Thus, affect enables children to enrich, solidify, and expand their ideas to the point of developing an enduring, coherent, characteristic personal philosophy. This hardening of ideology through affective commitment bypasses the use of affective experience for constructive interpersonal relations. Although the authors obviously intend for progress in the affective domain to assure humanitarian involvement (e.g., "We want the student to lead the good life and become a good man in all his parts"), the criteria for "characterization" (p. 172) (the highest level in the affective domain) could easily be satisfied by a well-organized dictator or fascist. If these standards alone are applied, Hitler, Mussolini, Machiavelli, and Stalin could easily be regarded as having achieved the ultimate in the affective domain.[3]

It is not our intent to depreciate the importance of Krathwohl, Bloom, and Masia's work, for it has stimulated an increased interest and regard for the affective aspect in education. This occurrence is extremely important; furthermore, we agree with the authors' statement that:

> The affective domain contains the forces that determine the nature of an individual's life and ultimately the life of an entire people. To keep the "box" closed is to deny the existence of the powerful motivational forces that shape the life of each of us. To look the other way is to avoid coming to terms with the real (p. 91).*

However, from our point of view, the meaning of teaching in the affective domain includes more than degree of investment in one's ideas or knowledge. It also includes awareness, acknowledgement, expression, and management of one's feelings; it includes constructive coping with the pain of inner life as well as experiencing the joy of sharing loving affect.

---

[3] "*Characterization By a Value or Value Complex.* At this level of internalization the values already have a place in the individual's value hierarchy, are organized into some kind of internally consistent system, have controlled the behavior of the individual for a sufficient time that he has adopted to behaving this way; and an evocation of the behavior no longer arouses emotion or affect except when the individual is threatened or challenged" (p. 184) (Krathwohl, Bloom and Masia, 1964).

*Used with permission of the publisher

"In-touchness" with self and others is what we all desire. Yet the forces within us which provide identity, uniqueness, and freedom also struggle to ward off the suffocation of mass living and depersonalized technology. Shocking reports of interpersonal callousness, deceit, and manipulation abound. In our age of powerful threats to existence, the rush to gain personal power and control sometimes seems unrestrained by more traditional norms for compromise and respect for others. Yet there are other rumblings as well. Never before have so many people sought out experiences of group intimacy. Never before have so many called for integrity in national leadership. And never before have so many yearned for reform in social institutions from government to industry to schools.

Many critics of today's societal happenings have become sufficiently disenchanted to give up on existing organizational systems. In education, we have heard cries of hopelessness from some of our colleagues about prospects for significant improvement in public education. A host of dramatic critiques have appeared, such as Goodman's *Compulsory Mis-Education* (1964), Hentoff's *Our Children Are Dying* (1966), Kozol's *Death at an Early Age* (1968), Silberman's *Crisis in the Classroom* (1970), and Reimer's *School Is Dead* (1971).

At the same time, moderate voices sincerely advocate the possibility of educational responsiveness, as exemplified by John Goodlad's proposal that curriculum change from "discipline-centered" to "total curriculum" to "humanistic curriculum" (1966). Moreover, there is evidence of a growing willingness to encourage innovation and experimentation in formulating humanistic educational goals and activities (Allen, 1971; Klopf, 1972; Shedd, Newberg, and Delone, 1971; Williams 1969; Ylvisaker, 1972).

Despite the current recognition of need, there continues to be a shortage of programmatic efforts to prepare children to cope with human emotions and interpersonal communication. Thus, Richard (1970) reports: "A recent survey of several curriculum guides for use with behaviorally disordered children showed less than five percent of their potential curriculum materials pertained to personal growth and human relations activities" (p. 3). And this paucity of emphasis exists in regard to the very children who need affective development the most!

There have been some encouraging attempts to provide learning situations which promote constructive affective expression (Borton,

1970; Brown, 1971; Lyon, 1971; Newberg, 1969; Stenhouse, 1971).[4] On the whole, however, direct introduction of affective events into the school day as a part of a purposeful program of instruction is still practically nonexistent.

The most logical reason for this lag between stated needs and programs of action resides in the fact that there are few educationally oriented professionals or parents who are both knowledgeable and comfortable in dealing with the sphere of feelings. Direct experience in this area is most likely to be found with clinicians or counselors, and these specialists generally are not available to invest time in curriculum development. In contrast, classroom teachers and university professors, while keenly interested in curriculum planning, typically have had only limited exposure to emotional expression. As a consequence, the classroom has not been perceived as an appropriate and comfortable laboratory for learning about the feelings of self and others.[5]

It is strikingly clear that ventures into the realm of affective experience in the classroom should be conceived carefully and explained fully to teachers *prior* to implementation. The gap between the recognized need for teaching constructive expression of affective experiences and implementation of programs to meet this

---

[4] Newberg (1969) and Borton (1970) describe a process-oriented approach used in the Philadelphia school system which attempts to meet three student needs: developing a positive self-concept, fostering meaningful interpersonal relations, and creating a sense of control and power over one's destiny. The Newberg-Borton affective education curriculum is remarkably consistent with our self-control curriculum in purpose but focuses on different specific processes.

Brown (1971) and Lyon (1971) offer a wide range of affective techniques for classroom use. Although most of the exercises suggested for increasing self-awareness seem more appropriate for older rather than younger children, the model for integrating affective experience with subject or lesson content is quite helpful.

In our terms, these innovations do represent psychoeducational curriculum efforts. In particular, the work of Newberg and Borton can readily be generalized to youngsters in elementary and junior high schools.

[5] A recent event in an in-service seminar illustrates this point well. During a visit by one of the authors to a teacher's classroom, he had occasion to lead the teacher's third-grade class into a semistructured discussion of prevalent fears in the pupils' lives, including anxieties regarding adult burglaries and violence. At a subsequent training session with teachers employing the self-control curriculum, several of the teachers animatedly expressed the feeling that they had always wanted to talk about such realities with their children but were reluctant to do so for fear of making matters worse. After seeing that such discussion was obviously important and helpful to the children, these teachers stated a desire to deal more directly with their students' feelings in the future.

need is symptomatic of educators' existing apprehensions about dealing with feelings in the classroom. Establishing a positive attitude toward building affective experience into the curriculum appears to be an essential first step. Such an outlook is more likely to exist when there is a clear understanding of the value in accepting and expressing feelings. Chapter 10, "Appreciating Feelings," and Chapter 11, "Managing Frustration," describe specific teaching activities and sequences which are designed to achieve constructive expression of affective experience.

The Value of Acceptance and Expression of Feelings

There are several important ways in which the acceptance and expression of affect carries value and significance.

Acceptance and expression of one's own feelings can provide an alternative to destructive behavior: As one's capacity to acknowledge and retain feelings consciously grows, there is a concomitant reduction in the need to depersonalize or "deindividuate." As Zimbardo (1969) has shown, human motivation includes powerful impulse- and disorder-prone forces which seek to find release under conditions of relative anonymity or group immersion. Groups often take on major importance as vehicles for expression of underlying impulses which individuals have difficulty managing alone.

For example, Paul is troubled by his destructive feelings toward school and knows that it would be wrong to damage school property. However, he suddenly finds himself in a group of boys who are roaming the school yard for excitement. One boy picks up a rock and hurls it through a window yelling, "Take that, mother. . . ." Soon the assault on windows, doors, and walls is being shared by all the group, including Paul. How comforting it must be to Paul to discover that other fellows harbor feelings of destructiveness toward school. Furthermore, in acting out against the school in a collective action, Paul's group gains cohesion.

Encouraging personal verbal expression of feelings connected with unacceptable behavior is a healthy alternative to group or individual acting out. The more one can "live with himself," the less he needs to release hidden parts of himself in deindividualized situations.

Acceptance and expression of one's own feelings can promote new, positive learning: By directly expressing emotions in words, the individual opens up possibilities for feedback and new assessment of information. In contrast, indirect manifestations and avoidance of feelings close off possibilities for new learning and set conditions for perpetuating old biases.

This point becomes particularly striking when emotion is considered from a cognitive or perceptual outlook. In this case, emotion is viewed as a result, not a cause, of cognitive activity and as being subject to change—providing that perceptions are assessed openly (Lazarus, 1966; Leeper, 1965). It is not that intellect and emotion are separate functions but, rather, that emotions inevitably accompany meaningful perceptions. Instead of thinking in terms of an emotional reaction as opposed to an intellectual one, Lazarus prefers to say that: "This is an irrational reaction, based on incorrect facts, or an incorrect assessment of the facts" (p. 252). A similar point is made by Leeper: ". . . it seems that all perceptual habits can be modified by learning and that sometimes such modifications can occur suddenly and dramatically. If emotional habits are perceptual habits, these same possibilities should exist for them" (p. 115).

Thus, direct expressions of feeling can provide data for responses from others which may alter existing cognitions. For example, Suzy says she's "mad because you lied to me." Following a brief dialogue with the teacher, Suzy learns she was mistaken in thinking that when the teacher said, "I'd be glad to have your help," she meant she would appreciate such help at any time, in any way (e.g., in marking the other students' papers).

A strong initial perception often precludes the development of alternative perceptions. For example, "I feel lonely because no one likes me" generates behavior which holds others at a distance and supports the initial perception, unless the reality of the belief is exposed so that different feedback becomes possible.

The acceptance of feelings which are expressed indirectly through nonverbal or obtuse means often can be facilitated by verbalizing a likely emotional response to that situation. Thus, a child who is reluctant to enter into noisy activities can be helped by such remarks as: "It's sometimes hard to get into new things"; "It takes a while to get used to a lot of noise"; or "Loud sounds can be scary sometimes." In this case, the initiative for building acceptance and expression of affect comes from outside the child having the feeling. Here, another person's appropriate expression of a feeling the child likely is having about that situation can accomplish two purposes: increase the child's acceptance of his affective reaction, since it is acceptable (understandable) to the other, or present new information which can lower any anxiety associated with the situation.

Acceptance and expression of one's feelings can allow for an awareness and increase of more constructive and satisfying affect: Negative or unacceptable feelings are common by-products of frustration in achieving positive desires. Rather than focusing on the defect or failure aspects of the situation, one's response to negative affect expression can highlight the constructive elements which originally created vulnerability. For example, the child might say: "I feel sad because I couldn't finish the book." The teacher's response could be: "Reading has really become very important to you, hasn't it?" Or the child might say: "I feel angry because nobody wanted to play with me." The teacher might respond: "It's hard to take being left out when you care about being with others."

Admittedly, the outcome of the feelings expressed in these examples depends upon the other person's response. As in all cases, if honest expression of feelings is followed by hostile remarks, the outcome will be increased defensiveness and mistrust. The main point, however, is that expressed feelings can reveal positive dimensions even when they are couched in the form of disappointment and discouragement. In addition there is an important corollary to this identification of frustrated positive desires in that children need help in seeing that life involves many unavoidable disappointments. Almost every negative affect has its roots in the thwarting of constructive human goals. Table 1 portrays this relationship between thwarted desire and feeling.

We are suggesting that exploration into the world of feelings can lead to the discovery of fundamental human desires which are continuously being partially attained and partially frustrated. Entangled with frustration is gratification; thus, in the revelation of one's negative affects lies a powerful source of concern for positive investments in self, others, and the environment.

Many educators and parents are fearful of providing school experiences which stimulate release of affective expressions. They are apprehensive that opening the classroom to affective expression will unleash destructive, uncontrollable impulses or disrupt learning by unproductive flights into fantasy. While it is essential that the stimulation of feelings be handled with care, there is an undeniable need to build in emotional education, for a total curriculum, one that

Table 1: *Relationship of Feeling States to Thwarted Desires*

Feeling	*Thwarted Desire for*
Resentment and feeling of neglect	Involvement with others
Withholding of effort and discouragement	Appreciation of effort
Rejection and coldness	Affection and warmth
Alienation and isolation	Friendship
Inferiority and despair	Mastery and competence
Helplessness and defeat	Autonomy and self-pride
Hostility	Love
Rebellion and defiance	Respect and inclusion

meets the human needs of all learners, must include knowledge and experience pertaining to things, symbols, self, and others. The concept of a psychoeducational curriculum requires that real time be provided for learning in each of these areas.

Certainly the work of Bessell and Palomares (1970); Borton (1970); Brown (1971); Raths, Harmin, and Simon (1966); Weinstein (1971); and others indicates that public education is slowly beginning to recognize the potential and feasibility of teaching to affective needs. Once we face up to the fact that verbal expression of feelings is not wrong or shameful and that our emotions hinge upon basic perceptions and beliefs about ourselves in relation to others, we will have cleared the way for truly meaningful education.

Acceptance and expression of feelings can facilitate mutual understanding and problem solving: A strong resistance to seeking out or listening to another's feelings about things often derives from anxiety about becoming overinvolved or being inadequate to help. This anxiety results from approaching listening to the expression of feelings with the expectation that listening means taking responsibility for altering circumstances. We think that when someone reveals his problems or concerns to us, especially if he does so by invitation, we need to be responsible for helping to work those problems out. Yet we are painfully aware of our own limited resources and may not want to sacrifice ourselves to somebody else or mistakenly take them down a path of false promises.

Defining the role of listening this way fosters an unwillingness to include exchange of feelings in teacher-child relationships. Teachers traditionally have perceived their role as one of imparting knowledge and facts to children, and they realize that informed, factual responses are not possible when dealing in the realm of feeling expressions. Instead, teachers must redefine their role so that facilitation of self-understanding and self-respect becomes a prized function.

Unpleasant feelings are an inevitable part of our reality. When it becomes permissible to share these feelings in the classroom, several possibilities open for new learning, none of which depends upon the teacher's taking over responsibility. For example, by providing the conditions for mutual listening to real feelings, the teacher permits: an increased likelihood of understanding the student, greater involvement by the student in the classroom, the possibility for modifying the environment so that it more closely meets the student's needs, student participation in suggesting or planning modifications, increased awareness and acceptance of reality frustrations, consideration of feedback which may modify initial perceptions and associated feelings, and possible shifts in student goals or desires to a more realistic and attainable level.

INTEGRATION OF COGNITIVE AND AFFECTIVE EVENTS

For any cognitive material to be acquired and retained, it must be incorporated as a desired personal possession. This point is emphasized by Long (1969): "Learning must be invested with feeling to give it interest, meaning, and purpose" (p. 370). This acquisition and application of cognitive information is enhanced by its personal relevance (i.e., by the nature of one's feelings in the learning situation). Thus, the relationship between feeling and learning seems to follow at least three general principles:

1. *Positive feelings about the subject matter enhance learning.* For example, if one desires to travel, explore the world, or

have a reunion with a distant relative, interest in geography might be keen (see Rhodes, 1965).

2. *Subjects associated with positive self-esteem are more easily learned.* For example, if a child thinks he is good at history or mathematics, he learns that subject matter best (see Purkey, 1970).

3. *Positive feelings about the teacher enhance learning of the material presented in that situation* (see Gorman, 1969).

There are many times when seemingly impersonal information cannot be learned because of painful feelings it arouses in the immediate situation. For example, suppose that a child's anxiety over aggression is strong. In such a case, any subject associated closely with aggression, such as war, hunting, fighting, or dissection, is likely to heighten already existing anxiety. Jones (1968) describes a classroom incident in which children were unable to attend to the instructional content of a lesson on hunting habits of the Eskimos after being exposed to some very bloody hunting scenes from *Man: A Course of Study*. It is to be expected that when students are struggling to resolve unsettling feelings or experiencing strong feelings which they are not allowed to express, learning will be impeded.

There is a difference between blocking the opportunity for affective release and offering material which the child is unable to accept. In both cases, learning of the material is impaired; however, the teacher can observe the effects of anxiety in the group when emotional expression is blocked (e.g., restlessness, widespread noise, silly antics, inattention) and alleviate these affects by seeking open reactions associated with the task or material being presented. In this situation, it is not the student who is avoiding the issue but the teacher; by providing for feeling expression, the teacher meets an existing need for that expression.

Some Guidelines for Stimulating Affective Responses in the Classroom

Many educators are concerned about instances where the teacher might open things up for discussion when a need for expression is not so obvious. We have heard much about the adverse outcomes of stripping away defenses and flooding people with emotional responses (see Back, 1972). This is a serious point to consider—one for which comfort must exist if emotional expression is to become a facilitating experience. Therefore, several guidelines need to be established in considering any process for stimulating emotional responses in the classroom:

Issues should be central enough to assure relevance to most members of the group: For example, one should be able to discuss topics that are of primary concern to the students, whether the feelings are about fighting, school rules, arrangement of furniture, or the bases for friendship. Goldman (1969) makes a similar point in saying that "schools become relevant only to the extent that they are able to establish a connection between a student's search for self and their own efforts in his behalf" (p. 154). Although it is not possible to identify in the abstract precisely which issues are central for a particular class or subgroup within a class (for that depends on the particular state of the learners), the point must be kept in mind.

No individual should be pressured to respond or to divulge his feelings: Teacher or peers might question one another out of interest, but an explicit norm should be established for the "right to privacy" or the "right to pass."

It should be recognized that participation by pupils may be verbal, nonverbal, or vicarious: Students can be learning without saying or doing anything. The right to be silent, to listen, and to observe should be respected at all times. The watchful member is often learning more about emotions and acceptance of them (including his own) than is the rapid talker.

Practice with more personal and less anxiety-laden issues should be provided before taking up any directly personal or high-anxiety issues: For example, feelings about television, the weather, sports, etc., can be introduced before beginning to talk about feelings about parents, teacher, or other students. In this way, students can first learn that differences are acceptable, that retaliation or hurt is not a consequence of honest expression, and that feelings are not right or wrong.

The teacher should continually reiterate that feelings can be pleasant or unpleasant and enjoyable or painful, but he should emphasize that they are never bad or wrong: A clear distinction should be made between a person's right to own any and all feelings and his responsibility to place limits on acting on his feelings.

Feelings are most usefully introduced by focusing on some present event, experience, or issue: Questions introduced by: "How do you feel when . . .?" or "What thoughts or feelings do you have . . .?" or "When do you feel that way?" are preferable to questions in the past tense.

Moments for expression of feeling should be interwoven with cognitive, recreational, or social activities in the classroom: Meaningful feelings can be expressed on any subject at any time of day. Although this self-control curriculum describes structured tasks for developing an appreciation for feelings and for managing feelings of frustration, we do not mean to imply that feelings should only be permitted during certain specific activities. Brief, structured activities which promote affective expression are particularly important at an early point in the introduction of feelings into the classroom. Gradually, however, children and teacher will want to explore feelings as they occur, either on a planned or spontaneous basis, within other parts of the program.

In *Fantasy and Feeling in Education,* Jones (1968) addresses himself to teacher concerns that stimulation of emotions in classrooms will be threatening to children. He notes that many lessons, particularly those in the humanities or social studies, can be intended to confront students with true reflections of life (e.g., the Boston Tea Party, the death of Lincoln) and will stimulate emotions and fantasies naturally. Going a step farther, Jones notes that in many cases, a lesson which *cannot* threaten children *will not* stimulate them. The following quotation from his book conveys a basic point of view which we share with him:

> . . . a feeling, or image, that cannot be controlled is frightening; a feeling, or image, that cannot be shared is estranging; a feeling, or image, that cannot be put to work is belittling. These conditions do threaten children. But do not blame these conditions, when they exist, on the stimuli. Blame them, instead, on the teacher who lets it be feared that anything transpiring under her guidance could get out of control; or who has failed to create an atmosphere in which the children may choose to share their feelings and private thoughts, free of the illusion that this must lead to acting them out; or, worse, whose command of her subject matter is so shallow as to be unable to see the relevance to it of all possible human feelings and images (p. 245).

SUMMARY

Much like the myth of Sir Launcelot and the dragon, formal education has perpetrated a myth of intellectual control which calls for extinguishing imagined, wild, and dangerous forces of emotion. This common fear of confronting feelings in ourselves and others has created an almost impenetrable barrier to self-other relations and the humanization of education. If we are to advance beyond our longstanding impasse with the world of feelings, there can be no further avoidance of dealing directly with the dragon of feeling—in our personal lives, in our interpersonal relationships, and in our classrooms.

In the past decade, a widening recognition of the critical need for humanizing teaching has occurred. Unfortunately, action to this end has lagged far behind philosophy and intellectual acceptance. The growing movement toward affective education promises to bridge this value gap between verbalization and action. However, the affective education thrust requires sensitive channeling into the realities of school environments, with full consideration for the needs of teachers and administrators.

We suggest that the concept of a psychoeducational curriculum can promote the desired balance and interaction between cognitive and affective priorities. Both the attributes of this psychoeducational concept and the need for psychoeducational curricula have been described in this chapter. In addition, the function of a psychoeducational curriculum has been described in terms of providing planned learning situations which stimulate two major personal developments: constructive expression of affective experience and integration of facts and feelings. The remainder of this chapter has been devoted to providing background, meaning, and purpose for building these two dimensions into school curriculum.

Progress toward inclusion of constructive expression of affective experience as an educational objective is enhanced by greater appreciation for the value of accepting and expressing feelings. The value of acceptance and expression was discussed in relation to four outcomes: increased personal security and stability; new, positive learning; more constructive and satisfying affect; and mutual understanding and problem solving.

The concluding portion of this chapter dealt with the importance of bringing about an integration of cognitive and affective events. Because of the existence of serious and valid concerns about irresponsible stimulation of human emotions, it is necessary to establish guidelines for professional behavior. Seven points were suggested as guidelines for any process to stimulate emotional responses in the classroom. While we do not regard *these* particular guidelines as inviolate or complete, we feel strongly that the myth of the dragon can only be dispelled after increased comfort and understanding is reached. In contrast to the masses of King Arthur's days who had their Sir Launcelot, we have only each other.

Part II of this book provides the content and activities which comprise the self-control curriculum.

REFERENCES

Allen, D. "The Seven Deadly Myths of Education." *Psychology Today* 4 (1971): 71–72; 100.

Back K. *Beyond Words: The Story of Sensitivity Training and the Encounter Movement.* New York: Russell Sage, 1972.

Bessell, H., and Palomares, U. *Methods in Human Development.* San Diego, California: Human Development Training Institute, 1970.

Bloom, B. *Taxonomy of Educational Objectives, Handbook I: Cognitive Domain.* New York: McKay, 1956.

Borton, T. *Reach, Touch, and Teach.* New York: McGraw-Hill, 1970.

Bowlby, J. "Maternal Care and Mental Health." *World Health Organization Monograph* Number 2, 1952.

Brown, G. *Human Teaching for Human Learning: An Introduction to Confluent Education.* New York: Viking Press, 1971.

Burton, Arthur, editor. *Encounter.* San Francisco: Tossey-Bass, 1969.

Combs, A. W. "Humanizing Education: The Person in the Process." In *Humanizing Education*, edited by R. R. Leeper, pp. 73–88. Washington, D.C.: Association for Supervision of Curriculum Development, 1967.

Fagen, S. A. "A Psychoeducational Approach to Specifying and Measuring Competencies of Personnel Working with Disturbance in Schools." Paper presented at the Council for Exceptional Children meeting, 1971, in Miami Beach, Florida.

Fagen, S. A., and Checkon, S. "Issues in Measuring Teacher Competence for Affective Education." Paper presented at the American Educational Research Association meeting, 1972, in Chicago, Illinois.

Fantini, M., and Weinstein, G. "Toward a Contact Curriculum." New York: B'nai Brith, 1969.

Gewirtz, J. L. "A Learning Analysis of the Effects of Normal Stimulation, Privation, and Deprivation on the Acquisition of Social Motivation and Attachment." In *Determinants of Infant Behavior*, edited by B. M. Foss, pp. 213–90. New York: Wiley, 1961.

Glavin, J. "New Directions in Research on Emotionally Disturbed Children." Paper presented to Special Study Institute on Planning Research on

Education of Disturbed Children, September 24–26, 1970, at Peabody College, Nashville, Tennessee.

Goldfarb, W. "Psychological Privation in Infancy and Subsequent Adjustment," *American Journal of Orthopsychiatry* 15 (1945): 247–55.

Goldman, S. "The Question of Relevancy." In *Designing Education for the Future*, edited by E. Morphet and D. Jesser, pp. 148–56. New York: Citation Press, 1969.

Goodlad, J. "Directions of Curriculum Change." *NEA Journal* 55 (1966): 33–37.

Goodman, P. *Compulsory Mis-Education*. New York: Horizon, 1964.

Gorman, A. H. *Teachers and Learners: The Interactive Process in Education*. Boston: Allyn & Bacon, 1969.

Hentoff, N. *Our Children Are Dying*. New York: Viking Press, 1966.

Jones, R. M. *Fantasy and Feeling in Education*. New York: New York University Press, 1968.

Kelly, E. "Editorial: The Place for Affective Learning." *Educational Leadership* 22 (1965): 455–57.

Klopf, G. "Preface to Leadership Roles in Educational Innovation." *Journal of Research and Development in Education* 5 (1972): 1.

Knoblock, P., and Reinig, J. *Special Project Report: Preparing Psychoeducators for Inner-City Teaching*. Syracuse, New York: Syracuse University, Division of Special Education and Rehabilitation, 1971.

Kozol, J. *Death at an Early Age*. New York: Bantam Books, 1968.

Krathwohl, D.; Bloom, B.; and Masia, B. *Taxonomy of Educational Objectives. Handbook II: Affective Domain*. New York: McKay, 1964.

Lakin, M. *Interpersonal Encounter: Theory and Practice in Sensitivity Training*. New York: McGraw-Hill, 1972.

Lazarus, R. S. *Psychological Stress and the Coping Process*. New York: McGraw-Hill, 1966.

Leeper, R. "Some Needed Developments in the Motivational Theory of Emotions." *Nebraska Symposium on Motivation* 13 (1965): 25–122.

Long, N. J., and staff. "Helping Children Cope with Feelings." *Childhood Education* 45 (1969): 367–72.

Long. N.J.; Morse, W.; and Newman, R., editors. *Conflict in the Classroom*. 2d ed. Belmont, California: Wadsworth, 1971.

Lyon, H. *Learning to Feel—Feeling to Learn*. Columbus, Ohio: Charles E. Merrill Publishing Co., 1971.

Maslow, A. *Toward a Psychology of Being*. Princeton: Van Nostrand, 1962.

Menlove, F. L. "Aggressive Symptoms in Emotionally Disturbed Adopted Children." *Child Development* 36 (1965): 519–32.

Morse, W. "Public Schools and the Disturbed Child." In *Intervention Approaches in Educating Emotionally Disturbed Children*, edited by P. Knoblock, pp. 113–28. Syracuse: Syracuse University Press, 1966.

Morse, W.; Cutler, R.; and Fink, A. *Public School Classes for the Emotionally Handicapped: A Research Analysis*. Washington, D.C.: Council for Exceptional Children, 1964.

Newberg, N. "The Impact of Affective Education in the Philadelphia School System." In *New Directions in Psychological Education* (Educational Opportunities Forum), edited by A. Alschuler, pp. 33–47. Albany: New York State Department of Education, 1969.

Otto, H. *A Guide to Developing Your Potential*. New York: Scribner's, 1967.

Provence, S., and Lipton, R. *Infants in Institutions*. New York: International University, 1962.

Purkey, W. *Self-Concept and School Achievement*. Englewood Cliffs, New Jersey: Prentice-Hall, 1970.

Raths, L.; Harmin, M.; and Simon, S. *Values and Teaching: Working with Values in the Classroom*. Columbus, Ohio: Charles E. Merrill Publishing Co., 1966.

Reimer, E. *School Is Dead: An Essay on Alternatives in Education*. Garden City, New York: Doubleday, 1971.

Rhodes, W. C. "Curriculum and Disordered Behavior." In *Conflict in the Classroom*, 2d ed., edited by N. J. Long; W. Morse; and R. Newman, pp. 405–10. Belmont, California: Wadsworth, 1971.

Richard, W. "Research on the Development and Use of Classroom Materials for the Improvement of Personal and Social Adjustment among Elementary School Children with Behavioral Disorders." Paper presented at Special Study Institute on Planning Research on the Education of Emotionally Disturbed Children, September 24–26, 1970, at Peabody College, in Nashville, Tennessee.

Rogers, C. *Freedom to Learn*. Columbus, Ohio: Charles E. Merrill Publishing Co., 1969.

———. "The T-Group Comes of Age." *Psychology Today* 3 (1969): 27.

Shedd, M.; Newberg, N.: and Delone, R. "Yesterday's Curriculum/Today's World: Time to Reinvent the Wheel." In *The Curriculum: Retrospect and Prospect*, Part I, Yearbook of the National Society for the Study of Education, edited by R. M. McClure, pp. 153–80. Chicago: University of Chicago, 1971.

Shostrom, E. *Man the Manipulator*. New York: McGraw-Hill, 1969.

Silberman, C. *Crisis in the Classroom*. New York: Random House, 1970.

Solomon, L., and Berzon, B., editors. *New Perspectives on Encounter Groups*. San Francisco: Jossey-Bass, 1972.

Spitz, R. "Hospitalism: An Inquiry into the Genesis of Psychiatric Conditions in Early Childhood: A Follow-up Report." *The Psychoanalytic Study of the Child* 2 (1946): 113–17.

Spitz, R., and Wolf, K. "Anaclitic Depression." *The Psychoanalytic Study of the Child* 2 (1946): 313–42.

Stenhouse, L. "The Humanities Curriculum Project: The Rationale." *Theory into Practice* 10 (1971): 154–62.

Torrance, E. P. *Encouraging Creativity in the Classroom*. Dubuque, Iowa: Brown, 1971.

Weinstein, G. "The Trumpet: A Guide to Humanistic Psychological Curriculum." *Theory into Practice* 10 (1971): 196–203.

Williams, F. "Models for Encouraging Creativity in the Classroom by Integrating Cognitive-Affective Behaviors." *Educational Technology* 9 (1969): 7.

Ylvisaker, P. "Beyond '72: Strategies for Schools." *Saturday Review of Education* 55 (1972): 33–34.

Zimbardo, P. G. "The Human Choice: Individualization, Reason, and Order versus Deindividualization, Impulse, and Chaos." *Nebraska Symposium on Motivation* 17 (1969): 237–307.

PART TWO

The Self-Control Curriculum

5

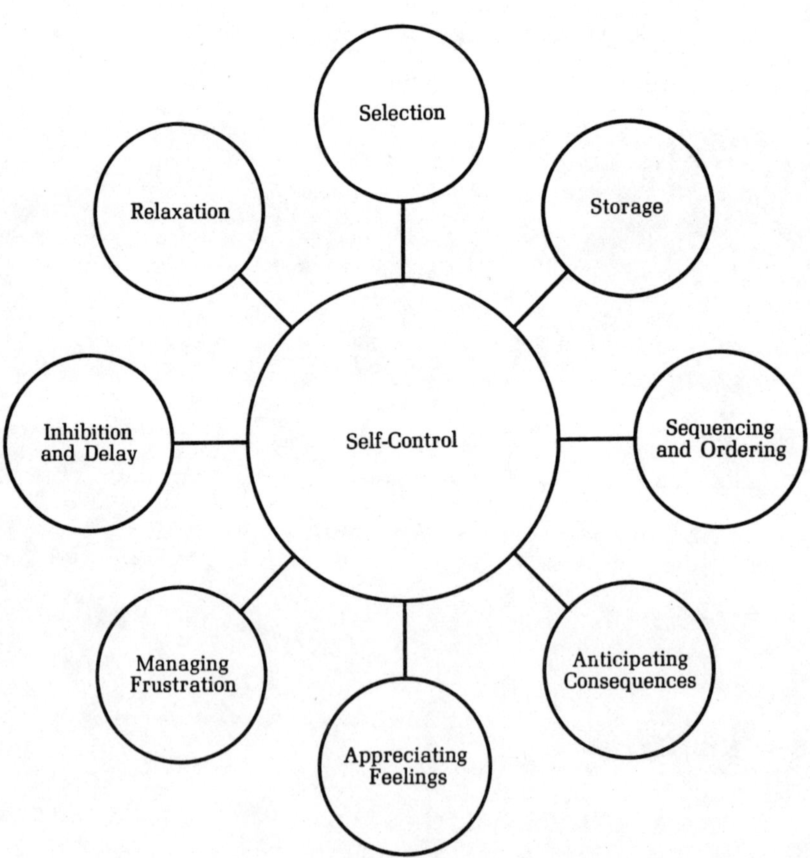
Selection
Relaxation
Storage
Inhibition and Delay
Self-Control
Sequencing and Ordering
Managing Frustration
Anticipating Consequences
Appreciating Feelings

Overview of the Self-Control Curriculum

INTRODUCTION TO THE SELF-CONTROL CURRICULUM

Frost and Rowland (1969), who consider the most appropriate function of an educator to be "a guide to knowledge," state, "The teacher is responsible for the ultimate behavior of his students, and therefore must see to it that his charges achieve the necessary behavioral controls and means of communication for ultimate assimilation into society" (p. 35). While we feel that this statement is overly possessive, we do agree that educators must concentrate more on learning which prepares students for real-life pressures.

The self-control curriculum seeks to develop skills which are necessary for confronting, making, and acting upon difficult decisions. By facilitating practice and reinforcement of the eight identified processes for self-control, it is expected that growth will occur in *one's capacity to direct and regulate personal action flexibly and realistically in a given situation.* However, by no means do we present this curriculum as a complete or definitive program of preparation. Instead, we are hopeful that by drawing attention to a fairly specific set of goals which mediate self-control and by offering model or prototype structured tasks for achieving these goals, we can be of help in making some progress toward a more "practical curriculum" (Schwab, 1970).

Organization of the Curriculum

The self-control curriculum consists of eight curriculum areas; each area is discussed in a separate chapter of Part Two of this book. The eight areas are: selection (Chapter 6), storage (Chapter 7), sequencing and ordering (Chapter 8), anticipating consequences (Chapter 9), appreciating feelings (Chapter 10), managing frustration (Chapter 11), inhibition and delay (Chapter 12), and relaxation (Chapter 13).

Each chapter contains an introduction, a statement of rationale, a description of the curriculum units and goals, and suggested learning tasks.[1] The introduction describes, in a thumbnail fashion, the importance of the skill area and the expectations that a teacher should establish for his pupils in that area. The rationale provides the justification of the skill as a necessary developmental area for children. The description of the curriculum units specifies teaching goals for each unit within that curriculum area, while the suggested teaching tasks or activities describe in detail the necessary instructions, materials, and procedures for teaching the skills in that unit.

It should be noted that the curriculum units contain statements of educational goals which lend themselves to an immediate translation into student-centered behavior objectives. For example, a curriculum unit goal might be stated as: "To teach the pupil to distinguish discrete parts of a stimulus arrangement from the remaining parts." This curriculum goal can be shifted easily into a behavior objective format: "Given a stimulus arrangement containing several parts, the student will be able to distinguish one part from the remaining parts" (Mager, 1962; Popham and Baker, 1970).

Table 2 presents an overview of the eight curriculum areas and the specific units within each of these areas.

---

[1]Our approach to curriculum language usage is consistent with a model which specifies that statements of instructional intent be called goals, aims, or purposes, while statements of student performance be referred to as behavior objectives (Goodlad, Steophasius, and Klein, 1966; Johnson, 1967; Payne, 1969).

Table 2: *The Self-Control Curriculum: Overview of Curriculum Areas and Units*

Curriculum Area	*Curriculum Unit*
Selection	1. Focusing and concentration 2. Mastering figure-ground discrimination 3. Mastering distractions and interference 4. Processing complex patterns
Storage	1. Developing visual memory 2. Developing auditory memory
Sequencing and ordering	1. Developing time orientation 2. Developing auditory-visual sequencing 3. Developing sequential planning
Anticipating consequences	1. Developing alternatives 2. Evaluating consequences
Appreciating feelings	1. Identifying feelings 2. Developing positive feelings 3. Managing feelings 4. Reinterpreting feeling events
Managing frustration	1. Accepting feelings of frustration 2. Building coping resources 3. Tolerating frustration
Inhibition and delay	1. Controlling action 2. Developing part-goals
Relaxation	1. Developing body relaxation 2. Developing thought relaxation 3. Developing movement relaxation

The curriculum may be implemented flexibly. While we have suggested an order for presenting the skill areas, this sequence need not be fixed. In general, all eight areas can be applied at the discretion of the teacher. It is suggested, however, that the appreciating feelings area precede managing frustration in order to build positive relationships before the child faces negative feelings about himself and others.

With regard to specific learning tasks, the teacher is free to adopt, modify, or discard any of the tasks we suggest. These tasks are presented as examples or models of activities that can be utilized; they are not sacred. The only limit on the number of relevant tasks for any skill area is the teacher's time and imagination.

A number of options are available for applying the curriculum during the school year as well as within any particular school day. Thus, a teacher may choose to use any one or a combination of four options for implementing the curriculum:

Option Number 1: The curriculum can be taught in one school year for eight months. Approximately one month should be spent in each curriculum area.

Option Number 2: The entire curriculum can be taught in one semester and then repeated, or recycled, in the second semester. Approximately two weeks should be spent on each curriculum area if this option is used.

Option Number 3: The entire curriculum can be taught during the first semester of the school year, with the teacher selecting specific areas for the second semester. In the first semester, approximately two weeks should be spent on each curriculum area, while time spent on any one area in the second semester depends on the needs of the class and the discretion of the teacher.

Option Number 4: Any area of the curriculum can be taught at any time of the year, depending on the needs or displayed weaknesses of the entire class or class members. The amount of time spent on any curriculum area is left to the discretion of the teacher.

In addition, the teacher may elect to follow an instructional schedule suited to her plan for implementing the curriculum. Several options exist for scheduling such curriculum activities:

Option Number 1: Thirty minutes each day. This application is designed to cover every segment of the curriculum and ensures teaching skills in each curriculum unit as well as providing regularity and gradual progression. Daily sessions also allow for individualized identification of pupil weaknesses.

Option Number 2: Throughout the day, in conjunction with academic subjects. Teachers should feel free to intersperse the content of the self-control curriculum with classroom academic material. Games or role-playing episodes in the curriculum can be coordinated easily with academic content.

Option Number 3: Periodically, to bolster interest or motivation. Periodic diversion to games in the curriculum can act as a stimulus for additional academic endeavors and teach a specific skill as well.

Option Number 4: Effectively during a free fun-play period. Indoor recess periods or free-time game periods can be utilized effectively to teach the curriculum. Games that require little or no preparation should be considered when filling this time slot.

Option Number 5: In conjunction with programs for physical education and aesthetic appreciation. For example, many activities for developing inhibition and delay skills can be related easily to physical education goals. Activities for building relaxation can be introduced in music, as well as physical education.

Figure 3, the self-control flow chart, shows the basic areas of the curriculum as an interconnected set of skills which contribute to competency for completion of any task assignment. The sequence of skills is not meant as a functional process by which self-control is attained, but, rather, as a convenient way of showing the relationship of skill areas to requirements for task completion. While all enabling steps are not necessary for completion of every task, any serious weakness in any one skill area will act as an impediment to desired task fulfillment.

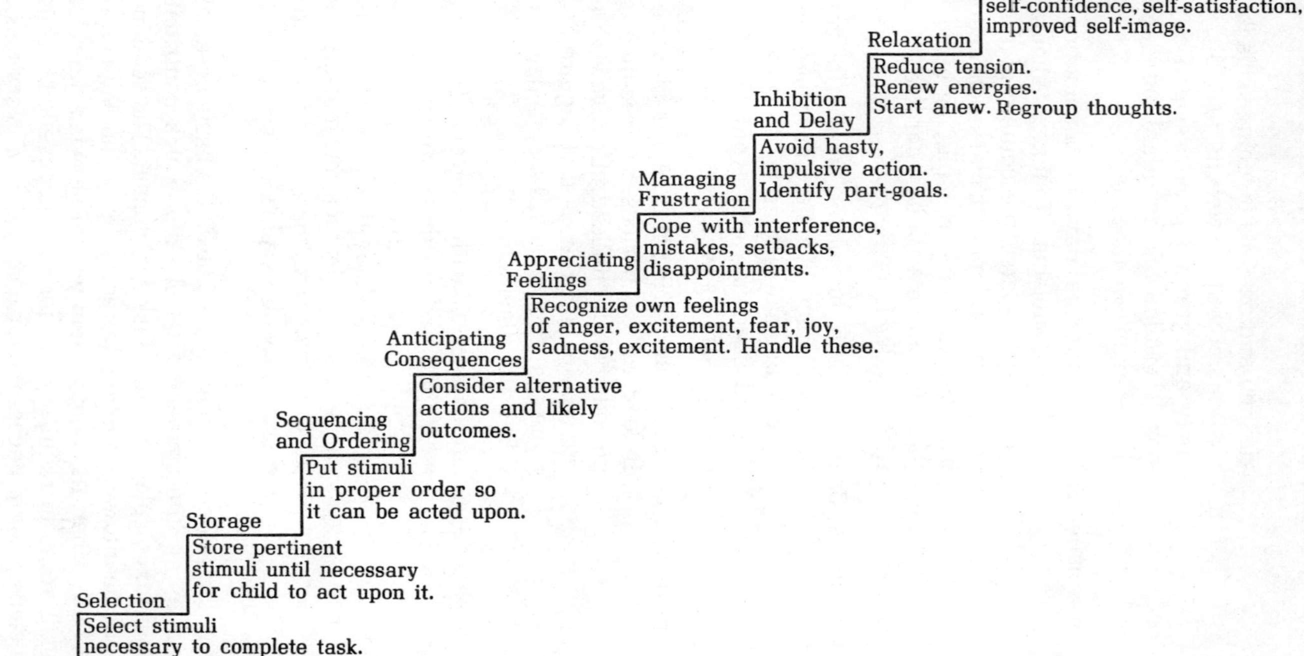

Figure 3: *The Self-Control Flow Chart as Enabling Steps toward Competency for Task Completion*

When teachers are able to evaluate the needs or identify the deficits of pupils in their class, they may select particular areas of the curriculum or units within areas and concentrate on those skills. This can only take place after a teacher has become thoroughly acquainted with the self-control curriculum and can make an accurate assessment of the needs of each individual pupil or pupils in his class (see Chapter 14 for section on planning for individualized instruction).

Aims of the Curriculum

The self-control curriculum is intended for all children, urban and suburban, regardless of ethnic, social, or racial background. The curriculum is programmed for a regular school setting but can also be used in recreational programs, summer camp programs, and neighborhood programs which are separate from the school setting. It can be taught very effectively to whole classes, small groups, or on an individual basis.

A major aim of the curriculum is to provide pupils with skills for coping flexibly and realistically with their life situations. Furthermore, by teaching children to have a better feeling towards themselves and an appreciation of the feelings of others, we can greatly enhance possibilities for satisfying interpersonal relationships. With this improved self-image comes security, a greater degree of happiness, and the confidence to master new tasks. In short, the curriculum strives to broaden the pupil's chances for success and fulfillment in life.

Teaching Strategies

The strategies used in teaching the self-control curriculum are threefold: *games, role-playing,* and *lesson or discussion.*

Games: Games are included more frequently than other strategies for a number of reasons. First of all, children enjoy games. In addition, there is a great learning potential involved, and games create lasting impressions.[2] Games can be modified or amended to suit the

---

[2] We might note here the enlightening study of children's games by Lora and Peter Opie (1971) which convincingly shows both the universality and permanence of ordinary street games, including such games as "Blind Man's Bluff" (which originated in the 1570s), Kick the Can (played in Surrey, England, as early as 1890), and "Statues Freeze."

wishes of the group and adapted to conform to space limitations or the class's level of ability. They also can serve as a basis for imaginative and exciting activity (Gordon, 1970). Finally, most skills learned in playing games have direct skill adaptation and application to the life cycle of the pupil.

Role-Playing: Skill areas, such as managing frustration, appreciating feelings, and anticipating consequences, that do not lend themselves easily to the game method can be taught dramatically by means of role-playing. Role-playing allows a pupil flexibility of actions and imaginative feelings as well as freedom of vocabulary in the role he assumes. Although the episode has been created for him, the words, manner, feeling, and actions he expresses are all his own and reflect his own thoughts, fears, wishes, and desires. The pupil often will identify with the role he is playing, thus making it a realistic as well as affective learning experience. At the same time, however, the child is well protected from direct confrontation or stress (Chesler and Fox, 1964).

As Shaftel and Shaftel (1967) point out, role-playing is quite useful for focusing on making decisions among alternatives and discovering consequences—factors which are closely related to aspects of self-control.

Lesson or Discussion: The third strategy for teaching the self-control curriculum involves a presentation of content or assignment. It might entail a brief presentation of information, group discussion, or individual seat work and academic exercises. The lesson format is the best method of conveying those parts of the curriculum which do not easily adapt themselves to games and role-playing. The presentation allows a teacher to take advantage of the student's current reservior of language arts, spelling, social studies and to review or reinforce other subject materials.

Thus, the self-control curriculum permits a wide spectrum of activities through structured classroom teaching. The dispersion of these three teaching strategies throughout the curriculum maintains high levels of interest, appeal, and involvement for all pupils.

Teaching Guidelines for Full Curriculum Application

For any teaching program to be successful, it must establish working conditions which enable the learner to experience satisfaction in the process of mastering tasks or developing new skills. Unless curriculum content is transmitted through a medium which supports interest and growth, the content remains a body of empty words on a printed page. The program ought to guarantee that the child will experience success if he makes a sincere effort. Any repeated successes the children achieve will help to motivate them to more difficult tasks and encourage them to attempt new learning situations.

The extent of curriculum planning for the entire program will depend upon the age and grade level of the students, their degree of self-control, and the extent of their knowledge. The pace should be determined largely by the children, especially when such fundamentals as lengthening attention span and visual and auditory skills are being taught.

To guide in the implementation of this self-control curriculum, several key procedures have been formulated. They are:

1. *Start at or below the functional level.* Always seek to proceed from a point that can be handled by the child. Work up to harder tasks gradually and avoid presenting tasks that do not allow for simplification or modification when necessary.

2. *Increase difficulty by small steps.* Try not to force big jumps in administering skill exercises, unless you believe that readiness and self-esteem are sufficient. It usually will be best to proceed by increasing difficulty gradually, placing harder requirements on top of successful earlier accomplishments.

3. *Place teaching tasks in developmental sequence.* Attempt to organize tasks so that higher-order skills follow upon development of more elementary skills. Break complex tasks into separate components and order them sequentially (e.g., kicking a ball requires left-right discrimination, balancing on one foot, freedom to move).

4. *Provide positive feedback.* Be sure to indicate through praise, gesture, pictures, charts, videotape, and other methods that progress is made. Do not overdo praise so that it sounds artificial or untrue, but do use it freely. Frequently remind the child of gains he has made since he started—this often offsets discouragement during plateau phases.

5. *Strengthen by repetition.* Return to earlier tasks often during the year and always repeat the last task performed at a prior session.

6. *Show appreciation for real effort.* Of critical importance is offering recognition for effort rather than the more usual practice of merely recognizing results. Work at converting appraisal methods so that success is defined relative to a child's baseline level and subsequent progress made (see Meacham & Wiesen, 1969). Appreciation for goal achievement is also important, but this should never be emphasized at the expense of real effort.

7. *Enhance the value of the skill area.* Unless the particular skill being taught is perceived as a valuable one by the child, meaningful change is not likely. The enhancement of value is therefore a *sine qua non* for effective teaching. We will expand upon this point later on in this chapter.

8. *Maintain flexibility and enjoyment.* The planned program is never sacrosanct and should always be subject to modification. Combat boredom, fatigue, restlessness with appealing activities that may or may not have teaching value. For example, a change of scenery through interesting trips, walks, or outdoor activities can be beneficial—and these may be used as rewards for hard work.

9. *Prepare for real-life transfer of training.* Keep in mind that learning tasks are not ends in themselves but serve, rather, as gateways to satisfaction in everyday life. For example, skills needed for walking a balance board are also important in climbing a fence in a game of follow-the-leader. However, the child may not realize that these skills are related, and stop at the fence, even though he can walk the balance beam. Transfer can be optimized by extending and generalizing the learning tasks to as many everyday activities as possible.

10. *Emphasize short, frequent, regular training sessions.* Hold sessions at the same place, daily if possible, and for short periods (e.g., one-half hour). It is always better to get sharp, energetic, complete attempts from children at a few tasks in a short session than half-hearted, apathetic tries at many different exercises.

Materials

The majority of the games and role-playing episodes which comprise the bulk of the self-control curriculum require no materials. On occasion, however, a lesson or discussion task will require mimeographing a list of words or duplicating a design. Or the teacher may want to enrich the curriculum with her own materials—to the degree that her time, imagination, and material resources will permit her.

A number of tasks are introduced by commercial games, such as, Snap, Crazy Eights, Old Maid, Dominoes, Checkers, Chutes and Ladders, and Candyland. These games not only provide a good method for teaching a specific skill but also give children an enjoyable pastime.

As is often the case, the amount and quality of materials a teacher constructs or assembles may greatly supplement her effectiveness in teaching the curriculum. Most skill areas and/or units can be further enhanced by creating a colorful poster with a suitable title depicting that particular skill. This can act as a reminder or reinforcer of current teaching areas.

Generally, tasks have been designed with a minimum of materials in mind. In many cases, the teacher has a choice of conducting the learning session orally, taking advantage of verbal-motor activity, using the chalkboard, or using paper-and-pencil seat work. We encourage as much preparation of materials as a busy teacher's schedule will allow.

Value Enhancement

In addition to skill objectives, it is critical that the teacher keep in mind the need for enhancing the value placed on self-control by the child. It is expected that self-control will become a personal goal or value to the extent it brings about inner satisfactions as well as material pleasure. Undoubtedly, though, many children who have learned to react impetuously have found this pattern to be of more immediate benefit and have never experienced the more enduring satisfactions that are possible through flexible control of behavior. Multiple sources of satisfaction or reward exist, however, and each of these are capable of serving as a mechanism for the enhancement of value. In seeking to develop alternative behaviors for impulsive youngsters, the intention is to assure success of the teaching program by incorporating several sources of individual gratification or positive reinforcement (see Becker, Thomas, and Carnine, 1969; Buckley and Walker, 1970). The forms of reinforcement include:

1. *Adult Respect, Approval, and Appreciation.* The relationship between instructors and children is crucial if value is to become attached to teaching objectives. A warm, trusting, supportive relationship is considered a prerequisite here. When these ingredients exist, it becomes possible for the child to feel and recognize the respect, approval, and appreciation offered by the adult. Ultimately, the child acquires an inner sense of esteem and respect as a result of positive reactions from the important adult.
2. *Attainment of Desirable Outcomes.* Since children gravitate towards those activities which bring them pride and pleasure, it will greatly facilitate investment in self-control skills if the exercising of these skills frequently leads directly to desired consequences. At least two broad categories of desirable outcomes are immediately apparent—material rewards and social recognition.
3. *Identification with Constructive Models.* Children push themselves to be like those people they like and respect. Once a child values the relationship between himself and a potential model, he is ready to incorporate the values and skills held by that model. A sense of satisfaction can arise from the expression of behaviors which are perceived as being similar to those of the liked model, and through practice, the child becomes able to more and more closely approximate that model.

SUMMARY

This self-control curriculum presents a challenge and an opportunity to the elementary school teacher. Through the application of this psychoeducational curriculum model, a teacher should be in a much stronger position to arouse and maintain the involvement of her pupils in meaningful, realistic learning experiences.

The self-control curriculum may be regarded as a supplementary process for promoting readiness for and integrating other academic challenges in the total school curriculum. By specifying clear instructional tasks and activities to promote development of self-control, we hope to prevent the occurrence of emotional and learning handicaps.

Wilson (1969) makes the point that school authorities have to decide whether desired learning elements should be taught through curriculum, left to the free experience of the child, or avoided completely. We are in agreement with him when he says, "A decision not to teach something in curriculum form is just as important as a decision to teach it" (p. ix). Our unequivocal decision is to teach the elements of self-control via a structured psychoeducational curriculum.

Games, role-playing, and presentations or discussions represent the main strategies for implementing the curriculum. Curriculum units may be applied in a flexible pattern with options to conduct special, short-period classes on self-control skills or to introduce units responsively within the regular school day. In addition, a variety of options exist for sequencing and managing time for the eight curriculum areas. Thus, the curriculum lends itself to the individualized needs of the teacher and her students.

REFERENCES

Becker, W.; Thomas, D.; and Carnine, D. *Reducing Behavior Problems: An Operant Conditioning Guide for Teachers.* Urbana: University of Illinois, Information Center, 1969.

Buckley, N., and Walker, H. *Modifying Classroom Behavior.* Champaign, Illinois: Research Press, 1970.

Chesler, M., and Fox, R. *Role Playing in the Classroom.* Ann Arbor: University of Michigan, Institute for Social Research, 1964.

Frost, J., and Rowland, G. T. *Curricula for the Seventies: Early Childhood through Early Adolescence.* Boston: Houghton Mifflin, 1969.

Goodlad, J.; Steophasius, R.; and Klein, M.F. *The Changing School Curriculum.* New York: Fund for the Advancement of Education, 1966.

Gordon, A. *Games for Growth: Educational Games in the Classroom.* Palo Alto, California: Science Research Associates, 1970.

Johnson, M. "Definitions and Models in Curriculum Theory." *Educational Theory* 17 (1967): 127–40.

Mager, R. *Preparing Instructional Objectives.* Palo Alto, California: Fearon, 1962.

Meacham, M., and Wiesen, A. *Changing Classroom Behavior: A Manual for Precision Teaching.* Scranton, Pennsylvania: International Textbook, 1969.

Opie, I., and Opie, P. *Children's Games in Street and Playground.* Oxford: Oxford University Press, 1971.

Payne, A. *The Study of Curriculum Plans.* Washington, D.C.: Center for the Study of Instruction, a division of the National Education Association, 1969.

Popham, J., and Baker, E. *Systematic Instruction.* Englewood Cliffs, New Jersey: Prentice-Hall, 1970.

Schwab, J. *The Practical: A Language for Curriculum.* Washington, D.C.: National Education Association, 1970.

Shaftel, F., and Shaftel, G. *Role-Playing for Social Values: Decision Making in the Social Studies.* Englewood Cliffs, New Jersey: Prentice-Hall, 1967.

Wilson, J. *Moral Education and the Curriculum.* Oxford: Pergamon Press, 1969.

6

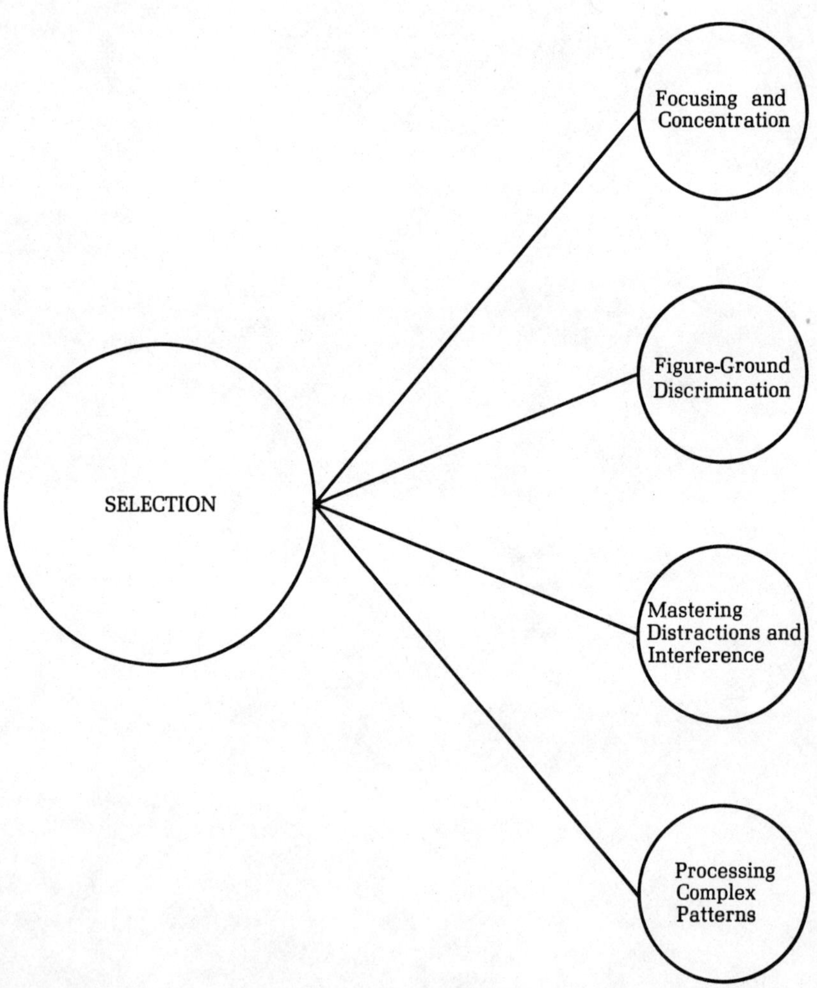

SELECTION
Focusing and Concentration
Figure-Ground Discrimination
Mastering Distractions and Interference
Processing Complex Patterns

Curriculum Area: Selection

INTRODUCTION TO SELECTION

Basic to effective learning are attentiveness, concentration, and perceptual integration toward the available information. Without these skills, a pupil is at a severe disadvantage. Nevertheless, pupils lacking these skills exist in every strata and group of our society, rich and poor, black and white, urban and suburban.[1] They are frequently our most vulnerable pupils.

For the average pupil to function effectively in his classroom setting, he must learn to devote a high degree of attentiveness to

[1]The importance of selection skills for effective behavioral and academic functioning has been emphasized in research on remedial approaches for conduct problem children. Thus, Quay, Werry, McQueen, and Sprague (1966) report: "[We] have been impressed by the very poor attention and hyperactivity of the pupils as a serious impediment, not only behaviorally, but also academically. Before they can be taught anything, whether it be social or academic, it is necessary to obtain their attention" (p. 512). Interestingly enough, defects in selection skills have also been reported in hyperactive, brain-injured, and economically disadvantaged children (Kallan, 1970). In discussing the latter, Kallan states, "He responds to all the stimuli in his environment simultaneously and is unable to filter out and discriminate between what is relevant to learning and what is not" (p. 73).

teacher instruction, classroom behavioral expectations, and curriculum requirements. This chapter is organized in order to help the pupil select stimuli from his environment which will contribute to satisfactory task completion. We also will emphasize the enhancement of skills that render the environment less threatening and assist in managing distracting or complex stimuli.

To select is to make a choice; to select effectively or accurately requires discrimination and concentration in making the choice. Since the purpose of a choice is to fulfill a requirement, satisfy a need or want, make a situation more acceptable, or acquire information which will contribute toward a desired goal, faulty or ineffective selection of stimuli creates a feeling of futility. If a pupil consistently makes faulty choices, he then resorts to avoidant behavior that protects him from failure (see Connolly, 1971; Kurlander and Colodny, 1969). Such behavior maintains the status quo but allows no room for growth or successive mastery of skill requirements. Perpetuation of such avoidant behavior, whether in the classroom or in society, often results in deviancy, defeatism, and a depreciating self-image (Bower, 1960; Haring and Phillips, 1962).

For example, William had reasonable success when working alone but was easily distracted by the sounds or actions of others in his class. When other children were present, he characteristically discarded his individual assignment in favor of involvement in the distracting behavior of his peers. Consequently, he fell farther and farther behind, thus making his return to academic tasks increasingly painful and the attraction to other, non-task activities even greater. The net result was an undermining of William's sense of accomplishment or ability. By responding to or initiating disruptive or distracting classroom behavior, the youngster could temporarily rid himself of painful feelings of inadequacy, even though doing so meant drawing negative attention to himself. Frequently, teachers or parents will state to a child, "You could do it if you'd only stop fooling around." What is not so obvious to these parents is that the "fooling around" is often a cover-up for the child's difficulty in meeting the challenge imposed by the task itself.

Because effective selection frees the pupil to attempt imaginative, exciting, and satisfying pursuits, we are impressed by the need to teach ways for improving selection skills. To accomplish this, we have developed games which may be played in or out of the classroom. These games incorporate basic functions which are necessary for effective selection of pertinent stimuli. The teacher should, however, feel comfortable adjusting or modifying suggested activities to better fit into the particular pupil's life situation.

Rationale

For children to perform in behaviorally and academically appropriate ways, they must be able to process accurately the information necessary to carry out a desired task. A child unable to identify correctly the relevant incoming stimuli—whether for reasons of poor concentration or faulty perception—must depend on personal hunches or reactions which come out of confusion and frustration. The process of successful living and behaving thus hinges on sound understanding and interpretation of objective inputs. By teaching children to more adequately select the essential aspects of stimulus presentations, a basic building block for effective learning is set into place.

TEACHING UNITS AND GOALS

The selection learning area consists of four teaching units: focusing and concentration, mastering figure-ground discrimination, mastering distractions and interference, and processing complex patterns. We recommend the units be followed in the order outlined, with clear progress made by the child in one unit before he proceeds to the next. Each unit is designed to strengthen and/or develop a particular element of the learning process. Within units, each task permits the teacher to present requirements which will move the pupil from the simple to the more complex.

Unit 1: Focusing and Concentrating

Goals: To improve the pupil's ability to focus attention on a specific task, increase attention span, and concentrate on task directed activities.

Unit 2: Mastering Figure-Ground Discrimination

Goals: To teach the pupil to distinguish discrete parts of a stimulus arrangement from the remaining parts and to separate the stimulus that has relevance.

Unit 3: Mastering Distraction and Interference

Goal: To develop a pupil's ability to concentrate his efforts on a given task despite extraneous or distracting stimuli.

Unit 4: Processing Complex Patterns

Goals: To develop an ability to perceive complex stimulus patterns and to be attentive to diverse stimulus arrangements.

UNIT 1. FOCUSING AND CONCENTRATING

Goals: To improve the pupil's ability to focus attention on a specific task, increase attention span, and concentrate on task directed activities.

Task 1: Slow Motion Tasks

Have a pupil make attempts to draw, walk, move, talk, etc., as slowly as possible in an atmosphere which is relatively free of distraction. Introduce tasks as "slow motion"; e.g., bowling, racing, baseball, basketball, etc. Having a pupil verbalize bits of action may support his attempts to slow down and add to his power of concentration. Tasks should proceed from simple movements to more complicated, imaginative actions in an effort to provoke thought on the part of the actor as well as on the part of the audience. For example, the slow motion tasks may be made part of a game of "charades."

Task 2: Hide the Bean Game

Seat the pupil in a chair facing a table with two, three, or four cups on it. Place a bean or button under one cup and begin to switch the cups around. Have the pupil try to locate the cup covering the bean. This task demand may be altered by using different or identical cups, increasing the number of cups, varying the amount of switching done, or increasing the number of beans.

Task 3: Find the Object Game

Describe an object in the room, telling approximately where it is and what it does. The pupils have to guess what the object is. For example:

1. "The object is round, hangs on the wall, and has two hands. It tells us when to go to lunch, but it can't talk." *Answer:* A clock.
2. "The object has four legs but can't walk, is square, is very hard, and holds things." *Answer:* A desk.
3. "The object is a rectangle, includes many stories, but can't talk, will stay where you put it, and is fun to look through." *Answer:* A book.
4. "The object is round and soft. You can throw it, kick it, catch it, roll it, or bounce it." *Answer:* A ball.

Difficulty may be increased by making the clues more vague. Variation can be achieved by having one pupil describe an object in the room. Whoever guesses the object first becomes the *leader* and, in turn, describes another object.

Task 4: Lengthening the Balance Beam

Stretch the child's attention span by having him walk boards which can be gradually lengthened. The board can be a balance beam or wooden planks set up as ramps or across blocks. Introduce minor obstacles along the beam (e.g., eggshells, paper cups) to emphasize the element of care and attention. Allow the child to walk the beam moving forward, backward, and sideways (from left to right). Difficulty may be increased by having a child attend to catching, throwing, or bouncing a ball while walking the beam.

Task 5: Location Exercises— Forms, Letters, Numbers, Symbols

Using a slide or overhead projector or chalkboard, present a series of forms, letters, numbers, or symbols (e.g., ⅄ + 3B). Ask pupils to "watch where the number (letter, form, etc.) is" in relation to position (e.g., end of window, end of door, middle of room). Positions may be indicated by visual cues for younger children, such as pictures of different animals. The teacher might then tell children to "watch what animal the number lands on." Expose presentation for three to five seconds and then remove it; then ask the children to recall the location of the key stimulus. Stimulus content, the number of stimuli, and exposure time may be varied to adjust difficulty of task.

Task 6: Find the Sound Game

A click, rattle, squeak, snap, or other sound object is passed from hand to hand around a circle while the pupil in the middle of the circle tries to guess who has the snap. The pupil can be blindfolded to increase the difficulty. Only one instrument for making noise should be used so that concentration can be centered on that object. If the child in the middle of the circle can correctly identify the person making the noise, he gets to exchange places with that person. The object is to move out of the middle by listening carefully to locate the sound.

Task 7: Silly Sentences

Using current classroom material or daily events, construct words or sentences that have all the letters running together, or capitalized when not necessary, or separated in an illogical manner. The teacher should start with simple words and phrases the pupils understand, not with new or complicated material. The words and sentences can be a review of the previous day's exercises. The purpose is to concentrate on saying or writing the phrase or sentence in proper form. For example:

1. Doyouthinkitwillsnowtoday?
   DoyOutHinKITwillsNoWtoDAy?
   Doy OutH inKitw iLLsN oWtoD ay?
   Answer: Do you think it will snow today?

2. Whattimeisit?
   wHAttIMeiSIt?

wHA ttIM ei SIt?

Answer: What time is it?

3. FlO wEr

   Answer: Flower

4. I cec Re aM

   Answer: Ice Cream

Task 8: Hangman

Put dashes on the chalkboard representing letters in a word or a short sentence. Draw a hangman's platform and noose in a nearby spot. The pupils then take turns guessing the letters in the words. If a pupil guesses a letter in the word, it is filled in above the dash(es). If the letter is not included in the word or sentence, it is listed and crossed out. In addition, when a letter is crossed out, some part of the body should be added to the figure to be hung. The object is to guess all the letters in the sentence before the figure is hung. Increase the amount of detail in the figure so that a hanging never takes place if you wish. The game will stimulate focusing, concentration, and imagination.

Task 9: Seat Exchange

The purpose of this task is to teach pupils to focus and concentrate on picture or word recognition. The entire class forms a circle with the exact number of chairs required for those to be seated. After one person is chosen to stand in the middle of the circle, cards are passed out to the children with one picture or word on them. All cards have one matching card somewhere else in the circle. Although you have a duplicate set of cards, no one else sees any other card.

The game starts when you give the person in the center a card and ask him to name the picture (e.g., "butterfly") or spell the word aloud. The pupils in the circle who have the picture or word on their card then have to expose their cards to everyone. The two pupils in the circle with the same picture or word then exchange places as quickly as they can. In the meantime, the person in the center tries to sit in one of their chairs.

If the pupil in the center succeeds in getting a seat, the last person to leave his seat goes to the center of the circle, and the card of the new person in the center is passed to the person who took his seat. If he doesn't succeed in naming or spelling the word, he goes back to the center, and the teacher supplies him with another picture or word to spell. The game continues until interest diminishes.

This game can be used to reinforce concepts, develop vocabulary skills, or improve spelling; it can also be varied to include math as well as science and social studies facts or concepts.

UNIT 2. MASTERING FIGURE-GROUND DISCRIMINATION

Goals: To teach the pupil to distinguish discrete parts of a stimulus arrangement from the remaining parts and to separate the stimulus that has relevance.

Task 1: Basic Concepts

Be certain that the child can discriminate basic concepts related to size, shape, color, and sound. Use puzzles, pegboards, form boards, common noises, and colored blocks. Develop problems requiring the child to discriminate between two or more objects which differ in size, shape, color, or sound.

Task 2: Position in Space

Develop a knowledge of position in space through the use of a chair in a room or a grid on the floor. Ask the pupil to jump forward or up, backward or down, to the left or right. Ask the pupil to stand on the right side of a chair, pointing out by tactile stimulation that the chair is on his left; reverse the position for the right side. Move the pupil around and ask him to indicate his position relative to the chair and where the chair is in relation to him. Ask the pupil to touch himself on his left, right, back, front, top, and bottom. To further enhance his understanding of the concept, ask him to verbalize his action as he moves and touches.

Task 3: Identifying Foreground Objects

Set out everyday objects on a table and ask the child to name those in front or closest to him; then switch the objects around and repeat. Introduce new objects, one at a time, and mix them into the existing table arrangement; ask the child to find and describe the location of the object (e.g., between spoon and ball, in back of glass, in front of the flowers, etc.). Gradually introduce two-dimensional pictures of table arrangements, asking the child to identify objects in foreground of the picture corresponding to foreground objects on the table. Vary the task by showing pictorial arrangements and asking the child to duplicate them with three-dimensional models. Enhance meaningfulness by taking photographs of the child's arrangements and using these photos as task stimuli.

Task 4: Hidden Figures Game

The child or teacher draws, cuts out, or finds any sort of object or figure (e.g., triangle, pencil, model car, etc.). With this object as discrimination or "figure" stimulus, the child or teacher tries to hide the figure, first, by drawing it on the chalkboard or paper and, then, by adding background parts. The child can be asked to find his own or the teacher's hidden figure after looking away for a short interval. Increase the difficulty by gradually making the "figure" stimulus fade while elaborating background factors.

UNIT 3. MASTERING DISTRACTIONS AND INTERFERENCE

Goal: To develop a pupil's ability to concentrate his efforts on a given task despite extraneous or distracting stimuli.

Task 1: Action orders

Give a pupil several things to do (e.g., add two plus three on the chalkboard; then walk around the chair twice; then hop on one foot across the room). While the pupil is carrying out the directives, interfere with their smooth performance by walking across his path, talking about numbers, asking him questions, moving furniture, etc.

Teach the pupil to concentrate on the orderly completion of the directives and to screen out extraneous incoming stimuli. Current academic material can be used as part of the directives in an effort to reinforce learning. To increase difficulty, add more directives and increase distractions.

Task 2: Distracting Questions

Assign a certain task to the class that must be finished in a specific time period. Announce that if the task is completed within the required time, the class will be given some reward (e.g., a fun-play period). For example, the task could be copying several words from the chalkboard, working a list of current arithmetic problems, or completing half-finished sentences. When the pupils start the assigned task, start asking interesting questions, such as, "What do you think we are having for lunch today?" "Who did something interesting on vacation last summer?" "Where should we go on our next class trip—any ideas?" You may remind the class periodically of the time left to finish the assignment, while, at the same time, asking interesting and thought-provoking questions. You should point out beforehand what you intend to do in order to establish readiness for the activity. At the end of the activity, review with the class what their primary goal was as well as your attempt to distract them.

Task 3: Academic and Humorous Actions

Assign directives to a pupil which mix academic content with humorous actions (e.g., add 3 + 7 on chalkboard; show an angry face; write CAT on chalkboard; pretend you are seven feet tall). While the first child is carrying out the directives, ask two other pupils to work math problems on the chalkboard. You might give a child three or four fun directives, only one of which is academic (e.g., soar like a bird; turn around twice; pretend you are driving a car; add 6 + 5 on the board). Ask two pupils to act like they are getting dressed in the morning. Difficulty may be increased by adding more directives and/or increasing the number of pupils engaged in other activities. The more discrepancy there is between the child's task and his classmate's behavior, the greater the challenge for mastery of distraction.

UNIT 4. PROCESSING COMPLEX PATTERNS

Goals: To develop an ability to perceive complex stimulus patterns and to be attentive to diverse stimulus arrangements.

Task 1: Flash Card Recalls

Use flash cards with two numbers, letters, or symbols in the center of the card and smaller numbers, letters, or symbols surrounding them in a circle. Flash the cards before the class for three to five seconds. Ask for recall of large numbers in the center first; then ask for recall of numbers, letters, or symbols surrounding the center.

Task 2: Symbol Flash Cards

Use flash cards with two or three symbols in the center of the card and smaller symbols surrounding the circle. Flash the cards before the class for three to five seconds. Ask for recall in writing or for an auditory response requiring the symbols in the center to be offered first. Difficulty can be increased by enlarging the circle and making the symbols smaller.

Task 3: Straight-Line Flash Cards

Arrange letters in a straight line, leaving ample distance between two or three center letters and letters on both ends of the line. Flash them for from three to five seconds and ask for written or auditory response. Ask the pupils to recall as many letters as possible without the restriction of first recognizing the center letters.

Task 4: Peripheral Vision Area: Right-Left

Ask a pupil to concentrate his vision on an object. As he does, ask him to describe everything he can see within the peripheral vision area on his right and left. In this manner, you can develop the pupil's awareness of surrounding stimuli.

Allow pupils to experiment with peripheral vision. For example, while one pupil concentrates on looking at an object, another moves until he is out of the peripheral vision area.

Or ask a pupil to look at an object for an extended period of time. During this time, write a number on the chalkboard six to eight feet to the child's right or left. After the number is erased, ask for recall.

Or within the peripheral vision area, have one pupil concentrate his vision on an object while another pupil moves parts of his body. Ask for a description of the movements from the first child. These exercises develop the child's ability to be aware of and process incoming stimuli while concentrating on a selected subject.

SUMMARY

Many pupils are often overwhelmed by a mass of incoming stimuli and are unable to establish any system of priorities for handling and processing such input. If the teacher can help the pupil to select the task-relevant stimuli and be aware of, but not threatened by, the irrelevant stimuli, he will insure a higher degree of emotional stability and successful task completion.

Selection skills taught in this chapter are fundamental to sound adjustment and learning, for mastery of distractive and interfering stimuli frees the pupil so that he can focus and concentrate on specific task assignments. Accurate identification of relevant stimuli provides a sound base that will enhance subsequent learning processes.

For tasks in this chapter to have relevance and purpose to the pupil, however, the teacher must continually attempt to relate them to real-life situations and the environment in which the pupil lives. The teacher should also clearly state the importance of these tasks for learning, mastery, and self-growth.

Table 3 provides a summary of the curriculum units and tasks comprising the area of selection.

Table 3: *Summary of Curriculum Units and Tasks for Curriculum Area: Selection*

Units	*Tasks*
Focusing and concentrating	1. Slow Motion Tasks 2. Hide the Bean Game 3. Find the Object Game 4. Lengthening the Balance Beam 5. Location Exercises—Forms, Letters, Numbers, Symbols 6. Find the Sound Game 7. Silly Sentences 8. Hangman 9. Seat Exchange
Mastering figure-ground discrimination	1. Basic Concepts 2. Position in Space 3. Identifying Foreground Objects 4. Hidden Figures Game
Mastering distractions and interference	1. Action Orders 2. Distracting Questions 3. Academic and Humorous Actions
Processing complex patterns	1. Flash Card Recalls 2. Symbol Flash Cards 3. Straight-Line Flash Cards 4. Peripheral Vision Area: Right-Left

REFERENCES

Bower, E. *Early Identification of Emotionally Handicapped Children in School.* Springfield, Illinois: Charles C. Thomas, 1960.

Connolly, C. "Social and Emotional Factors in Learning Disabilities." In *Progress in Learning Disabilities,* Vol. 2, edited by H. R. Myklebust, pp. 151–78. New York: Grune & Stratton, 1971.

Haring, N., and Phillips, E. L. *Educating Emotionally Disturbed Children.* New York: McGraw-Hill, 1962.

Kallan, C. "Privation or Deprivation." *Journal of Learning Disabilities* 3 (1970): 24–27.

______. "Rhythm and Sequencing in the Intersensory Approach to Learning Disability." *Journal of Learning Disabilities* 5 (1972): 69–74.

Kurlander, L., and Colodny, D. "Psychiatric Disability and Learning Problems." In *Learning Disabilities: Introduction to Educational and Medical Management*, edited by L. Tarnopol, pp. 131–53. Springfield, Illinois: Charles Thomas, 1971.

Quay, H. C.; Werry, J.; McQueen, M.; and Sprague, R. "Remediation of the Conduct Problem Child in the Special Class Setting." *Exceptional Children* 32 (1966): 509–15.

ADDITIONAL RESOURCES

Cratty, B. *Developmental Sequences of Perceptual-Motor Tasks*. New York: Educational Activities, 1967.

Cratty, B., and Martin, M. *Perceptual-Motor Efficiency in Children: The Measurement and Improvement of Movement Attributes*. Philadelphia: Lea & Febiger, 1969.

Fairbanks, J., and Robinson, J. *Perceptual-Motor Development*. Boston: Teaching Resources, 1967.

Fitzhugh, K., and Fitzhugh, L. *The Fitzhugh Plus Program*. Gulien, Michigan: Allied Educational Council, 1966.

Frostig, M., and Horne, D. *The Frostig Program for the Development of Visual Perception: Teacher's Guide*. Chicago: Follett, 1964.

Karnes, M. *Helping Young Children Develop Language Skills: A Book of Activities*. Arlington, Virginia: Council for Exceptional Children, 1968.

Marzollo, J., and Lloyd, J. *Learning through Play*. New York: Harper & Row, 1972.

Stephens, T. M. *Directive Teaching of Children with Learning and Behavioral Handicaps*. Columbus, Ohio: Charles E. Merrill Publishing Co., 1970.

Valett, R. *The Remediation of Learning Disabilities: A Handbook of Psychoeducational Resource Programs*. Palo Alto, California: Fearon, 1967.

Van Witsen, B. *Perceptual Training Activities Handbook*. New York: Columbia University Teachers College Press, 1967.

Wedemeyer, A., and Cejka, J. *Creative Ideas for Teaching Exceptional Children*. Denver: Love Publishing Co., 1970.

Young, M. *Teaching Children with Special Learning Needs*. New York: John Day, 1967.

7

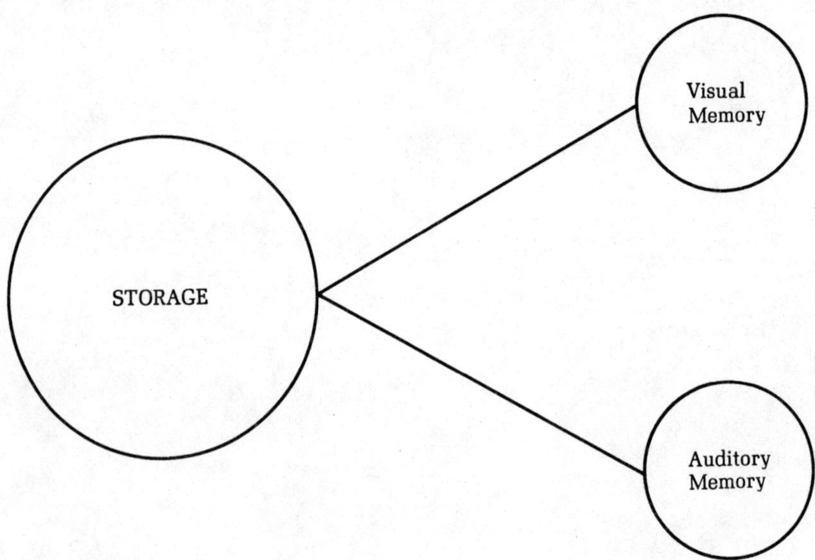

Curriculum Area: Storage

INTRODUCTION TO STORAGE

Chapter 6 was directed toward teaching pupils to *select* stimuli relevant for task completion, but, after this selection of relevant stimuli, the pupil must be able to store and recall this input in order to take purposeful action.

Memory is commonly defined as "the power or process of reproducing or recalling what has been learned or retained" (Chalfant and Scheffelin, 1969, p. 161). The degree of retention is evidenced by the amount and accuracy of recall and recognition. In other words, the retention process must function efficiently after the stimulus has been removed and then produce accurate recall when a task requires the use of that stimulus. For efficient learning, a pupil must be able to store information rapidly and automatically, although, unfortunately, many students do not believe themselves capable of memory, and many others simply do not care to remember. While faulty or inaccurate recall permits a pupil to function in school and society, it impedes the learning process and results in a knowledge base that is both narrow and ineffectual.

It should be noted that storage functions can be distinguished in terms of being either short or long term. Short-term, or immediate, memory refers to situations where recall is expected within seconds. Long-term memory, on the other hand, requires that information be retained and stored for hours, days, or even longer. There is some evidence to suggest that short- and long-term memory are relatively independent functions which are located within different brain structures (Howe, 1970; Magoun, 1967). Because of the clear relevance of short-term memory to completion of classroom task requirements, we will confine our attention to that function; therefore, all tasks suggested in this chapter will require immediate rather than long-term memory.

We are aware that there is inconclusive evidence regarding the possibility of improving storage functions (see Hunter, 1957; Vergason, 1968; Wiseman, 1965). It does appear, however, that children can be helped to develop better techniques for responding to incoming information (see Chalfant and Flathouse, 1971), as well as for gaining confidence in their ability to retain information through such techniques as rehearsal, coding, and organization. Given the significance of storage to the process of self-control and the extent of professional interest in remediation of memory deficits, we believe it important to attempt skill enhancement in this area.

Rationale

The ability to retain a symbolic image after the stimulus is withdrawn and use this memory trace to guide actions is a necessary adjunct to the learning process, for a pupil who is unable to recall information (e.g., instructions, facts, pictures) also will be unable to meet the expectations of others—in the classroom or elsewhere. Adequate storage, however, enables the pupil to proceed accurately from the point of task presentation to the point of satisfactory task completion.

TEACHING UNITS AND GOALS

This chapter has been divided into two basic units—visual memory and auditory memory. Visual and auditory processes are the main channels through which an individual receives information to be stored or retained for use in the learning process.

Unit 1: Visual Memory

Goals: To improve ability to remember visual material and to reconstruct presented material through words or motor expression; to enhance one's capacity to store information for later use and to broaden the knowledge base of the individual.

Unit 2: Auditory Memory

Goals: To improve ability to remember auditory material and to reconstruct presented material through words or motor expression; to enhance one's capacity to store information for later use and to broaden the knowledge base of the individual.

UNIT 1. VISUAL MEMORY

Goals: To improve ability to remember visual material and to reconstruct presented material through words or motor expression; to enhance one's capacity to store information for later use and to broaden the knowledge base of the individual.

Task 1: Identifying a Withdrawn Object

Present a box of objects to a pupil. Allow him ample time to look at the objects and touch each if he wishes. Then, while his eyes are closed, withdraw an object and place it in another box of objects. Ask the pupil to identify the withdrawn object by looking at either box, if he wishes. The pupil may identify the withdrawn object either verbally or by locating it in the box of other objects. Vary the number and similarity of objects in each box to increase the difficulty of the task.

Task 2: Verbal Memory Recall

Use verbal recall tasks, such as describing a cow or flower in detail, closing the eyes and describing another pupil's clothes, or reviewing a TV or movie picture scene or program. Emphasize memory recall and how valuable and important it can be in daily living.

Task 3: Trick Your Partner Game

Partners stand opposite one another. One is told to examine the other carefully and then turn around while trying to remember how the partner looked. The first partner changes three things on his person and then the other pupil turns back and tries to identify what is different. The number of items changed can be varied in order to point out more clearly the importance and value of careful observation.

Task 4: Touch Game

Use objects in the classroom or in pictures. The first pupil touches some object and names it; the second pupil touches the same object, names it, and adds another object. Pupils and teachers are added to the game. When a pupil cannot recall all objects, the next person tries to complete the recall. The game can be started again after two or three pupils have been unable to recall all objects. A variation can be employed by using teams of children, awarding points for each correct recall, and alternating players on each team.

Task 5: Picture Recalls

Using a projector or flash cards, expose a picture for ten seconds, remove it, and then ask the pupil to describe, draw, or write what was seen. The pictures can be varied to include people, objects, colors, or designs. The number of pictured items, the length of exposure time, the type of response, and the amount of recall may all be varied to increase or decrease difficulty. The purpose is to train the pupil to observe with a purpose, use discrimination in his observation, and store knowledge in his memory bank.

Task 6: Pattern Reproduction

Arrange a pencil, ruler, and eraser or similar items on a desk or table. Allow a pupil to view them for a few seconds and then cover them. After a delay, ask for reproduction of the original pattern. Vary the complexity of the pattern, exposure time, and delay intervals for increased difficulty.

Task 7: Chalkboard Recalls

Write numbers, letters, words, designs, or shapes on the chalkboard; erase them and ask for recall (which can be either drawn or recited). Gradually toughen the requirements by adding more of same or mixing units; for example, add number-word-design-number or words together to form a thought.

Have pupils put their own material on the board for others to recall. For example:

1. 64 Q AN
2. BB C 6
3. TAC 9
4. C 9 A 10 T
5. CBS NBC

Task 8: Chalkboard Letter Removal Game

Play this game by writing a word on the chalkboard. As pupils close their eyes, remove a letter from the word and ask a pupil to identify the missing letter and fill it in. Then pronounce the word, ask the group to close their eyes, and remove the first letter in addition to another letter. The game continues until all letters of the word have been removed. Do not remove additional letters unless the pupil can fill in all the missing letters to that point. This game can be used in conjunction with a spelling lesson or any academic subject the teacher wishes to reinforce.

Task 9: Checkerboard Placements

After exposure to the set for approximately ten seconds, ask a child to duplicate patterns set up on a checkerboard. The number of checkers used and the complexity of placement will increase the difficulty. Vary the game by replacing some of the checkers with dominoes, small flat objects, etc.

This game can be played with the whole group by mimeographing sheets with a checkerboard format and distributing them to each child. Teacher or child may mark on a chalkboard or overhead projector a checkerboard arrangement for group to reproduce after the model is covered.

Task 10: Stop-Action Game

A pupil is given a chance to perform some action (e.g., bowling, building, jumping rope) and then is instructed to "freeze." Another pupil tries to duplicate the "freeze" position after a period of delay and with the model unavailable (e.g., the model may be covered or shielded, or the pupil attempting the recall may turn around so that he does not see the model). This game not only requires accurate recall of the position of the person but also demands that a pupil be able to interpret the position in a visual-motor modality.

Task 11: Do What I Do

Here, a pupil gets a chance to do something which others then try to remember. A pupil might perform a simple act (e.g., hopping, skipping, jumping, imitating a teacher) or write on the chalkboard. After completion of the act, the writing is covered, and another pupil is asked to recall the total act. The first one who recalls the action or set of actions (not necessarily in correct order) gets the next chance.

UNIT 2. AUDITORY MEMORY

Goals: To improve ability to remember auditory material and to reconstruct presented material through words or motor expression; to enhance one's capacity to store information for later use and to broaden the knowledge base of the individual.

Task 1: Sound Identification with a Picture or an Object

Sound with Picture: Provide sounds of various animals and/or everyday objects and have a pupil identify the sound. Strengthen the child's memory by associating sounds with pictures and having the pupils imitate sounds in the presence of the picture. For example, have a pupil "make like a clock, a chicken, a fire engine," etc.

Sound with Object: Such sounds as a whistle, small bell, buzzer, snapper, stick-hitting can, metal-hitting bottle, file on metal, paper tearing, rag tearing, telephone dialing, pencil tapping on a table, twig breaking, bicycle horn, or nail pounding are made and the items are hidden. As each item is used, ask for its identification. As each is correctly identified, allow the pupil to see the object.

Task 2: Repeating Musical Sounds

Play or hum popular records or melodies and have the pupils repeat them. Give the pupils the opportunity to create original tunes or hum their favorites, while other students try to reproduce. Tap out sequences of numbers or rhythms for pupils to repeat. Make the tapped-out sequences into a game, either by the student's tapping out immediately what the teacher taps or repeating the last tap and adding another, etc.

Task 3: Morse Code Talk

Send simple messages of short and long sounds; first, have pupils try to repeat the sound pattern (e.g., "dot, dot, dash," or "bip, bip, beep"). Then, ask students to hold an auditory trace in order to find a visually corresponding decoded letter (e.g., "dot, dot, dash" equals the letter "b"). Further elaborate sending messages with the aid of a written code. Ultimately, the pupils may be sending and receiving by auditory memory alone. Then, you may send simple known words to the pupils or names of pupils or even silly words in an attempt to maintain interest and fun. This task may be associated particularly usefully with a science project.

Task 4: Gossip

A pupil gets a chance to say something which others try to remember. Sentences, numbers, jargon, or sound imitation can be spoken, and another pupil repeats what was said. You should participate when you are needed. For example, whisper a short statement to one pupil and have him walk across the room and whisper it to another pupil. That pupil in turn passes the message on. Let the message be passed through several pupils and then compare the final statement with the original. The statement can be said only once by each messenger, and then not loud enough for others to hear. Some sample sentences are:

Kick on the fourth down.

A foot race is fun.

A fly ball to right field.

Jumping rope is neat.

Get ready for the big dance.

Task 5: Add-a-Word Game

As a pupil states a word, the next pupil repeats the word and adds another word. The game continues until the chain of words becomes too long for most children to handle. To add to the attention of the group or class, do not take turns as one would normally do. Instead, skip around the room so that anyone can be called upon at any time to repeat and add a word. A team variation can be used, with points awarded for number of correct recalls.

Task 6: Humorous Additions

In reading short nursery rhymes or familiar childhood poetry to pupils, allow the pupils to finish the last line or add an additional line with some humorous rhyming sentence. For example:

Jack be nimble,
Jack be quick,
Jack jump over the candlestick,
And look like a toothpick.

When the last line is added by a pupil, ask him to repeat the entire rhyme, including the line he added.

Task 7: Lost and Found

A pupil is told that he has lost something (e.g., piece of candy or a pencil) and has to find it. With verbal direction from a helper, the pupil tries to follow directions to the lost object. The directions can be varied to include numbers (e.g., two steps forward), letters (e.g., go to the sign marked B-A-L-L), objects (e.g., "It's under the thing that rhymes with fox." "It's near the thing that turns on the light").

Task 8: Buzz Game

Any number of pupils form a circle. The first pupil starts with the numeral 1, and, in succession, each pupil counts the next number. However, when a number ends in the numeral 5 or 0, the pupil must say, "Buzz." If a number is stated instead of "buzz," the pupil sits down. The task can be varied by counting by twos or threes. The last person standing wins the game. To increase difficulty, the sequence may be speeded up by substituting an additional word for numbers ending in zero (e.g., "Ding"). This task may be especially helpful in arithmetic.

Task 9: False Statement

Make two, three, or four short statements, one of which is wrong. The pupils identify the wrong statement and then correct it. For example, you might say, "The water is warm. School is out. Dogs can fly. He is funny." Or you might say, "Cars are nice. The sun is hot. Fish have toes. The sea is salty." Difficulty can be increased by requiring accurate recall of *all* the statements.

Task 10: Bounce-Count-Tap

Have pupils face the front of the room. When the class is quiet, bounce a rubber ball at the back of the room. The pupils must listen carefully and count the number of bounces. Arithmetic skills can be utilized by bouncing the ball three times, hesitating, then bouncing three times again. A pupil then has to give the equation ($3 + 3 = 6$ or $3 \times 3 = 9$) or simply recite the product.

Difficulty can be increased by lengthening the time span between the bounces and the requested answer. Also, you can make the game more complex by requesting that numbers be subtracted or divided. If a ball is not available, the loud tapping of a pencil on a desk will work just as well.

Task 11: Word Category Game

State the category of words to be used (e.g., household items, weather, clothing, body parts, foods, animals, etc.). State the sentence and name the first word. The first pupil repeats the sentence and word and then adds another word in the category.

Example:

Teacher: "We moved last week and took with us a chair."
First Pupil: "We moved last week and took with us a chair and a bed."
Second Pupil: "We moved last week and took with us a chair, a bed, and a table."

Shift the game to another category when difficulty peaks. The class can be divided into two, three, or four teams. A point is scored each time a team member completes the sequence. If a team member cannot recall the named objects, proceed to the next team. Difficulty may be increased by lengthening the sequence. Current academic material may be used such as states, spelling words, names of continents, mountains, rivers, etc.

Task 12: Listening for Fact or Fantasy

Divide the class into two groups. One group is designated as the "fact" group and the other as the "pretend" group. After explaining the difference between fact and pretending, reality and unreality, read a story and inject fantasy at certain points in the story. When a fact is stated, the members of the group designated "fact" raise their hands and identify the fact. When fantasy is stated the "pretend" group members raise their hands and identify the fantasy. Points are scored for each group on the basis of identification and explanation. The roles then can be reversed. Difficulty may be increased by using factual information with a pretend twist. For example, the story might say, "He pitched the ball to me and I hit it with my toothpick."

ADDITIONAL SUGGESTIONS

Teaching storage to children in the classroom requires that you draw on your mastery of many skills in order to meet the specific requirements of individual pupils. You may want to use several of the following methods for presenting material: repetition of same information; diverse presentation of information (e.g., loud-soft voice, print-script); association of material with an object, picture, or situation; asking pupils to provide the stimulus; variation in mode of recall (e.g., recognition, motor, verbal, etc.); presentation of key words, phrases, ideas, and word combinations.

The delay introduced between the time a statement is made and recall asked for will stretch memory as well as increase attention span. Many classes seem to enjoy the challenge created when the teacher states a fact at the beginning of the period and asks for recall of it at the end.

Random guessing should be discouraged, although hints or clues may be given to build prospects for success. Teachers should always offer encouragement and praise for partial accurate recall and be sure to show appreciation for real efforts.

SUMMARY

The tasks in this chapter were designed to sharpen and build the pupil's resources for retaining information made available through visual and auditory channels. In addition, these tasks should facilitate effective sensory discrimination and strengthen concentration and attention span. Improvement in memory skills should help immeasurably in children's efforts to remember instructions and directions and thereby derive pleasure from the satisfactory completion of a given act. One might consider the storage function as being similar to the purpose of a steering wheel—necessary to insure accurate movement from point of departure to destination.

For tasks in this chapter to have relevance and purpose to the pupil, however, the teacher must continually attempt to relate them to real-life situations and the environment in which the pupil lives. Clearly state the importance of these tasks for learning, mastery, and self-growth.

Table 4 summarizes the curriculum units and tasks for the storage area.

Table 4: *Summary of Curriculum Units and Tasks for Curriculum Area: Storage*

Units	*Tasks*
Visual Memory	1. Identifying a Withdrawn Object
	2. Verbal Memory Recall
	3. Trick Your Partner Game
	4. Touch Game
	5. Picture Recalls
	6. Pattern Reproduction
	7. Chalkboard Recalls
	8. Chalkboard Letter Removal Game
	9. Checkerboard Placements
	10. Stop-Action Game
	11. Do What I Do
Auditory Memory	1. Sound Identification with a Picture or Object
	2. Repeating Musical Sounds
	3. Morse Code Talk
	4. Gossip
	5. Add-a-Word Game
	6. Humorous Additions
	7. Lost and Found
	8. Buzz Game
	9. False Statement
	10. Bounce-Count-Tap
	11. Word Category Game
	12. Listening for Fact or Fantasy

REFERENCES

Chalfant, J., and Flathouse, V. "Auditory and Visual Learning." In *Progress in Learning Disabilities*, Vol. 2, edited by H. R. Myklebust, pp. 252–92. New York: Grune & Stratton, 1971.

Chalfant, J., and Scheffelin, M., editors. *Central Processing Functions in Children: A Review of Research.* Bethesda, Maryland: U.S. Department of Health, Education, and Welfare, Monograph Number 9, 1969.

Howe, M. *Introduction to Human Memory.* New York: Harper & Row, 1970.

Hunter, I. M. *Memory: Facts and Fallacies.* Baltimore: Penguin Press, 1957.

Magoun, H. "Commentary." In *Brain Mechanisms Underlying Speech and Language*, edited by F. Darley and C. Millikaw, pp. 199–201. New York: Grune & Stratton, 1967.

Vergason, G. "Facilitation of Memory in the Retardate." *Exceptional Children* 34 (1968): 589–94.

Wiseman, D. E. "A Classroom Procedure for Identifying and Remediating Language Problems." *Mental Retardation* 3 (1965): 20–24.

ADDITIONAL RESOURCES

Bannatyne, A. *Language, Reading, and Learning Disabilities*. Springfield, Illinois: Charles C. Thomas, 1972.

Buist, C., and Schulman, J. *Toys and Games for Educationally Handicapped Children*. Springfield, Illinois: Charles C. Thomas, 1969.

Bush, W., and Giles, M. *Aids to Psycholinguistic Teaching*. Columbus, Ohio: Charles E. Merrill Publishing Co., 1969.

Frostig, M. "Visual Perception, Integrative Functions, and Academic Learning." *Journal of Learning Disabilities* 5 (1972): 1–15.

Karnes, M. *Helping Young Children Develop Language Skills: A Book of Activities*. Arlington, Virginia: Council for Exceptional Children, 1968.

Knights, R., and Thompson, A. *Training Suggestions for Children with Perceptual Deficits*. Toronto: Canadian Association for Children with Learning Disabilities, 1966.

Valett, R. *The Remediation of Learning Disabilities: A Handbook of Psychoeducational Resource Programs*. Palo Alto, California: Fearon, 1967.

Young, M. *Teaching Children with Special* Needs. New York: John Day, 1967.

8

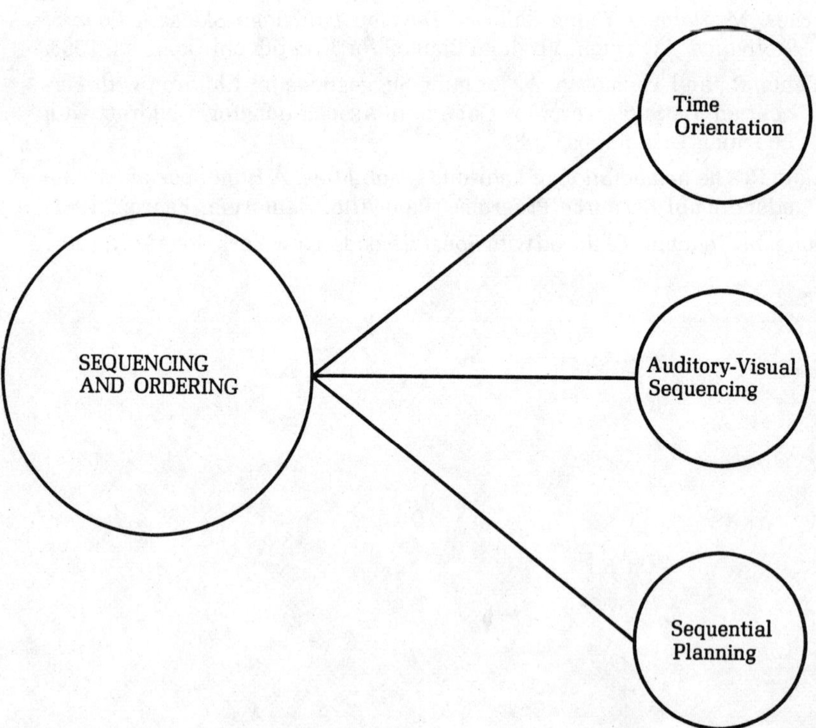

SEQUENCING AND ORDERING
Time Orientation
Auditory-Visual Sequencing
Sequential Planning

Curriculum Area: Sequencing and Ordering

INTRODUCTION TO SEQUENCING AND ORDERING

It is a common classroom expectation that children will be able to move from the point of receiving information or instructions to the successful completion of a task. Often implicit in this expectation is the requirement for carrying out a sequence of behaviors in a planned and orderly fashion. For example, a teacher may specify that the group is to work silently in their books, attempt only a certain number of problems or pages, and then proceed to a different activity or check with the teacher.

As the influence of "open" schools, learning centers, and self-directed activity increases, the skills for guiding one's own behavior within time and space boundaries become even more crucial. Many youngsters, however, are poorly equipped to impose such order on themselves (see Bannatyne, 1972; Barsch, 1967; Hewitt, 1968; Silver and Hagin, 1967). For these children, more specific instruction or remediation is indicated. This chapter focuses on teaching pupils to sequence and order the stimuli received so that their actions are appropriate to a given norm or standard.

The games and activities presented in this chapter are intended to help children acquire an awareness of themselves in relation to time and space and to foster a sense of regularity and "anchoring" (Torrance, 1965) within these dimensions. In addition, suggested tasks are designed to facilitate self-organization and planning.

Rationale

To feel comfortable and in control of one's inner resources, one needs to view life situations within a framework of order and planning. Events cannot be regarded merely as being random, inexplicable happenings or separate, disjointed phenomena. Organization into time and space dimensions creates a manageableness, predictibility, and mastery which are vital to a child's sense of strength and security.

TEACHING UNITS AND GOALS

Three skills are involved in the teaching units in this chapter—time orientation, auditory and visual sequencing, and sequential planning.

Unit 1: Time Orientation

Goal: To increase ability to place things and events into time and space relationships.

Unit 2: Auditory and Visual Sequencing

Goals: To promote the recognition that a total act may consist of a series of smaller steps, with each step having a relationship to the one preceding and following it; to improve ability to accurately arrange or reproduce a sequence of auditory or visual stimuli.

The point needs to be made that our combining of auditory and visual processes under one unit is not meant to imply a functional interdependence between these processes. In fact, research indicates that auditory and visual processes may be differentially intact, both for storage and for sequencing functions (Johnson and

Myklebust, 1967; Lerner, 1971). Thus, a youngster may be quite capable of sequencing visual stimuli yet demonstrate a weakness in auditory sequencing. The same is true for memory operations.

Teachers need to be alert to these possibilities. Through close observation of a child's obvious difficulty in accomplishing a visual or auditory-mediated task, the teacher can often confirm a specific learning disability or at least raise an important question which can then be referred to a resource or diagnostic-prescriptive teacher.

Unit 3: Sequential Planning

Goal: To teach pupils to place limits on their behavior so that discrete actions become part of an overall plan.

UNIT 1. TIME ORIENTATION

Goal: To increase ability to place things and events into time and space sequences.

Task 1: Metronome Exercises

Teach the pupil to coordinate body movements to beats of a metronome by walking, jumping, marching, or running. Call out the name of a part of the child's body and ask the pupil to touch the body part while keeping the beat. Bounce, roll, hit, and throw a ball to the beat. Play jump rope or patty cake. Jump up and down on trampoline springs. Extend the exercises with records, piano, and other musical instruments.

These exercises can assist in helping the child to perceive himself and his actions in relation to external movement (i.e., the passage of time). Regulating self-movements against an external time frame forces one to exert energy and awareness into setting limits on one's own behavior.

Task 2: Time in Action Play

Present pictures or names of seasons, months of the year, day and night, and time of day (e.g., pictures of planting and harvesting or summer and winter sports). Ask class to act out or describe things that can be done during those periods (e.g., in winter, ice skating, sledding, skiing, building snowmen, throwing snowballs). Reverse the procedure and have pupils name season or time shown in scenes of happenings (e.g., the World Series, Miss America contest, Election Day).

Task 3: Drawing Time Circles

Season-of-Month Circle: Using large unlined sheets of paper (newsprint, wrapping paper, etc.), ask children to make a big circle. The floor might be a good place to work. Then show the pupils how to divide the circle into twelve parts, one for each month of the year. Using different colors or heavy dividing lines, have children identify the months within a given season.

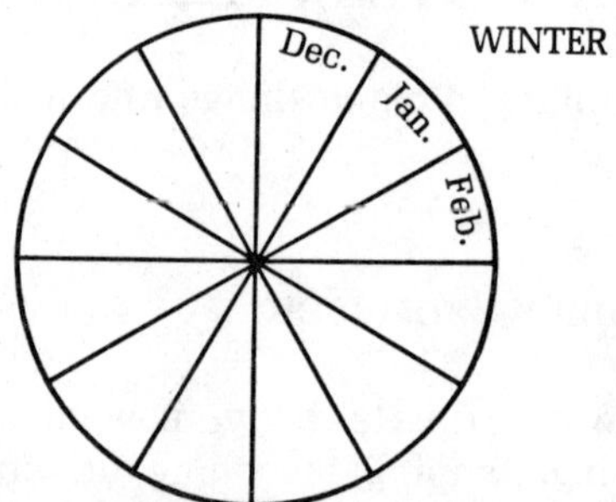

Figure 4: *Season-of-Month Circle*

Ask the children to cut out, describe, or draw pictures of things they do or would like to do during each month and season.

Days-in-Week Circle: As a follow-up to the season-of-month circle, have pupils draw a circle with seven parts, one for each day of week. Again, ask them to cut out, describe, or draw pictures of things they do or would like to do during each day of the week.

Time-of-Day Circle: As an additional follow-up, have pupils draw a circle and divide it into meaningful parts (e.g., before school, morning, afternoon, after school, night). Again, ask them to cut out, describe, or draw pictures of things they do or would like to do during these parts of the day. Try to develop as many time-oriented concepts, such as before, after, early, late, now, then, etc., as possible.

Asking about ways the children feel during the various time segments often enhances the relevance and impact of these activities.

Task 4: "One-Two-That's You" Game

Seat the children in a circle and assign each a number in sequence. To the beat of a metronome (which is speeding up gradually), have players clap their hands for first two counts, then hit right knee for third count, and hit the left knee for the fourth count. When everyone can do this, teach them to call numbers on the third and fourth counts, using their own number on third and anyone else's on the fourth. The game is played by calling different numbers until the last single player who has not erred is left. The game may be simplified by using names for numbers (e.g., count-count-me-Sylvia).

Task 5: Stopwatch Games

With the others watching, time a pupil who is asked to do one of the following type things: run around the room, crawl across the floor, say the alphabet, stand on one leg while writing his name, perform the potato race, etc. Explain how time measures actions and how seconds lead to minutes and minutes to hours. Have pupils begin to estimate the time required for themselves or others to do everyday things, such as putting on a jacket, writing one's name, drinking a glass of milk, etc. Appoint a pupil as a timekeeper for the events and record the estimated time on the chalkboard, checking this approximation later against the correct time.

Lay out a simple course on the classroom floor. Using a stopwatch to measure his attempt, ask a pupil to walk the course in ten seconds. Record the actual time on the chalkboard.

Task 6: My Day Game

A pupil describes a typical day into the tape recorder. Events are then sorted into various time periods, with drawings depicting scenes, and the material is made into child's own storybook. The object is to establish clear, personal referents for the concept of time.

Task 7: Time Puzzles

Present the following sentences which contain verbal puzzles involving time. Ask the class to indicate what is wrong with these or similar statements:

1. I got up early this morning, had supper, and went to school.
2. The sun is just coming up when I go home from school.
3. During June, July, and August, I wear a heavy coat and gloves to school.
4. I like the fall when flowers start blooming.
5. If I plant seeds today, tomorrow they should be flowers.
6. The first day of school each week is Saturday.
7. It takes us five hours to eat lunch.
8. My birthday comes once each month.

Task 8: Hickory Dickory Dock

The class is divided into two groups. One group is assigned the numbers one to six and the other group numbers seven through twelve. Draw the face of a clock on the chalkboard, indicating where the numbers will be placed. Taking turns in questioning one team or the other, make the following statement, "Hickory, Dickory, Dock, the clock struck ______." As a number is called, a pupil is selected to go to the chalkboard and write the number in its proper place. Different colored chalk may be used for each team. The first team that completes its six numbers wins. The game can be lengthened and made more difficult (after the numbers have been written) by requiring hour and minute hands to be drawn in denoting a specific time. The hands are then erased before the next person is required to show a time. The first team completing six correct requests wins the game.

UNIT 2. AUDITORY AND VISUAL SEQUENCING[1]

Goals: To promote the recognition that a total act may consist of a series of smaller steps, with each step having a relationship to the one preceding and following it; to improve ability to accurately arrange or reproduce a sequence of auditory or visual stimuli.

Task 1: Basic Auditory Sequence Game

Present material via auditory means. The purpose of the game is to train the pupil to keep auditory stimuli in the same sequentially ordered arrangement in which they were received. Use simple, commonplace activities, such as repeating letters in alphabet, singing words of songs, giving the days of week and months of year, counting numbers, following directions, repeating sentences and digits (forward and backward), repeating nonsense sounds or phrases, repeating rhythmic patterns tapped out on table, and spelling simple words. Increase difficulty gradually by lengthening sequences. Pupils may be divided into teams, with players earning points for correct sequencing, or the game may be individualized with each pupil striving to reach a specified number of points.

Task 2: Basic Visual Sequence Game

Present material via visual means. The purpose of the game is to train the children to keep visual stimuli in the same sequentially ordered arrangement in which they were received. The material can be fed back by verbal or by visual-motor means on the chalkboard. Use simple, commonplace activities, such as writing letters in the alphabet, copying numbers, spelling simple words, reproducing shape patterns (circle, square, triangle, etc.), reproducing color patterns, reproducing size patterns (big, small, larger, smaller,

---

[1] Auditory and visual sequencing is closely related to storage skills in that performance often requires a recall or reproduction of information initially presented. In fact, Guthrie and Goldberg (1972) have studied the relationship of visual sequential memory to reading disability. We feel, however, that memory is different enough from auditory and visual sequencing to warrant separate consideration. One such difference is that with storage *per se*, the information does not have to be recalled in a precise order. Instead, it can be reproduced in terms of main ideas or content. In addition, visual sequencing skill can be tapped without requiring a memory component, as in the case of Task 7: Picture Sequencing.

greater, lesser, etc.), or reproducing arrangements of objects. Increase the difficulty gradually by lengthening the sequences. Pupils may be divided into teams with players earning points for correct sequencing, or the game can be individualized, with each pupil striving to earn a specified number of points.

Task 3: Sequence Drawing and Word Game

The students take turns repeating a preceding student's sequence and adding another. For example, the first student puts a circle and the numeral 3 on the board, and this sequence is covered; the second student then repeats the circle and the numeral 3 but also adds a sketch of car, etc. Or, in another example, the first student might say, "Hit the ball"; the second student repeats this sentence and adds another sentence of his own, etc. The game may be played in teams with any of the basic sequence activities in auditory or visual modalities. Points may be scored for each team which completes a correct sequence. The team with the most points wins.

Task 4: Action Sequencing

Pupils repeat signs given by teacher or classmate, adding another sign after each round. For example:

1. Hands on head, hands on ears, shoulder, hips, elbows, etc.
2. One step forward, turn around, one step backward, one-half turn, etc.
3. Clap hands, hands over head, hands behind back, arms folded, etc.

The game can be played with all the pupils imitating one leader until only one or two are left who can repeat the sequence correctly, or a variation might be to "pass" the action around the room, with each child getting a chance to copy and initiate an action containing a specified number of steps (e.g., making three gestures while staying in the seat).

Task 5: Action Orders

Request that a pupil carry out a sequence of acts representing multiple response skills [e.g., finding the ball (visual); then, throwing it in the waste basket (motor); then, walking a balance beam (motor); and, finally, picking out a pencil from the feely bag (tactile)]. The directions must be carried out in the order in which they are given. To improve memory, you may wish to delay execution of the directions or inhibit a pupil's actions by talking about other things while he is carrying out the task.

Task 6: Mix Ups

Randomly line up objects or pupils; then reshuffle them, and have a pupil try to place them as they were originally. Allow approximately a ten-second observation of the original order. Start with two to three children and gradually increase to five or six. Point can be awarded for arranging the children in the original order.

Task 7: Picture Sequencing

Mount pictures that show some kind of sequence—sports activities, household duties, school events during the day, building a house, planting a garden, going camping, etc. Place the pictures on a desk or tray in random order and ask a pupil to put them in sequence or in order of occurrence. Extend the activity to such things as knowing the alphabet, counting sequences, completing sentences (current language arts material), spelling words, knowing seasons of the year, etc.

UNIT 3. SEQUENTIAL PLANNING

Goal: To teach pupils to place limits on their behavior so that discrete actions become part of an overall plan.

Task 1: Maze Tracing

Provide graded series of paper and pencil mazes or have one pupil attempt to "steer" another verbally through blackboard or floor mazes by giving "left" and "right" commands. Interest may be enhanced by placing pictures of animals at the start and finish lines of the maze.

Task 2: Number Tracing

Use a simple "Connect the Dots" booklet. Allow the pupils to connect the sequentially numbered dots to form a picture. Then after they have connected all dots, permit them to color imaginatively within the lines. For lower elementary grade children, lay out a series of dots (numbered sequentially) that will form a letter when connected. As a variation, provide a series of dots which are alphabetized so that a number will be formed when the dots are connected.

Task 3: Treasure Hunting

A pupil seeks to find a hidden reward by following an ordered series of clues or instructions, with each clue directing the pupil to the next clue until the treasure is found. For example, the clues might include the following:

1. Look near the window.
2. Very good. Now stand under the flag.
3. That's the way. OK, look in the clothes closet.

Gradually the hunt may be made more challenging by drawing maps to guide the search. Figure 5 provides an example.

Treasures that often please the children include such ordinary things as paper clips, rubber bands, pencils, chalk, paper, crayons, etc. Simple treasures please children, for the main thrill is in the search, not the treasure itself.

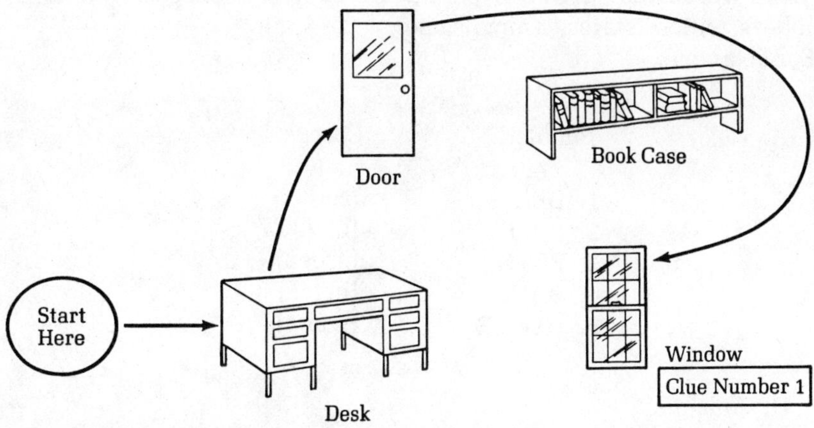

Figure 5

Task 4: Jumbled Words

Use words the pupil knows, such as his name, city, street, state, school, etc. Jumble the letters and then have the pupil place them in proper order of spelling. Current classroom content materials can be used from such subjects as language arts, geography, or science.

For example, ask the class to make as many words as they can using the jumbled letters given in the following list:

1. TPO — top, pot
2. AER — are, ear, era
3. EMTA — tame, mate, team
4. ASEV — save, vase
5. APNS — span, naps, pans
6. OEHS — shoe, hoes, hose
7. AREC — care, race, acre
8. ETPS — step, pets, pest

As a variation, present separate jumbled lists of words to the class. Then instruct the class to form new words or rearrange the letters to form words that are in a particular category, such as colors, numbers, cities, states, animals, etc.

For example:

A. *Colors:*	*Jumbled*	*Correct*
	1. DER	(red)
	2. EULB	(blue)
	3. EENGR	(green)
	4. BACLK	(black)
	5. HWTIE	(white)
B. *Animals:*		
	1. TAC	(cat)
	2. OGD	(dog)
	3. IBRD	(bird)
	4. NASEK	(snake)
	5. TAR	(rat)

Task 5: Scramble Sentences

Scramble the word order in simple sentences only. Then have the class place the words in order so that a complete sentence is constructed.

For example:

1. The look at snow.	(Look at the snow.)
2. Over is school.	(School is over.)
3. Cold weather is the.	(The weather is cold.)
4. I ice skate can.	(I can ice skate.)
5. Weekend this fun have.	(Have fun this weekend.)

Jumble letters and scramble words within one sentence. Use a few words in the proper spelling as clues, such as *in, on, up, down, and, the,* etc. Have the class put the letters and words in proper order so that a complete sentence is constructed.

For example:

1. Ice eamrc is doog.	(Ice cream is good.)
2. Kickllab we ylap.	(We play kickball.)
3. Witre yoru mean.	(Write your name.)
4. I ekil keoc.	(I like coke.)
5. He si my dirfen.	(He is my friend.)

Task 6: Action Planning

Have the class think through a task that requires assembling and ordering objects. For example, present the following problems: "In order to get dressed for school, what clothes would you need and in what order would you put them on?" "If you were going to build a house, what tools would you need and in what order would you use them?" List the needed objects for each problem in the proper order on the chalkboard so additional observation takes place.

Task 7: Origami

Cut pieces of thin white paper into approximately six-inch square pieces. Supply each pupil with one piece of paper. As the pupils follow your directions and demonstration, have each of them fold the paper into an origami figure. Carefully oversee each folded step so that every child finishes a recognizable figure. When the figure(s) are completed, allow the pupils to paint them with water colors or color with crayons. Discuss and analyze what would have happened if the proper steps had not been followed.

Task 8: Story Telling

Introduce the theme of a story involving the whole class. For example, "We are going to make up a story about activities yesterday." Make the first statement concerning some activity of the previous morning and then choose the first pupil to add to the statement. Continue in the same fashion. For example, "Yesterday we decided to learn some new words." (Second Person) "Then we got our papers and pencils." (Third Person) "We ate lunch." (Teacher) "Can you think of something or make up something that fits better with the story about learning new words?" (Third Person) "We wrote down—clown." (Teacher) "That's the idea." Random choosing of pupils will stimulate more careful listening by the entire class as well as encourage all of the children to think in terms of a sequentially developed story. As a variation, the story can be tape recorded and played back upon completion so that children can review the statements made in terms of how they fit the overall development.

Task 9: Following Plans

Have the children attempt to build or assemble something from a prepared plan (blueprint). (Simple models with accompanying diagrams can often be obtained commercially.) Or draw up a simple plan yourself and have the pupils attempt to follow its directions. Consider the following illustrative model, which uses toothpicks or popsicle sticks and some glue:

Step 1 — Line the sticks up like this (see Figure 6).

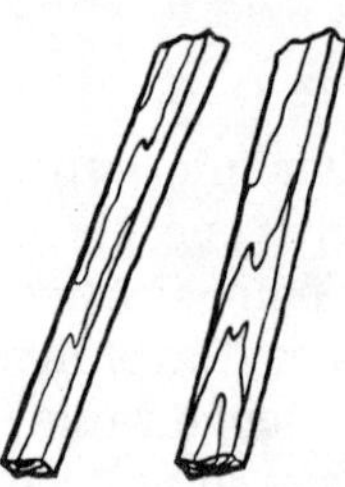

Figure 6

Step 2 — Place a new stick across the others (see Figure 7).

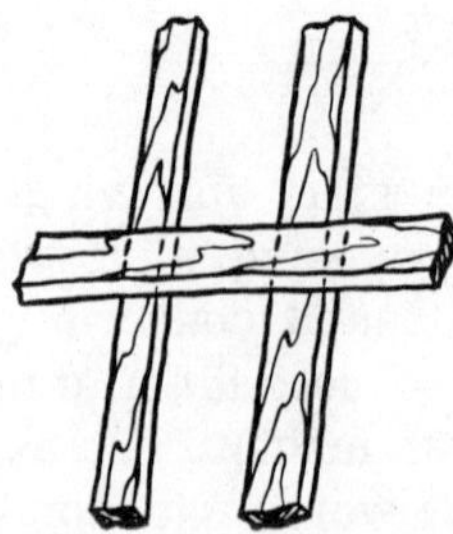

Figure 7

Step 3 — Make a roof with 2 new sticks—like an upside down letter V (see Figure 8).

Figure 8

Table 5: *Summary of Curriculum Units and Tasks in Curriculum Area: Sequencing and Ordering*

Units	*Tasks*
Time Orientation	1. Metronome Exercises 2. Time in Action Play 3. Drawing Time Circles 4. "One-Two-That's You" Game 5. Stopwatch Games 6. My Day Game 7. Time Puzzles 8. Hickory Dickory Dock
Auditory and Visual Sequencing	1. Basic Auditory Sequence Game 2. Basic Visual Sequence Game 3. Sequence Drawing and Word Game 4. Action Sequencing 5. Action Orders 6. Mix Ups 7. Picture Sequencing
Sequential Planning	1. Maze Tracing 2. Number Tracing 3. Treasure Hunting 4. Jumbled Words 5. Scramble Sentences 6. Action Planning 7. Origami 8. Story Telling 9. Following Plans

Difficulty level can be increased later on by adding more steps to the plan.

SUMMARY

The ability to sequence and order incoming information as well as one's own actions is an important resource for coping with the demands and expectations of personal responsibility. Pupils are often expected to process and complete tasks without step-by-step direction, but to succeed, many need specific instruction in the skills of time orientation, visual and auditory sequencing, and sequential planning.

For tasks in this chapter to have relevance and purpose to the pupil, however, the teacher must continually attempt to relate them to real-life situations and the environment in which the pupil lives. You also should clearly state the importance of these tasks for learning, mastery, and self-growth.

Table 5 summarizes the chapter units and tasks.

REFERENCES

Bannatyne, A. *Language, Reading, and Learning Disabilities*. Springfield, Illinois: Charles C. Thomas, 1972.

Bannatyne, A., and Wichiarajote, P. "Relationships between Written Spelling, Motor Functioning, and Sequencing Skills." *Journal of Learning Disabilities* 2 (1969): 4–16.

Barsch, R. *Achieving Perceptual-Motor Efficiency*. Seattle, Washington: Special Child, 1967.

Guthrie, J., and Goldberg, H. "Visual Sequential Memory in Reading Disability." *Journal of Learning Disabilities* 5 (1972): 45–49.

Hewett, F. M. *The Emotionally Disturbed Child in the Classroom*. Boston: Allyn & Bacon, 1968.

Johnson, D., and Myklebust, H. *Learning Disabilities: Educational Principles and Practices*. New York: Grune & Stratton, 1967.

Lerner, J. *Children with Learning Disabilities: Theories, Diagnosis, and Teaching Strategies*. Boston: Houghton Mifflin, 1971.

Silver, A., and Hagin, R. "Specific Reading Disability—An Approach to Diagnosis and Treatment." *Journal of Special Education* 1 (1967): 109–18.

Torrance, E. P. *Mental Health and Constructive Behavior*. Belmont, California: Wadsworth, 1965.

ADDITIONAL RESOURCES

Bateman, B. *Temporal Learning*. San Rafael, California: Dimensions, 1968.

Emberly, E. *Ed Emberly's Drawing Book of Animals*. Boston: Little, Brown, 1970.

Frostig, M., in association with Maslow, P. *Movement Education: Theory and Practice*. Chicago: Follett, 1970.

Karnes, M. *Helping Young Children Develop Language Skills: A Book of Activities*. Arlington, Virginia: Council for Exceptional Children, 1968.

Robins, F., and Robins, J. *Educational Rhythmics for Mentally and Physically Handicapped Children*. New York: Association Press, 1968.

9

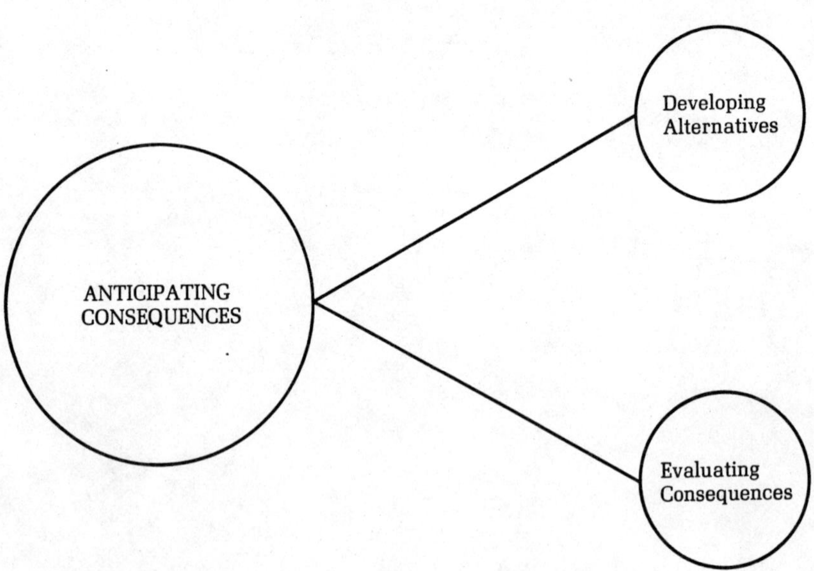
ANTICIPATING CONSEQUENCES
Developing Alternatives
Evaluating Consequences

Curriculum Area: Anticipating Consequences

INTRODUCTION TO ANTICIPATING CONSEQUENCES

At the core of the meaning of self-control is the degree to which an individual exercises personal choice over the alternatives for his own actions. To exercise such choice, one first must conceive of personal behavior in terms of options of action, each with different consequences. For example, at the very least, every child in the classroom can opt either to follow instructions or to resist them. If he follows instructions, he can anticipate teacher approval, parent satisfaction, and some peer reinforcement. On the other hand, if he resists, he may gain self-confidence by standing in opposition to something, some enthusiastic peer support (as well as a few negative or taunting comments), and unfavorable reactions from adults.

Since self-esteem is forged from the responses of significant others to the individual (see Cooley, 1922; Mead, 1934), it is critical that a child have the ability to anticipate the effects his behavior will have on these others. It is one thing to say, "Who cares what they think?"; it is another to say, "Yes, I know they won't like it and will reject me for it, but I'll make that choice." The first attitude suggests a rigidity and insensitivity that is bound to become self-defeating. The second position, however, is based on a weighing of personal values in relation to those held by others and indicates a degree of self-control within a social order. Our goal is not to teach children to sacrifice their uniqueness to social conformity but to build their personal integrity with responsibility.

This chapter will provide suggested activities for teaching children that any problem they may face will have several alternative methods of solution, each with its own probable consequences. The capacity to generate these alternatives or to see things in a new light has been found to be central to creative thinking (Barron, 1969; Davis and Scott, 1971; Torrance, 1971). Furthermore, as Parnes and Noller (1971) report:

> Our bibliographic search has uncovered over forty studies evaluating programs for teaching students to improve their sensitivity, fluency, flexibility, originality, elaboration, and related abilities. . . . Approximately ninety percent of the total number indicate that subjects' creative-productivity levels were significantly increased by deliberate educational programs (pp. 65–66).

To anticipate the consequences of one's behavior, one must first be able to see alternatives; only under those circumstances will the element of choice exist. Thus, helping youngsters to develop alternatives is an indispensable first step toward the behavior of making responsible choices. Once alternatives can be imagined, it becomes possible to evaluate the likely consequences of different alternatives.

Much of the promising work by Ralph Ojemann (1972) and the Educational Research Council of America (1969, 1971, 1972), which applies a "causal" orientation to self and interpersonal behavior, is founded on creating alternative ways to understand human behavior and training to appraise probable consequences. The following quotation from the Council's curriculum publication *Understanding Human Behavior: Student Book* (1972) conveys the approach:

> Up to this point, we have been concerned primarily with trying to find out how and why a behavior or a situation develops. . . . This is something we need to do—become aware of possible causes, the reasons why people act the way they do.
>
> But this is only part of the story. We cannot stop here, for behavior not only has causes, it also has consequences. Every behavior, every action, has some result or effect (p. 32).

Griggs and Bonney (1970) conducted a study of the impact of Ojemann's "causal" orientation curriculum on fourth- and fifth-grade children. Data indicated highly favorable results in that children who had received one semester of instruction in understanding human behavior became significantly more accepting of each other and themselves than the control-group youngsters.

Systematic role-playing methods have been found to be effective for considering the consequences of behavior (Chesler and Fox, 1966; Shaftel and Shaftel, 1967). By structuring the particular role and—if desired—the possible alternatives to be enacted, the teacher can bring out reactions that pupils might otherwise avoid. For example, a role-playing situation mentioned by Chesler and Fox involves a boy and girl who are not speaking to one another. When asked how they might feel or act in the "player's" shoes, each student responded relatively more freely than if he had been asked how he would deal with girls or boys who do not like him.

A considerable body of research has been developed regarding the cognitive dimension of reflection-impulsivity (Drake, 1970; Kagan, Moss, and Sigel, 1963; Kagan, Pearson, and Welch, 1966; Messer, 1970; Reali and Hall, 1970; Ward, 1968; Yando and Kagan, 1968). This research indicates that there are clear and consistent differences in the style of conceptualization, for both children and adults, which can be characterized in terms of a reflective style as opposed to an impulsive style. Thus, reflective individuals take longer to make cognitive decisions, consider more response alternatives, and make fewer errors (Drake, 1970; Kagan, Moss, and Sigel, 1963; Reali and Hall, 1970). Messer (1970) found that impulsive children evidenced lower school achievement and language skills at first- and third-grade checkpoints in addition to missing important cues for reading.

The most fascinating aspect of the research on reflection-impulsivity is the apparent modifiability of cognitive style within the context of otherwise stable differences. Ward (1968) has shown that impulsive decision making can be altered by giving immediate reward for correct responses and withholding reward after errors, while Kagan, Pearson, and Welch (1966) found that impulsive first-grade students can be tutored to use a more reflective approach. Yando and Kagan (1968) have reported a direct influence of teacher tempo on reflection-impulsivity in their finding that, in contrast to their peers with more impulsive teachers, pupils with more reflective teachers became more reflective themselves during the academic year. This research clearly indicates that decision-making behavior can be modified to include consideration of alternatives and their consequences.

Individual differences in interests, values, and personality require that teachers respect the pupil's right to solve problems by more than one acceptable method. Teachers may want to point out a preferred method of solution as one of several choices available but they also should emphasize the possibility of other choices. A pupil will not always know the preferred method when confronted with a real-life situation, but if he has been taught to think in terms of alternatives, he will be in a stronger position to resolve the situation adequately. In addition, if faced with responsibility for one's own choice—be the outcome right or wrong—the student will adopt a more careful and considered attitude in alternative choice selection.

Rationale

Flexible control implies that a choice of response exists so that behavior is not fixed or irrational. Impulses or action dispositions ordinarily are aroused and pointed toward specific targets through preferred and habitual response modes. Rational behavior, however, depends upon one's capacity to respond in a variety of ways at a given time as well as to judge which of those ways is most likely to achieve satisfactory results. A child equipped with multiple alternatives for behavior and an ability to consider the impact of his actions on others is in a favorable position to function effectively.

TEACHING UNITS AND GOALS

This chapter contains two units—developing alternatives and evaluating consequences. The word *alternatives* denotes choices available for solution of a task, while *consequences* denotes an evaluative procedure of reflective thinking concerning those choices.

Unit 1. Developing Alternatives

Goal: To increase the ability to create alternative choices or methods for solving a task or problem situation.

Unit 2. Evaluating Consequences

Goals: To improve the ability to evaluate choices of action in terms of their probable outcome (consequences); to establish some degree of responsibility for the probable outcome of these choices.

UNIT 1. DEVELOPING ALTERNATIVES

Goal: To increase the ability to create alternative choices or methods for solving a task or problem situation.

Task 1: Action Stunts ("Show me" Situations)

Usual way: Ask a child to perform a number of actions in his usual or preferred way. Include emotional as well as physical processes. For example, ask a child to sing, jump, say "hello," laugh, show anger, throw a ball, show sadness, sit on a chair, and show fear in his usual way.

Different ways: Following a demonstration of the usual way, ask the child to show you how many different ways he can perform the same actions. Different expressions of a given action by a number of children should create an atmosphere for consideration of alternative choices available for almost any task.

Task 2: Thought Stunts ("Think of" Situations)

Usual way: Ask a child to describe how he would do the following: ask a parent for a household job, make a birthday party, build a house, cook dinner, clean his clothes, repair a bicycle.

Different ways: Following his description of a preferred way, ask the child to describe a number of different ways he could do the same tasks. Contrasts between the usual way and a different way will indicate many of the acceptable alternative choices available.

Task 3: Role-Playing Alternatives

Present students with a situation and ask for someone to *make believe* he is taking a certain role. For example, a child can be asked to make believe he is asking for a job, trying to teach another child to do something, trying to point something out to his parents which they did not know about previously. Then ask others to comment on the method or approach the student chose and to offer a different one.

Task 4: Simple Charades

Organize a game of charades in which the actor illustrates different sets of movements to demonstrate the same charade. Allow the child who is guessing to show other ways the actor could have performed the same charade. These games will point up the fact that many choices exist for a solution to a task, many of which are acceptable and sanctioned both by peers and by adults.

Task 5: Word-Change Games

Letter addition game: Choose a short word. Ask the students to make as many new words as possible from that word by adding a letter to the end. For example:

car — cars, card, care, Carl, cart, carp

bar — bars, Bart, barn, barb, bare, bard, bark

pin — pins, pine, ping, pink, pint.

Substitute word-letter game: Using a short word, ask the children to make as many new words as possible by changing the first letter only of that word. For example:

cod — rod, sod, mod, God, hod, pod

map — cap, gap, lap, nap, rap, sap, tap

bar — car, far, jar, mar, oar, tar, war

Using the same words, reverse the order and change the last letter only. For example:

cod — cob, cog, con, cop, cot, cow, coy

bar — bad, bag, bah, bam, ban, bat, baw

map — mad, mam, man, mar, mat, May

Scrabble word game: Choose simple words. Ask the children to make as many words as possible using only the letters in the original word. For example:

nose — no, so, one, son, eon, on

spin — pin, pins, in, sip, sin, nip, nips

care — race, arc, car, are, ace, ear, acre

read — dear, red, ad, are, dare, ear

These simple word games are intended to illustrate some of the alternatives available in assembling words. A rearrangement of the letters creates an entirely different meaning.

Task 6: Devising Methods ("What Methods")

Ask the students to think of ways or methods they might employ to do the following: Build a house; find a job; catch a butterfly; change a wheel on a wagon; get someone to do something for them; trade with a friend; ask for help; tell the teacher they haven't done their homework. Ask the students to express their methods through words and/or actions, and encourage alternative suggestions from the class.

Task 7: Structured Independence ("What's your way?")

The goal here is to help the pupil to recognize that his own approaches to performing a task are worthwhile and that there are multiple ways to succeed in a task. The teacher performs an act and the child performs the same act in another way. For example:

Teacher sits on the floor with knees bent and crossed.

Child sits on the floor with legs stretched out and straight.

Teacher erases the chalkboard from top to bottom.

Child erases the chalkboard from side to side.

Teacher throws the ball underhand.

Child throws the ball overhand.

Task 8: Structured Divergence ("Doing Opposites")

Ask the children to do the opposite of what the teacher does. For example:

Teacher stands up.

Child sits down.

Teacher runs in place.

Child stands still.

Teacher laughs.

Child is sad.

Teacher walks backwards.

Child walks forward.

UNIT 2. EVALUATING CONSEQUENCES

Goals: To improve the ability to evaluate choices of action in terms of their probable outcome (consequences); to establish some degree of responsibility for the probable outcome of those choices.

Task 1: "What Could Happen If" Situations

In an attempt to build capacity for thought before action, show the pupils pictures depicting potential hazards or accidents. For example: an open manhole cover, a glass on the edge of a table, a child leaning against a door, a parked car on a hill, a ball rolling into the street, crossing the street against a red light, running down steps, riding a bike at night without a light, catching a hard ball in front of a large glass window, forgetting to turn the fire off on the stove, running on a slippery floor, tearing another person's paper, pulling a chair out from under someone, playing with matches. Each statement will warrant discussion in reference to the consequences of such a hazard or aggressive behavior.

Task 2: Booby Trap Game

Use the commercial game involving the removal of various sized circular forms in such a way as not to release a spring. The child has to anticipate what will happen if a given form is removed.

Task 3: Reactions to Social Situations (Deciding "What or How")

Ask a student to think of a puzzling social situation, what course of action he would take, and its possible consequences. For example: what to do after being hit by a ball; what to do after being knocked down in a game; how to tell your best friend you broke his toy; how to tell your mother you didn't go to school; how to earn money to buy a toy. Conduct a discussion about the probable consequences of the responses offered by the child, getting the children's ideas as much as possible.

Task 4: "Hot and Cold"

Hide an object in the room so that the searcher does not know where it is although other class members do. As the searcher gets nearer the object the class says, "hot"; the farther away he goes, the response becomes "cold". Vary the game by using other terms such as "near" and "far" or music with loud and soft tones or fast and slow tempos. The pupil thus must learn to evaluate his movements in terms of the consequent responses from the class. This task adds an additional element, namely, the consequences of motor activity. It should be thought-provoking in evaluating one's own physical moves and how others perceive them.

Task 5: Understanding Feedback ("What's the Action?")

Ask a child to leave the room while those remaining decide what the child is to do when he returns. The task can be either positive or negative. The child must take his clues, which are all nonverbal, from the class. The clues may be facial or in gestures, including nonvocal expressions of laughter, sadness, anger, disgust, happiness, etc. The purpose is to demonstrate sensitivity to the feelings of others as a consequence of one's own action and the evaluation of clues in determining subsequent action. For example, the class may decide they would like the child to sit in the middle of the circle. As behavior is exhibited that moves toward this goal, the class shows pleasure; evidence of opposing behavior creates dissatisfaction among the class members.

It is useful to discuss the clues and interpretations after the game to clarify the meaning of reactions shown. The discussion may be expanded to include thoughts on how children learn and perceive.

Task 6: Mazes

Allow each child to trace a maze, using a soft lead pencil without an eraser. If the child takes a wrong route, realizes his mistake, allow him to try another route but not to erase his first error, even though no penalties are assessed for taking the wrong route and no points are scored for completion of the maze. The purpose of these maze exercises is to encourage the child to think ahead and anticipate where he will end up if he takes a particular route. You may want to buy commercial maze books or make up your own, although if you decide to make up your own mazes, you should start on a single route and then come to a point where three routes become available, two of which are incorrect. Mazes may be round or square; they may have a goal in the middle or on the opposite side from the starting point.

Task 7: Crossword Puzzles

Use crossword puzzles designed specifically for elementary school children. Several companies have developed such crossword puzzles which are reusable. Crossword puzzles cause the pupil to think before he puts down the missing letters in a word; since he has several words which could fit the definition, he has to select the most suitable alternative.

ADDITIONAL SUGGESTIONS

In this chapter, we have included several tasks directly related to language arts development; these tasks allow the teacher to make modifications in work usage to fit her particular grade level. Arithmetic content may also be used to develop the idea of alternatives. For example, ask the pupils to list as many different ways as possible for solving an equation (4 + 4 = 8, 2 + 2 + 2 + 2 = 8, 7 + 1 = 8, 6 + 2 = 8, etc.). Furthermore, if alternative views are encouraged in the classroom, the teacher may discover that she can develop a lively program for review and restudy of curriculum content.

SUMMARY

Effective functioning in today's environment is often contingent upon the development of several alternative methods of solution for a given problematic situation. If a child is not aware of alternatives available, his solution is fixed and based on habitual modes of action. The purpose of this chapter is to teach the child that there are acceptable and satisfying alternatives for behavior in given situations. Furthermore, the child needs to realize that in the selection of an alternative, he must be responsible for the consequences of that choice and that, therefore, careful evaluation must precede choice. Reflective or empathic thinking in terms of another's reaction will assist the child in predicting the probable outcome of his choice.

For the tasks in this chapter to have relevance and purpose to the child, however, the teacher must continually attempt to relate them to real-life situations and the environment in which the child lives. Also, clearly state the importance of these tasks for learning, mastery, and self-growth.

The curriculum units and tasks presented in this chapter are reviewed in Table 6.

Table 6: *Summary of Curriculum Units and Tasks in the Curriculum Area: Anticipating Consequences*

Units	*Tasks*
Developing Alternatives	1. Action Stunts 2. Thought Stunts 3. Role-Playing Alternatives 4. Simple Charades 5. Word-Change Games 6. Devising Methods 7. Structured Independence 8. Structured Divergence

Table 6 (continued)

Units	*Tasks*
Evaluating Consequences	1. "What Could Happen If" 2. Booby Trap Game 3. Reactions to Social Situations 4. "Hot and Cold" 5. Understanding Feedback 6. Mazes 7. Crossword Puzzles

REFERENCES

Barron, F. *Creative Person and Creative Process*. New York: Holt, Rinehart & Winston, 1969.

Chesler, M., and Fox, R. *Role-Playing Methods in the Classroom*. Chicago: Science Research Associates, 1966.

Cooley, C. H. *Human Nature and the Social Order*. New York: Scribner's, 1922.

Davis, G., and Scott, J., editors. *Training Creative Thinking*. New York: Holt, Rinehart & Winston, 1971.

Drake, D. M. "Perceptual Correlates of Impulsive and Reflective Behavior." *Developmental Psychology* 2 (1970): 202–14.

Educational Research Council of America. *Education in Human Behavior: Learning to Decide Program*. Cleveland, Ohio: Educational Research Council, 1969.

———. *Education in Human Behavior: Learning to Decide Program*. Cleveland, Ohio: Educational Research Council, 1971.

———. *Program in Mental Health and Human Behavior: Understanding Human Behavior, Student Book*. Cleveland, Ohio: Educational Research Council, 1972.

Griggs, J., and Bonney, M. "Relationship between 'Causal' Orientation and Acceptance of Others, 'Self-Ideal Self' Congruency, and Mental Health Changes for Youth and Fifth-Grade Children." *Journal of Educational Research* 63 (1970): 471–77.

Kagan, J.; Moss, H.; and Sigel, I. "Psychological Significance of Styles of Conceptualization." *Monographs of the Society for Research in Child Development* 28 (1963): 73–112.

Kagan, J.; Pearson, L.; and Welch, L. "The Modifiability of an Impulsive Tempo." *Journal of Educational Psychology* 57 (1966): 359–65.

Mead, G. *Mind, Self, and Society from the Standpoint of a Social Behaviorist.* Chicago: University of Chicago Press, 1934.

Messer, S.B. "Reflection-Impulsivity: Stability and School Failure." *Journal of Educational Psychology* 61 (1970): 487–90.

Ojemann, R. *Brief Description of the Program of Education in Human Behavior and Potential.* Cleveland, Ohio: Educational Research Council, 1972.

Parnes, S., and Noller, R. "The Creative Studies Project: Raison d'Être and Introduction." *Journal of Research and Development in Education* 4 (1971): 62–66.

Reali, N., and Hall, V. "Effect of Success and Failure on the Reflective and Impulsive Child." *Developmental Psychology* 2 (1970): 240–46.

Shaftel, F., and Shaftel, G. *Role-Playing for Social Values: Decision-Making in the Social Studies.* Englewood Cliffs, New Jersey: Prentice-Hall, 1967.

Torrance, E. P. "Creativity and Infinity." *Journal of Research and Development in Education* 4 (1971): 35–41.

Ward, W. C. "Reflection-Impulsivity in Kindergarten Children." *Child Development* 39 (1968): 867–74.

Yando, R., and Kagan, J. "The Effect of Teacher Tempo on the Child." *Child Development* 39 (1968): 27–34.

ADDITIONAL RESOURCES

Davis, G. A. *It's Your Imagination: Theory and Training of Problem Solving.* New York: Basic Books, 1972.

Meeker, M. *The Structure of Intellect.* Columbus, Ohio: Charles E. Merrill Publishing Co., 1969.

Parnes, S. J. *Creative Behavior Guidebook.* New York: Scribner's, 1967.

Porteus, S. *Porteus Maze Test: Fifty Years Application.* Palo Alto, California: Pacific, 1965.

Torrance, E. P. *Encouraging Creativity in the Classroom.* Dubuque, Iowa: William C. Brown, 1970.

Williams, F. E. *Classroom Ideas for Encouraging Thinking and Feeling.* Buffalo, New York: D.O.K., 1970.

10

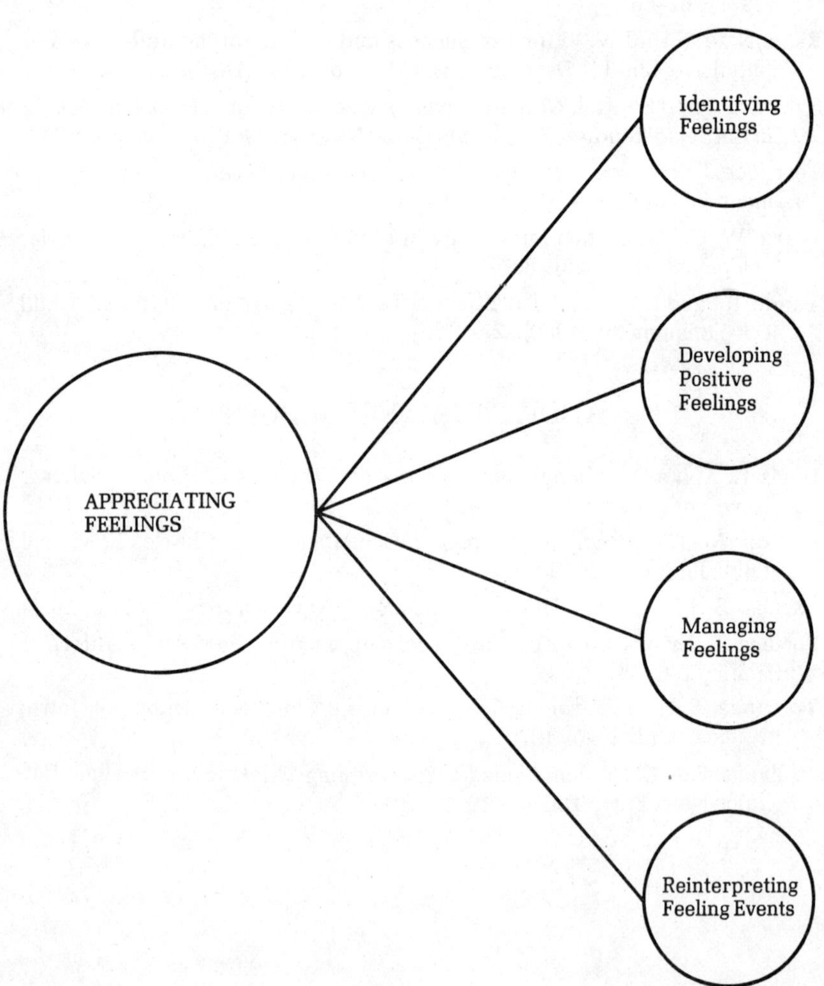
APPRECIATING FEELINGS
Identifying Feelings
Developing Positive Feelings
Managing Feelings
Reinterpreting Feeling Events

Curriculum Area: Appreciating Feelings

INTRODUCTION TO APPRECIATING FEELINGS

A major assumption in our approach to self-control is that awareness and mastery of feelings is necessary for the optimal development of self-control. Unexpressed or unresolved feelings create strong urges toward impulsive behavior, which, in turn, results in heightened anxiety about loss of control. Thus, an important function of the self-control curriculum is the provision of planned learning situations which stimulate constructive expression of affective experience as well as a balanced utilization and expression of facts and feelings.

This chapter brings the dimension of feelings directly into the classroom. We not only believe it possible to help children appreciate and constructively manage feelings systematically and according to a deliberate plan; we also are deeply convinced that such help is an educational priority. Earlier we spoke of a child's right to own his feelings as contrasted with the importance of placing limits on his actions. The critical challenge for all of us involves finding positive means for helping children to use feelings to promote constructive actions. Inlow (1966) calls for a similar thrust into the school curricula, if children are to be prepared to cope successfully with the challenges of today's world. "Because the key to the future lies in man's understanding of himself, education is remiss not to consider seriously every avenue which might lead to that outcome . . . . The time may well be ripe for education to try out new approaches. One of these logically is the direct instructional approach to mental health" (p. 60).

In the past few years, many psychologist-educators have responded to this call for direct instructional mental health programs. Limbacher (1969, 1970) has written several elementary texts on the theme of "Dimensions of Personality." These texts promote pupil study and discussion of a variety of human development topics, including: "My Feelings Are Real," "When I Cried for Help," "The Body I've Inherited," "Feelings and the Family," "The Need to Belong," and "Learning to Work Together." Wrenn and Schwarzock (1970) have developed a series of books for adolescents which deal with problems of coping with the stresses of reality (e.g., loneliness, cliques, social rejection). In addition, there are also a few social studies curricula which employ role-playing and guided inquiries as means of exploring causes and consequences of human behavior (LaRue, LaRue, and Hill, 1972; Lippitt, Fox and Schaible, 1971; Shaftel and Shaftel, 1967).

Bessell and Palomares (1970) have developed a particularly noteworthy human development program for preschoolers through intermediate-grade youngsters. This program consists of a thirty-six-week course of instruction which concentrates to an equal degree on awareness (of self and others), mastery (self-confidence and effectiveness), and social interaction (interpersonal comprehension and tolerance). The teaching strategy for this program calls for guided small-group discussion (in a "Magic Circle"), including opportunities for peer leadership. Complete lesson guides have been developed which include a statement of objectives, the activity, materials, and procedure.

There are also a number of guides or handbooks which seek to foster a classroom atmosphere that stimulates, encourages, and supports the constructive expression and appreciation of feelings (Alschuler, 1973; Brown, 1971; Canfield, Wells, and Hall, 1972; Lederman, 1969; Lyon, 1971; Randolph, 1971; Raths, Harmin, and Simon, 1966; Synectics, 1972; Weinstein and Fantini, 1970; Williams, 1970).

It should be obvious from this brief review that much progress has been made in efforts to promote mental or emotional health in the classroom. Yet we are just on the threshold of discovery in this field. The years ahead promise a period of emotional education; it may even become the moment in history when the human side of man catches up with the technological and scientific.

As indicated in Chapter 3, the self-control curriculum treats affective processes as being amenable to skill development in much the same way that cognitive processes have usually been regarded. However, to proceed in developing affective skills it is necessary to define *the nature of these skills, the characteristic outcomes that such skills promote, and the types of experiences or activities that may facilitate development of such skills.* In this curriculum, each of the major affective components or skills for self-control (i.e., appreciating feelings, managing frustration, inhibition and delay, and relaxation) is analyzed into *curriculum units* (corresponding to the nature of the skill area), *unit goals* (corresponding to characteristic outcomes mediated by the skill), and *unit tasks* (corresponding to experiences which facilitate skill development).

This curriculum unit on appreciating feelings is based upon four main teaching units: identifying and accepting feelings, developing positive feelings, managing feelings, and, reinterpreting feeling events. Tasks which assist children in acquiring the skills needed to effectively master their affective experiences are described in each of these areas. In approaching the teaching of these units, it is important to understand the theory underlying the organization and sequence of instruction which we advocate. This is of particular significance because of the relative lack of research and experience available for reference in promoting mastery of affective events through classroom procedures. Furthermore, we are acutely aware of the widespread discomfort and apprehension associated with emotional experience. Therefore, the central importance of this area to the self-control curriculum as well as to effective teaching in general makes it essential that our approach be clear-cut and convincing.

In considering the way into teaching an appreciation for feelings, we need to grasp several conceptual lines. No teacher should employ any task in this chapter without first understanding the following concepts: (1) directness of affective expression; (2) target of expression; (3) locus of responsibility; (4) medium of expression; and, (5) social acceptability of expression.

Directness of affective expression: A personal feeling may be handled in one of three basic ways: by keeping it private, by expressing it indirectly, or by expressing it directly. For our purposes, keeping a feeling private refers to a personal reaction or awareness which is not displayed to others.

Indirect expression consists of nonverbal behavior which reflects the emotional experience or verbal behavior which derives from the basic feeling yet does not acknowledge the feeling directly. Examples of indirect expression might be lowering one's eyes, hanging one's head, or slumping down in a chair when feeling ashamed or embarrassed; kicking over a chair, breaking a pencil, or scratching a desk when feeling resentful of another's treatment; screaming "You're a stupid idiot" or "Get the hell out of here" at someone else when feeling discouraged about one's own abilities. Thus, indirect expressions may be passive or active, socially acceptable or unacceptable, nonverbal or verbal. In all cases, however, the actual feeling either is disguised in some way, or the verbal expression of it is not congruent with the nonverbal reactions to it.

Direct expressions of affect occur when one's personal reaction is clearly and congruently identified in words and actions. Verbal statements must be phrased in terms of "I feel . . ." or "I am . . ." in order to reflect affective experience directly. Other "I" statements, such as "I wish . . .", "I think . . .", "I believe . . .", "I like . . .", and "I don't care . . .", also are reflections of an inner reaction. In addition, such direct statements of feeling should match the nonverbal aspects of behavior. There are times, however, when a direct affective expression will not be possible (e.g., when subjective awareness does not exist), and indirect statements represent the closest possible expression of an emotional reaction.

As direct expression increases, it is helpful to expand the "I" statement to include factors relating to the affect aroused. For example, "I feel . . ." can be expanded to "I feel . . . when you . . ." or "I am . . . because the class . . . ." *Identification of the perceived conditions which stimulate an emotional response provides an opportunity for presentation of new information necessary for correcting or modifying perceptions associated with particular affective reactions.*[1]

---

[1]This point is extremely critical and one which heavily influences our construction of tasks and desired learning experiences, especially in the curriculum areas of appreciating feelings and managing frustration. In effect, we are affirming the value of a perceptual or cognitive base for emotional education. We have been particularly impressed by the work of Ellis (1962); Lazarus (1966, 1970); Leeper (1965, 1970); and Peters (1970) in this area.

Ellis's (1962) advocacy of a rational-emotive approach to psychotherapy is based upon a similar premise; namely, that irrational ideas are responsible for emotional disturbance.

Target of expression: A personal feeling is aroused only in relation to a particular source, whether that source be human, animal, or natural. Thus, a child may become angry when his teacher yells at him, a dog grabs his ball, or it rains on the day of a field trip. Where *directness* of expression refers to the clarity and congruence of the feeling expressed to the feeling experienced, *target* of expression involves the correspondence between the *source* of the feeling and the *object* of the feeling. For example, a youngster who is sad because his father has to go away sobs in school when he misplaces a book; although the source of his sadness is his father, the target of the feeling he expresses is the lost book.

The target of expression dimension may be viewed as a continuum from responses expressed toward the *original* source of the feeling aroused, to responses expressed toward a target *close* to the original source, and, finally, responses expressed toward a target *distant* from the original source. In the previous example of the father and the little boy, the original target would be the father and direct expression would be evidenced if the son cried in his father's presence. A close target might be the mother or a substitute father figure, while a distant target might be anything associated with loss or absence but not closely related to the father (either by kinship or physical resemblance), such as the misplaced book. This dimension of feeling has traditionally been recognized through the concepts of "displacement" and "generalization."

Lazarus (1966) considers emotional responses as deriving from a primary cognitive appraisal of a situation. When stimuli are viewed as threatening, negatively toned affects result. In an effort to cope with this affective stress, secondary appraisal of situational constraints and consequences occurs. This secondary appraisal, in turn, determines the specific coping-reaction pattern (i.e., the actual emotional expression, such as anger, fear, depression, etc.).

The essence of Lazarus' analysis is that emotions, whether experienced as general anxiety or specific affective states, are consequences rather than causes of cognition. This formulation does not deny the reality or significance of emotion but does emphasize the rational-attitudinal aspects of emotional arousal.

Leeper (1970) presents a motivational-perceptual theory in which emotions are regarded as "especially important motives" for producing goal-directed behavior and mental activity" (p. 152). These emotional motives are "the individual's perceptions or representations of what he regards as the most significant realities in his life" (p. 164). In other words, one's perceptions of a given situation provide a signal for goal-directed action to obtain pleasure (creating happiness) or avoid pain (creating fear and anxiety). Leeper points out that emotions are direct results of how we view things and can be modified as a function of new or changed perceptions.

Peters (1970) carries this line of reasoning forward in a recent article on the education of emotions: ". . . a logically necessary condition for the use of the word 'emotional' is that some kind of appraisal should be involved, and that the different emotions must involve different appraisals. In other words, emotions are basically forms of cognition. It is because of this central feature which they possess that I think there is any amount of scope for educating the emotions" (p. 188).

Locus of responsibility: In addition to their relationship to directness and target of expression, feelings may be considered in relation to how responsibility for that feeling is perceived. Thus, the locus of responsibility may be perceived as external (outside oneself) or internal. For example, a child who has broken a window, when asked what happened, may reply: "It broke. The ball hit it." This reply shows that he perceives an external locus of responsibility. If he says, "I broke it when I threw the ball," he is indicating an internal locus of responsibility.

Medium of expression: Feelings may be expressed through verbal and/or nonverbal means. Children are sensitive to facial and bodily reactions and often know when adults are verbalizing one feeling while showing another (e.g., "Jimmy, I am glad you are here today," while clenching fists and grimacing). In teaching youngsters to appreciate feelings and how they may be managed and expressed, it is important to recognize both of these mediums for expression.

Social acceptability of expression: In teaching about feelings, it becomes essential to make the children aware that different forms of expression are likely to have different consequences. Although there are no absolutes for predicting consequences, since norms and attitudes vary within and across cultures and subcultures, flexibility and control of expression can be facilitated by promoting understanding about social acceptability.

It is convenient to view social acceptability of emotional expression along a continuum from acceptable to marginal to unacceptable. Socially *unacceptable* expressions are likely to include: actions which are violent, injurious, indecent, or conflicting with the rights or dignity of another person; and verbal responses which are slanderous or abusive to the character of another person. *Marginal* expressions are likely to be actions or verbal responses which are highly aggressive, provocative, powerful, or confronting. *Acceptable* expressions are likely to be: actions which are lawful, unattacking, constructive, and reflective of self-responsibility; verbal responses which are nonabusive and thoughtful; nonverbal expressions which are passively aggressive, evasive, or indirect.

The five dimensions to keep in mind when teaching appreciation of feelings are summarized in Table 7.

Each of the dimensions in Table 7 may be appraised in terms of a specific category of affective response. While conditions for categories along the left-hand side of each category of response are generally preferable response modes, it is our belief that optional

Table 7: *Basic Dimensions for Teaching Appreciating Feelings*

Dimension	*Category of Response*
1. Directness of Expression	Direct—Indirect—Private
2. Target of Expression	Original—Close—Distant
3. Locus of Responsibility	Self—External
4. Medium of Expression	Verbal—Non-verbal
5. Social Acceptability of Expression	Acceptable—Marginal—Unacceptable

self-control requires both the availability of all of these response modes and the capacity to choose flexibly between and among them at any time.

Success or failure of a classroom teacher depends to a great extent on whether he can identify and appreciate different feelings as they are expressed by students and how he handles or treats these feelings once they are recognized. Nor should the teacher ignore his own feelings that are aroused many times during the day and the way he reflects these feelings toward the class.

Teachers can be very helpful to children by identifying their own feelings and the feelings of the class; they can also guide and foster expression of feelings in an acceptable and appropriate manner, for a classroom devoid of expressed feeling is a classroom where the little learning which does take place is dull, boring, and ineffectual. A student who is denied the expression of feelings ultimately will have difficulty expressing his ideas, thoughts, and convictions; this is tantamount to negating the educative process.

For the implementation of most of the tasks in this chapter, it is advisable to group the children in a circular or semi-circular arrangement. Such an arrangement has been found to enhance the meaningfulness, involvement, and communication desired in these affective experiences (see Bessell and Palomares, 1970; Glasser, 1969). It is also *important to keep in mind the guidelines for stimulating affective responses presented in Chapter 4, pp. 65–67,* before introducing class discussion of emotionally laden experiences.

Rationale

Physical and motor reactions constitute a basic and powerful mechanism for expression of feelings and impulses. Developmentally, however, children, if they are to behave in a socially acceptable manner, must learn to use language and ideation to mediate between undifferentiated impulses and gross biological responses. Establishing a language channel for expression which can substitute for sheer physical release adds an indispensable dimension of flexibility and self-control.

Feelings are of profound importance in life, yet they too often are sources of pain, conflict, and confusion. For a person's growth to be full and adaptive, he must appreciate feelings as natural and viable parts of himself and others. And to appreciate the range and nuance of feelings requires an ability to identify and describe, accept, interpret, use, and enjoy one's affective life. Unfortunately, the affective world largely has been viewed as a pit of wild, ominous forces, better ignored or entrapped than appreciated. The teaching of an appreciation for feelings will, we hope, open the door to fulfillment through effective management and creative expression of one's emotional life as well as through deepening relationships with others by fostering possibilities for understanding, empathy, sharing, and forgiveness.

TEACHING UNITS AND GOALS

The goals in teaching children about feelings are contained in four units: identifying and accepting feelings, developing positive feelings, managing feelings, and reinterpreting feeling events.

Unit 1. Identifying and Accepting Feelings

Goals: To teach children to identify feelings and associate them with words; to teach children to recognize different types and sources of feelings; to teach children to accept the existence of feelings in themselves and others as being normal and valuable, not good or bad, right or wrong.

Unit 2. Developing Positive Feelings

Goals: To increase comfort, acceptance, and use of affection and the positive dimensions of human relationships; to help children develop positive feelings about themselves and others; to enhance the value and worth of the self.

Unit 3. Managing Feelings

Goals: To develop the ability to substitute verbal or ideational responses for tendencies to act impulsively; to create alternatives to automatic, non-reflective, impulsive action in situations which arouse emotions.

Unit 4. Reinterpreting Feeling Events

Goals: To develop the children's ability to find potentially positive elements in an emotionally disappointing event; to develop the awareness that feelings are related to perceptions or interpretations, and, thus, may be shifted from unpleasant to satisfying states with changes in cognitive understanding.

UNIT 1. IDENTIFYING AND ACCEPTING FEELINGS

Goals: To teach children to identify feelings and associate them with words; to teach children to recognize different types and sources of feelings; to teach children to accept the existence of feelings in themselves and others as being normal and valuable, not good or bad, right or wrong.

Task 1: Developing Emotional Responsiveness

Given the widespread uneasiness about bringing emotion into the classroom and the vast set of differences in attitudes and comfort about feelings, it is important that the teaching of feelings follow a structured, developmental approach. The approach to teaching feelings ought to proceed systematically according to several of the dimensions described earlier. Table 8 presents a model for a first sequence of instruction in identifying and accepting feelings. This sequence is viewed as a *prerequisite* for teaching the remaining units in this curriculum area.

Table 8 indicates that labeling pictures and enacting feelings in the introductory sequence will create the conditions for indirect expression of feelings with an external agent of responsibility. In other words, merely by labeling or enacting feelings shown in pictures, the pupils will not obtain personal ownership of those feelings; consequently, these initial tasks promote an exposure to use of feelings in the classroom in a safe and personally unthreatening manner.

Having the child suggest feelings to others and having him enact feelings suggested to him requires more self-ownership of feelings and feeling-related actions. In addition, as the teacher shifts from having the child suggest feelings to having him enact feelings, directness of feeling expressed increases to the point where a child is instructed to state his own feelings while carrying out a related action.

Table 8: *Introductory Sequence for Teaching Identifying and Accepting Feelings Using Two Dimensions of Affective Expression*

Locus of Responsibility	Directness of Feeling		
	Private	*Indirect*	*Direct*
External	X	1. Child labels pictures (see p. 163). 2. Child enacts feelings from pictures; other children identify feeling (see p. 163).	X
Self	3. Child suggests feelings to others (see p. 163).	4. Child enacts feelings suggested to him (see p. 163).	5. Child verbalizes feelings while they are being enacted (see p. 164).

Labelling pictures: Present a variety of pictures of facial and body expressions depicting emotional responses to outside events. Ask children to identify verbally the feelings of person depicted (e.g., "mad," "happy," "tired," "sad," "afraid," etc.). List the feeling labels suggested by the children on the chalkboard under the heading: "Feeling Words." Summarize the responses to bring out the fact of differences in interpreting feelings. For example, you might say, "You can see that Tim, Jane, and Richard thought the man in the picture was angry; Mary and Ken felt he was afraid; and Paul thought he was lonely. People get different feelings, even from looking at the same thing. That's because we can all be different in our feelings about things."

Enacting pictures: Tell the children that they will now try to guess the feeling being play-acted by one of their classmates. Call a child up to the front of the room, show him a picture containing an emotional expression, and ask him to whisper to you what feeling he obtains from it. Ask him to note body posture as well as facial expression. The child is then made the class leader and given the job of displaying the emotional expression shown in the picture and calling on classmates who think they can identify the emotion. After several classmates have replied (e.g., "sad," "mad," "proud"), ask the leader what feeling he was displaying and then praise him by pointing out either how much the imitation looked like the picture or how clear the play-action was for his classmates. It is important to help the child to understand that his display of affect is welcome and appreciated, even when he is merely imitating a model. Gradually, as children practice their emotional play-acting, the leader should generate an increasing degree of consensus in his classmates' guesses.

Suggesting and enacting feelings: When children appear at ease and familiar with displaying emotions from pictures, shift the task to displaying a feeling suggested by a whispered signal from either the teacher or another classmate. For example, one child might be called to the front and instructed to whisper a feeling (the suggestion) to another child (the actor) whose job it is to display that feeling to the class. Several classmates can be called up to play-act the feelings whispered by one child (suggestor-actors format), *or* several children can be requested to whisper feelings to one child, who is then responsible for enacting all of the feelings for the class (suggestors-actor format).

This procedure is valuable in establishing a beginning realization among the children that their real feelings can be expressed and accepted in their classroom. By shifting from posed expressions in pictures to the play-acting of classmates' feelings, the children bring the world of personal affect directly into the classroom—and in a pleasant, socially acceptable format. In addition, the procedure of passing a suggested feeling from one child to another facilitates the display of a wide range of feelings, since the responsibility for the play-action is shared and self-consciousness thus reduced. It should be noted that this procedure builds in flexibility, for several subgoals may be satisfied, depending upon the teacher's interest. In particular, the suggestor-actors format offers the following advantages: it offers safety to the suggestor in that he does not have to enact what is imagined; it maximizes chances of a wide range of actions by involving several children as actors; and it reduces anxiety about action by requiring only one expression per child actor. On the other hand, the suggestors-actor format provides these benefits: it insures variety of suggested affect; it gives one child practice in displaying a range of feelings; it allows the children who are more open to facilitate the expression of feelings; it allows children who are more reserved to share experience by making only one suggestion.

Enacting and verbalizing feelings: Present a variety of situations (through role-playing or use of tape, films, or pictures) which could arouse feelings and ask the children to describe their reactions and what they probably would do in that situation (e.g., "being selected for an award"; "being yelled at by teacher"; "father forgetting to take son to ball game"; "getting teased by other kids"). Guide the children in the use of "I" statements for their feelings while they simultaneously carry out an action and use nonverbal gestures or expressions.

Task 2: Interpreting Pantomime Behavior

Have the children observe a pantomime sequence of affective behavior which is spontaneously developed from a general starting situation (e.g., entering a store, boarding a plane, eating at a restaurant); then have the children attempt to describe what transpired between the people involved in the pantomime. Identification of feelings and learning to interpret feelings more flexibly and accurately can be facilitated by having some sequences on film or videotape so that episodes may be shown again and discussed.

Task 3: Understanding Name-Calling

Within the class setting, ask the children to list names and words that make them angry, hurt, or unhappy. Write the words on the board and then discuss each word in terms of the feeling it creates and what the person who would use the word might be feeling. Ask the group to provide more socially acceptable words which express similar meanings or give illustrations of such words to them. For example, "You dumb idiot" might express disappointment with how another child has performed, but the same feeling could have been stated as "I don't like the way you did that."

Shift the focus from the children as the "victims" of name-calling to them as the initiators of name-calling. Ask students to give examples of words they use to make others unhappy, hurt, or angry. Discuss each word in terms of what the person who used it may have been feeling at the time and the feeling it created in the victim. Ask the group to identify other words that could have been used to express the same feelings. Encourage verbal expressions of feelings which represent "I" messages (e.g., "I'm mad at you for taking my pen"; "I don't like it when you try to boss me around"; "I don't want to be with you when you start yelling a lot"). Contrast these messages with "you blaming" messages—those which attack and put the entire blame on the other person (e.g., "You stink"; "You are a real baby"; "You messed up the whole game").

The purpose of this activity is to teach children that name-calling is an attempt to express feelings and that acceptance of feelings will help to prevent feeling attacked or attacking with words.

Task 4: Feeling Questions

As important as it is that children recognize and deal with feelings within themselves, it is equally important that they recognize the feelings of others and the alternatives available for expressing acceptable feelings. Without creating an atmosphere of soul-searching, you might pose questions involving the use of feelings to clarify the understanding of feelings and to identify helpful, acceptable, and empathic feeling responses. The following questions can be introduced for class discussion and might become the basis for classroom charts or posters.[2] These questions also give an excellent opportunity to

---

[2] Teacher discussion skills become very important to the implementation of many tasks in the areas of Appreciating Feelings and Managing Frustration (see Hill, 1969; Stanford and Stanford, 1969).

reinforce honest, responsible expression of feelings through praise and recognition. Illustrative questions for discussion are:

1. If someone did not agree with you, how would you want him to tell you? How could you tell someone that you don't agree with him, in a way that is not mean?
2. If someone did not like what you did, how would you want him to tell you? How could you tell someone that you don't like what he did, in a way that is not mean or hurtful?
3. If someone did not like what you said, how would you want him to tell you? How could you tell someone that you don't like what he said to you, in a way that is not mean?
4. If you were not sharing, how would you want someone to tell you? How could you tell someone that he is not sharing?
5. If you lost a game, what could someone say to make you feel better? What could you say to someone who has lost a game?
6. If you made a mistake, what could someone say to make you feel better? What could you say to someone who has made a mistake?
7. If you got into trouble, what could someone say to make you feel better? What could you say to someone who has gotten into trouble?
8. If someone were angry with you, how would you want him to tell you? What could you say to someone who has made you angry?
9. If you were afraid, what could someone say to make you feel better? What could you say to someone who is afraid?
10. If you were crying, what could someone say to make you feel better? What could you say to someone who is crying?

Each of the preceding questions can be developed into a role-playing situation in which pupils take turns trying out the various methods of communicating appreciation of feelings to each other. In addition, questions can be posed in terms of "What can you say or *do* for someone who . . ." so that non verbal communications can be practiced. By checking out the impact of expressed words or gestures on the person addressed, it is possible to obtain immediate feedback on the effectiveness of a particular response.

UNIT 2. DEVELOPING POSITIVE FEELINGS

Goals: To increase comfort, acceptance, and use of affection and the positive dimensions of human relationships; to help children develop positive feelings about themselves and others; to enhance the value and worth of self.

The tasks in this unit are intended to introduce the value as well as the reality of positive feelings. We recognize that many children and adults find it difficult or embarassing to allow themselves to express warm, empathic feelings toward others. In particular, social norms and expectations generally have been shaped to avoid or impede public expression of love or love-equivalents. It is important, therefore, to assist the children in believing that a classroom can become an honest context which fosters a climate of positive interchange.

Task 1: The Compliment Game

Ask two children to go to the front of the class and face each other. One child tells the other two things he likes about him; the roles are then reversed. Some illustrative compliments are: "you have nice hair"; "I like your shirt"; "you have pretty eyes"; "he is good in arithmetic"; "I like your pretty dress"; "you have a nice smile." The purpose of the game is to teach the children to verbalize positive feelings toward others and to promote positive relationships within the class-group. You may have to assist those students who are shy or reluctant to compliment one another by elaborating and pointing toward the positive statements and by indicating that statements are not to be derogatory or embarrassing.

Task 2: The Teacher Compliment Game

As you call the pupils to line up for the rest room, recess, lunch, or dismissal, intentionally compliment a number of children. By choosing different children each time, you can compliment almost everyone in the class by the end of the day. For instance:

> "First in line is [name of pupil] who has on a pretty blue shirt today."

"Second in line is [name of pupil] who combed her hair so nicely."

"Third in line is [name of pupil] who tried so hard on the arithmetic assignment."

"Fourth in line is [name of pupil] who helped someone else in the reading assignment."

"Fifth in line is [name of pupil] who won the race yesterday at recess."

"Sixth in line is [name of pupil] who did her work very quietly without bothering anyone."

By noting a positive deed performed or some aspect of appearance or person that is appealing, it is possible to say something nice about every child. This type of game should enhance the child's self-image as well as provide a model for expressing positive attitudes in interpersonal relationships. The game can be extended to the point where the children themselves are selected to line up the class and state the compliments.

Task 3: Self-Praise

Allow the children to go to the front of the class and announce one or two things they like about themselves. Let them boast, brag, and take credit for what they are or what they can do. Some examples may be: "I'm good at kicking a ball"; "I'm strong"; "I'm good at writing"; "I can cook and sew"; "I'm wearing a neat shirt"; "My hair looks nice," etc. Positive self-esteem is based on liking oneself, and this task can help children become more able to see good in themselves. Some assistance, such as suggesting or encouraging peers to express some positives, may be in order for those children who are shy or lacking in self-esteem. It is important to establish a rule that no one be laughed at—regardless of what they say. This task can be very significant for children who have suffered many failures or who have a negative attitude about themselves.

Task 4: Good Moves—Self

Ask a child to describe some good act or deed that he has performed in the last few days. For example, he might say: "I learned to write my name"; "I learned a new word"; "I helped my mother"; "I ate all my lunch"; "I dressed myself," etc. The purpose is to make the child aware of good, positive things he may be doing each day. If he can verbalize bits of positive information about himself, his thinking in terms of his own self-worth and self-esteem will improve. In time, this improved self-image will encourage him to attempt new tasks in the classroom and elsewhere.

Task 5: Good Moves—Others

Just as the children verbalize positive bits of information about themselves and their good deeds, acts, and habits, let them do the same in reference to their peers or other people in the school or neighborhood. For example, a child might say: "I saw the policeman help a man into the ambulance"; "I saw the fireman try to put out the fire"; "I saw a boy give another boy part of his ice cream"; "I saw my friend helping his mother"; "I saw one student helping another," etc. The main theme here is to look for the positive things others do. The old adage "one good deed deserves another" can be fostered in a classroom to the extent that the children start helping one another and, in turn, build more positive relationships. Attempt to guide the information about others away from adults and authority figures and toward peers, preferably those within the same classroom.

Task 6: Recognizing Good Intent

In addition to actual good moves, deeds, and acts, consideration of the intention behind the deed is an important source for identification of positive feelings. Intention is the thought, purpose, or idea behind an act. Role-playing situations where the person intends to do some good act or deed but never succeeds because of an accident, obstacle, or interruption by an authority figure are good examples to consider (e.g., one child offers part of his dessert to another but drops it in the process of passing; one child offers another help in arithmetic but works the problem incorrectly himself; one child attempts to sharpen a pencil for another but then is restricted from doing so by the teacher; one child offers his crayons to another but a third child steps in and takes the crayons.) Children are prone to look only at the completed act or deed, judging the act in terms of what they did or did not receive; however, children can be taught to recognize the positive feelings and thoughts of another who is attempting to render a good deed. They can come to see that the intent can often become as important as the act itself.

Task 7: Relating Positively

Role play situations that include positive verbal relationships between two children; emphasize verbalization that is complimentary and sensitive toward the other person. For example, one child might say when meeting a new person, "How *nice* it is to meet you"; or if a persons asks a favor of him, he might say, 'I'll be *glad* to do it"; or, in asking for help, one might say, "I know you are *good* at this, would you help me?" In offering help, one might say, "You seem to be having a *little trouble;* may I help you?" Relating positively means using positive, hopeful words. It also requires using a degree of sensitivity that recognizes the feelings of another. In their relationships with one another, children can be taught to be honest, helpful of others, humble in seeking help, and able to allow another to *save face* when needing help.

Task 8: Bill of Rights and Freedoms

Lack of respect for the rights of others results in abuses of individual rights and freedoms, and interference with individual rights and freedoms creates feelings of frustration, anger, and resentment. One of the main objectives of the classroom teacher involves bringing respect for the rights of others into clear focus for children. To help accomplish this, form discussion groups to establish the rights and freedoms of people in the class. Discussion should include what is meant by respect for these rights, how one recognizes a right, and how one acts in respecting a right of another. The subject could range from respect for property, to ideas, to feelings. As children identify the rights of everyone in the classroom, a Bill of Rights and Freedoms can be drawn up for the class. For example, a Bill of Rights and Freedoms for an elementary school class might contain the following:

Rights

To be assured that we will protect each other's property.

To be assured that we will protect each other's school work.

To be assured that we will protect each other from physical harm.

To be assured that we will protect each other from threats.

To be assured that we will protect each other from mean teasing or insults.

To be assured that we will treat everyone fairly.

Freedoms

Freedom from fear.

Freedom from being bullied.

Freedom from being laughed at.

Freedom from being disturbed.

Freedom to move politely about the room.

Freedom to talk and be heard (with permission).

UNIT 3. MANAGING FEELINGS

Goals: To develop the ability to substitute verbal or ideational responses for tendencies to act impulsively; to create alternatives to automatic, non-reflective, impulsive action in emotionally arousing situations.

Tasks Promoting Substitution of Words

Task 1: Life Cycle Samples (Own or Others)

Have the pupils recall examples from their own or others' lives in which words have been substituted for physical action (e.g., a policeman talking to two boys about to fight; a minister talking to an angry crowd; one child talking to another who has taken his toy; a child objecting to an umpire's decision). These examples are discussed within the class group, with the teacher emphasizing the importance of substituting words to accomplish a peaceful solution to the problem.

Task 2: Hero Success Stories—Rationale Element

Try to arrange for film strips, tapes, or radio interviews by famous figures in sports, show business, or politics. Personal appearances by local celebrities also might be arranged. Organize the presentation so that the thinking, planning, and verbal reasoning elements in the "hero's" success story are clearly visible. For example, Johnny Bench might talk about his way of catching and preventing runners from stealing bases; O.J. Simpson could explain the role of thinking and planning in football; Sidney Poitier might speak about the reflective element in acting; a local fireman might talk about fighting fires; the state legislator might discuss politics. Children can pick out their personal hero and obtain samples of how that person does his work through newspaper articles, books, and films.

Task 3: Sharing Emotional Reactions

Establish a group period for sharing sad, unhappy, joyful, and fearful feelings. During this period, allow the children to relate their experience but give very little interpretation to the feelings expressed. For example, a child might want to talk about how sad he was when his pet died or when he broke his favorite toy. Unhappiness may take the form of being disappointed by a parent or cheated by a friend. Joy might be expressed by family plans for a birthday party. Fears such as fear of darkness, strange noises at night, criminals breaking and entering, ghosts, death, illnesses, etc., elicit strong emotional reactions from children.

Emphasize the feelings connected with the incident the child describes and with the sharing of these feelings with others. Remember that verbalizing bits of information tends to lessen the intense emotional feelings surrounding the incident for the child. Take care to allow the children to enter into the sharing at their own pace and on their own terms. The right to pass or remain quiet must be basic.

In the event that a child becomes obviously upset in recounting any emotional reaction, a comforting and supportive remark such as "It is very hard to lose something we love" or "Things like burglaries are very frightening for us all" and an understanding arm around the shoulder or back rub should help considerably. Since any one child's upsetting experience is invariably shared in some way by the other children, it is important to seek group support for the child who is most upset. Group support can be developed by giving the others a chance to share their upsetting experiences. For example, you might say, "I know that someone else has probably been sad at losing something important" or "What other things have made you scared, children?" Convey a sense of calm and understanding while assuring the children that although feelings may be upsetting for everyone (including the teacher) at times, it is "OK" to have such feelings and that talking about them often helps.

Tasks Promoting Alternative Actions

Task 1: Private Cussing

You may want to suggest to certain students that they resort to private cussing in situations which arouse strong emotional feelings. This often acts as a safety valve in lieu of physical action or expression of angry words, yet it takes place within the person's mind, so no one hears it and is offended. Thus, the child is free to use any language he chooses. This type of expression often may be enough to defuse the intense feeling connected with an anger-producing incident.

Task 2: Reading as Emotional Support

Arrange books, stories, and incidents in a corner of the bookshelf in the room, so that a child can go to that corner to read a story reflecting a feeling that he has encountered. A bibliography can be established with headings related to managing anger, fear, sadness, hurt, loneliness, etc. The reading material can include incidents that happened to members of the class, with the characters and scene changed to conceal identities. References should be included in the bibliography which contain a satisfactory resolution so that the children can become aware that emotionally upsetting incidents often have a strengthening or positive consequence. Reading about an experience similar to one's own can offer support, hope, and useful suggestions for managing difficult emotions.

Task 3: Regulated Release

Permit certain students to manage strong feelings by providing an acceptable means for emotional release. For example, on a prearranged basis, you might allow a child to do such things as go to a corner and punch a bag, throw rubber darts at a board, smash playdough with his fists, cut up paper, throw a ball against a wall, or smear paint. These activities should be supervised carefully by an adult. Their purpose is to allow the student to give vent to his emotions when he has reached the saturation point by channeling those feelings into an acceptable substitute feeling-based activity.

Task 4: Cool-Off Signals

An effective means of avoiding a "blow up," a tantrum, or acting out behavior is to establish a system of signals with students who find it hard to control their actions in the classroom. When such a child gives a prearranged signal and receives a return sign of permission, he may proceed with a prearranged course of action. Use of this system should be permitted only after the child comes to feel that he can no longer endure the present situation. Any peaceful action that would terminate the present unbearable situation and allow the child a chance to cool off would be valuable. Some examples could be getting a drink, going to the bathroom, sitting in the hall, putting his head down on his desk, or looking out the window. By developing cool-off signals (e.g., raising his hand, tapping a pencil, saluting) for the child, you provide the upset youngster with an internal means of bringing about orderly change before his disturbance results in a possible explosion.

Task 5: Work-It-Out Corner

Many children need a motoric means of working out destructive feelings. A corner of the room, equipped with materials that lend themselves to working out such feelings, can be set aside for this purpose. This corner could contain, for example, nails to be hammered, paper to be torn, pencils, crayons and chalk for drawing, and clay or foam rubber to be squeezed and jabbed. Once the child has worked out his feelings in this corner, he may return to his seat. Care should be taken that the items placed in the corner not harm a child and that the noise level be acceptable for that classroom situation. As a child establishes acceptable methods of working out destructive feelings, his self-image will improve and he will need to use the corner less frequently.

Task 6: Travel Orders

As a safety valve for a child who is about to lose control of his impulses, you might elect to send him on a trip. The emphasis here is not on managing the child's behavior for him, but, rather, on establishing a mutual plan for helping the child to cope with overly stressful situations. Thus, the pupil must agree to *initiate* a clear signal when he feels a trip is necessary to prevent disruption (e.g., a hitchhiking motion of thumb or a salute). Prepare a list of specific errands which need to be done and draw from the list when a child signals appropriately.

UNIT 4. REINTERPRETING FEELING EVENTS

Goals: To develop the children's ability to find potentially positive elements in an emotionally disappointing event; to develop the awareness that feelings are related to perceptions or interpretations, and, thus, may be shifted from unpleasant to satisfying states with changes in cognitive understanding.

Task 1: Happy-Unhappy Seesaw

During a class discussion session, list a number of things on the chalkboard that make the children happy and a number that make them unhappy. For example, eating ice cream makes one happy because the ice cream tastes good and is cold. Losing a race because someone cheated makes one feel unhappy because he lost and because it was not a fair race. A person can do several things to take the hurt out of the unhappy feeling: (1) feel confident that he could win in a fair race; (2) be proud that he did not cheat; and (3) prove to others that he is a good loser.

The goal is to take the negative elements of unhappiness and turn them into strengths. We often can learn more from a loss than from a win and more from an unhappy event than from a happy event. Have the children role play both situations that make them happy and those that make them unhappy in an attempt to increase their skill in reinterpreting unhappy events. Skits may include one person's taking the role of the happy person and another's taking the role of the unhappy person and then reversing the roles.

Task 2: Finding the Positive

Children can be helped to manage upsetting feelings if they are provided with opportunities to identify supportive feelings which counter forces toward self-blame or lack of worth. These countering or "antidotal" feelings should bolster the child's self-concept and enhance the likelihood of his performing socially acceptable actions.

Ask the children to describe some school situations where they have felt upset, annoyed, or unhappy. Clarify the feeling experienced and the source of the feeling aroused (i.e., who "caused" the feeling). List a few of these situations on the chalkboard using the following format:

Unhappy/Upset Feeling	*Who Did It*	*Happier Feeling*

Then have the class give their ideas about what better or happier feeling might also be present in unhappy situations. For example:

Unhappy Feeling Experienced	*Happier or Antidotal Feeling*
Anger	Feeling secure that won't lose control of self.
Hurt	Feeling proud of self for being brave.
Sad	Feeling good, knowing you did all you could.
Abused	Not retaliating, being kind.
Cheated	Feeling proud of being honest.
Injured	Feeling proud that you are gentle.
Insulted	Feeling self-assurance in curbing one's language.
Embarrassed	Having the ability to laugh at one's self.

Task 3: I Like My Way

Develop role-playing situations that have several solutions or several different methods of arriving at the same goal. For example, the task might be to build a wagon which has three wheels, using a tinker toy set. Another child might attempt to help but then tell the first child he was wrong in his approach. Or a child might be told to write his name on the chalkboard in the fanciest way he knows, while another child interferes and attempts to show him he is wrong. Finally, a child might be asked to move two stacks of books from one side of the room to another, while another child attempts to show him how and ultimately tells him he is wrong.

Ask the children how it feels when someone says they are wrong. Discuss whether all tasks they have role played have right and wrong solutions and whether a good job is one that is "right" or one done with care and effort. Replay the role situations building in a new response for the child who has been told he is wrong (e.g., "I did my best and I like it"). Have the children practice asking themselves the question: "Can I like my way even though someone else thinks it's wrong?" and verbalizing: "I know how I'm doing this even if you don't think it's right."

Task 4: Distinguishing Thoughts and Feelings from Actions

Inform the class that the purpose of this activity is to help them understand the difference between thinking or feeling something and doing it. Ask the question: "*Do you ever think of doing something but don't do it?*" Call for examples and list them in simple words on the board. After listing a few examples, inquire as to why these thoughts were not carried out in action and record the reason next to the thought:

Thought	*Reason Not Done*
Run away	Would get lost
Hit teacher	Would get mad at me
Read to class	Might laugh at me

Praise the class for being able to give clear and honest examples. Let them know it is really important to see that thoughts are not the same as actions, that thoughts can be private property.

At another class session, ask the question: "*Do you ever have feelings that you try not to show?*" Call for examples, and list them in simple words on the board. Repeat the process previously indicated for thoughts, recording comments under two columns:

Feelings	*Reason Not Shown*
Afraid, scared	Embarrassed, ashamed.
Sad, unhappy	Ashamed to cry
Angry	Might get in trouble

As before, praise the class for being able to give clear and honest examples. Reiterate that feelings are not the same as actions and that feelings can be private and free.

Follow up this discussion (either at the same or a subsequent session, depending on age and attention span of children) by asking: "*Is it bad to have certain thoughts or feelings?*" or *Are there any thoughts or feelings which are bad or wrong?*" Paraphrase and reflect student comments to increase clarity and to demonstrate understanding and acceptance of their ideas.

Next, ask if there are *behaviors* that are wrong or bad to do and draw out the youngsters' ideas. Using examples given by the class, the following points may be brought out, in this and subsequent discussions:

1. All thoughts and feelings are OK and normal to have.
2. Thoughts and feelings can be private property; complete freedom is possible for thoughts and feelings.
3. All actions or behaviors are not OK; some are illegal, harmful to self or others, or against the rules.
4. Behaviors or actions cannot be private property; complete freedom is not possible for behavior.
5. Thoughts and feelings are different from behavior; you can think and feel things without needing to do them or without blaming yourself for having mean or "bad" ideas.

SUMMARY

The teaching of appreciation for feelings is critical for two reasons: unless feelings are subject to conscious, voluntary control, they are apt to erupt into destructive actions; and advances in human relations are unlikely to be made without effective management and positive regard for feelings. Appreciating feelings in oneself and others is a gateway to human compatibility.

Four teaching units were presented in this chapter: identifying and accepting feelings, developing positive feelings, managing feelings, and reinterpreting feeling events. A basic intructional sequence was outlined which required proceeding gradually from private to direct and from external to self-expression of feeling. The following five dimensions for appraising and organizing the teaching of appreciating feelings were stressed: directness of affective expression, target of expression, locus of responsibility, medium of expression, social acceptability of expression.

Regulation of more primitive, physical expressions of underlying impulses is greatly facilitated by the development of language and ideation as substitute channels for expression of feeling. This chapter has described teaching tasks which promote discrimination and verbal identification of emotions and strengthen the use of words to express feelings. In addition, tasks have been presented which will help children to develop more positive and supportive feelings toward themselves and others and to gain security about their own strength and control in the face of emotional stress or upset. However, before introducing class discussion of emotionally laden experiences, review the important guidelines for stimulating affective responses that were presented in Chapter 4.

For tasks in this chapter to have relevance and purpose to the child, the teacher must attempt continually to relate them to real-life situations and the environment in which the child lives. The teacher should also clearly state the importance of these tasks for learning, mastery, and self-growth.

The units and tasks contained in this chapter are summarized in Table 9.

Table 9: *Summary of Curriculum Units and Tasks in the Curriculum Area: Appreciating Feelings*

Unit	*Tasks*
Identifying and Accepting Feelings	1. Developing Emotional Responsiveness 2. Interpreting Pantomime Behavior 3. Understanding Name-Calling 4. Feeling Questions
Developing Positive Feelings	1. The Compliment Game 2. The Teacher Compliment Game 3. Self-Praise 4. Good Moves—Self 5. Good Moves—Others 6. Recognizing Good Intent 7. Relating Positively 8. Bill of Rights and Freedoms
Managing Feelings	*Tasks Promoting Substitution of Words* 1. Life Cycle Samples 2. Hero Success Stories—Rationale Element 3. Sharing Emotional Reactions *Tasks Promoting Alternative Actions* 1. Private Cussing 2. Reading as Emotional Support 3. Regulated Release 4. Cool-Off Signals 5. Work-It-Out Corner 6. Travel Orders
Reinterpreting Feeling Events	1. Happy-Unhappy Seesaw 2. Finding the Positive 3. I Like My Way 4. Distinguishing Thoughts and Feelings from Action

REFERENCES

Alschuler, A., editor. *New Directions in Psychological Education.* Middletown, Connecticut: Education Ventures, 1973.

Bessell, H., and Palomares, U. *Methods in Human Development.* San Diego, California: Human Development Training Institute, 1970.

Brown, G. *Human Teaching for Human Learning: An Introduction to Confluent Education.* New York: Viking Press, 1971.

Canfield, J.; Wells, H.; and Hall, L. *100 Ways to Enhance Self-Concept in the Classroom.* Upper Troy, New York: Values Associates, 1972.

Ellis, A. *Reason and Emotion in Psychotherapy.* New York: Lyle Stuart, 1962.

Glasser, W. *Schools without Failure.* New York: Harper & Row, 1969.

Hill, W. *Learning thru Discussion.* Beverly Hills, California: Sage, 1969.

Inlow, G. *The Emergent in Curriculum.* New York: Wiley, 1966.

LaRue, W.; LaRue, S.; and Hill, S. *Understanding Our Feelings: An Adventure in Classroom Role-Playing.* Chicago: Century Consultants, 1972.

Lazarus, R. *Psychological Stress and the Coping Process.* New York: McGraw-Hill, 1966.

Lazarus, R.; Auerill, J.; and Opton, E. "Towards a Cognitive Theory of Emotions." In *Feelings and Emotions,* edited by M. B. Arnold, pp. 207–32. New York: Academic Press, 1970.

Lederman, J. *Anger and the Rocking Chair: Gestalt Awareness with Children.* New York: McGraw-Hill, 1969.

Leeper, R. "The Motivational and Perceptual Properties of Emotions as Indicating Their Fundamental Character and Role." In *Feelings and Emotions,* edited by M. B. Arnold, pp. 151–69. New York: Academic Press, 1970.

———. "Some Needed Developments in the Motivational Theory of Emotions." *Nebraska Symposium on Motivation* 13 (1965): 25–122.

Limbacher, W. *Dimensions of Personality: Here I Am.* Dayton, Ohio: Pflaum, 1969.

———. *Dimensions of Personality: I'm Not Alone.* Dayton, Ohio: Pflaum, 1970.

Lippitt, R.; Fox, R.; and Schaible, L. *Social Science Laboratory Units.* Chicago: Science Research Associates, 1971.

Lyon, H. *Learning to Feel — Feeling to Learn.* Columbus, Ohio: Charles E. Merrill Publishing Co., 1971.

Peters, R. "The Education of the Emotions." In *Feelings and Emotions,* edited by M. B. Arnold, pp. 187–203. New York: Academic Press, 1970.

Randolph, N., and Howe, W. *Self-Enhancing Education: A Program to Motivate Learners.* Palo Alto, California: Stanford University Press, 1971.

Raths, L.; Harmin, M.; and Simon, S. *Values and Teaching: Working with Values in the Classroom.* Columbus, Ohio: Charles E. Merrill Publishing Co., 1966.

Shaftel, F., and Shaftel, G. *Role-Playing for Social Values: Decision-Making in the Social Studies.* Englewood Cliffs, New Jersey: Prentice-Hall, 1967.

Stanford, G., and Stanford, B. *Learning Discussion Skills through Games.* New York: Citation Press, 1969.

Synectics, Inc. *Making It Strange.* New York: Harper & Row, 1972.

Weinstein, G., and Fantini, M. *Toward Humanistic Education: A Curriculum of Affect.* New York: Praeger, 1970.

Williams, F. E. *Classroom Ideas for Encouraging Thinking and Feeling.* Buffalo, New York: D.O.K., Inc, 1970.

Wrenn, G., and Schwarzock, S. *The Coping with Books.* Circle Pines, Minnesota: American Guidance Service, 1970.

11

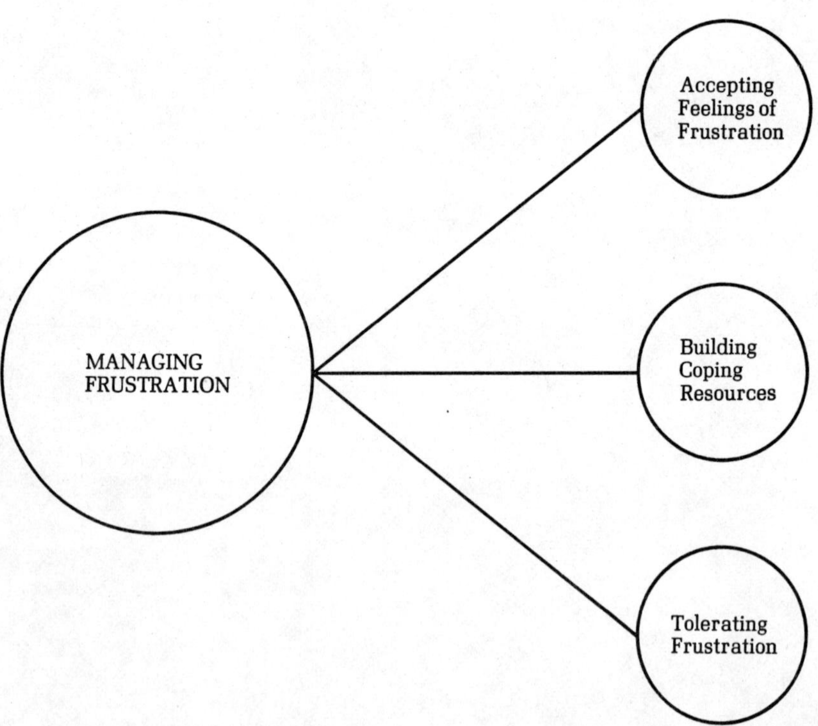
MANAGING
FRUSTRATION
Accepting
Feelings of
Frustration
Building
Coping
Resources
Tolerating
Frustration

Curriculum Area: Managing Frustration

INTRODUCTION TO MANAGING FRUSTRATION

Frustration is a natural, frequent, and inevitable element of the human condition which exists whenever a wish, desire, or goal is obstructed. The term implies both the thwarting of a stimulus and an associated set of negative emotional responses. Although there is little that can be done to prevent reality from placing obstacles in the way of immediate goal satisfaction, children can be taught to manage their negative feelings resulting from the stress of frustration.

Most Americans feel a deep sense of shock and dread when reminded of the widespread occurrence of violent reactions to frustration in this country. Yet we have not found effective alternatives to violent and destructive outpourings of frustration. Nonetheless, in writing on violence and American society, Iglitzen (1970) states that aggressive reactions are learned, not inborn.

> Carefully controlled studies of primates. . .lend support to the thesis that aggression is a learned response. In fact, no definitive proof exists to date that aggression *must* be exercised regardless of what happens in the external environment (p. 173).

Sanford and Comstock (1971) scream out the same affirmation in their sobering book *Sanctions for Evil.* They powerfully indict mankind for having cultivated sanctions which allow people to "feel they have some kind of permission (for social destructiveness) even to the point of feeling righteous, and who commonly regard their victims as less than human or otherwise beyond the pale" (p. ix). In drawing conclusions from their book, which represents the views of leading spokesmen in a variety of fields, Sanford and Comstock state:

> Unlike "instincts" such as the aggression described by some popular writers, the disposition of destructiveness is not inborn but is generated out of experience and learning in a social environment. . . . *Fundamentally, its source is inner conflict, which leads to a need to get rid of what is all too human in oneself.* If this badness is felt to be located in the self, a person may become self-destructive; but often he may ascribe the badness to other people upon whom the conflict is then played out (p. 331).

Hurting others when one himself is in pain is apparently a self-reinforcing behavior, particularly for those with little basic trust or caring for others. The violent action reduces pain and satisfies the need to avenge one's misery. Of course, since it is a self-reinforcing behavior, the more violence is used to satisfy these needs, the more addictive it becomes (Toch, 1969). We can no longer tolerate this form of conflict resolution, yet for us to angrily smash back at violent behavior with more of the same would be ludicrous, and—even more distressing—it would also be an admission of defeat.

Schools have had to accept responsibility for intervening in other areas besides violence where abusive or self-defeating behavior is prominent. For example, drug and sex education programs and curricula have infused school systems rapidly, moving to younger and younger age levels all the time. The knowledge and experience inherent in risking the movement into uncharted educational territory is slowly but surely being acquired. Schools must now take one more step—into the realm of those affects which are potentially explosive. Education in the constructive management of frustration and its accompanying negative emotions has to be attempted. Too much is at stake to wait any longer.

A Model for Focusing Interventions on the Frustration Process

Hollister (1965) first introduced the concept of "strens" and advocated preventive interventions in schools. He defined a "stren" as "an experience in an individual's life that builds strength into his personality" (p. 31). In relation to hostile-aggressive impulses, the concept of "stren-building" has more positive implications than do strategies for managing aggression *after* it has erupted (see Trieschman, 1969). What is needed, however, is a model for providing interventions or experiences which can and do add strength for coping with frustration without violence. The present approach to teaching management of frustration offers one such model.

In discussing frustration, Yates (1962) distinguishes between the state of frustration and the tolerance for frustration. As we interpret this distinction, the state of frustration refers to the degree of upset or stress experienced in immediate reaction to the blocking of a desired goal. Tolerance of frustration, on the other hand, means "the individual's ability to withstand a particular degree of frustration" (p. 198). Thus, when an obstacle is placed in the path of a desired goal, a state of frustration results which, in turn, challenges the individual's capacity to tolerate frustration.

One final concept is needed to round out the frustration process; namely, that of "coping." Murphy defines coping as "the steps or sequences through which the child comes to terms with a challenge or makes use of an opportunity" (p. 6). The emphasis is on the process of developing ways of dealing with new and difficult situations. Thus, the frustration process includes coping behavior which occurs after frustration is aroused (state) and processed (tolerance).

Table 10: *Focusing Interventions on the Frustration Process*

Process	*Process Level*	*Focus of Intervention*
Obstacle to Goal		
Frustration State	Level 1	Perceptual reappraisal
Frustration Tolerance	Level 2	Emotional desensitization, relaxation, counter-conditioning; perceptual reappraisal
Coping Behavior	Level 3	Cognitive awareness; reinforcing constructive behaviors

Table 10 depicts the frustration process in the left-hand column. The right-hand column relates the focus of our teaching efforts to the frustration process. Thus, we regard the state of frustration to be basically mediated by perceptual functions and, therefore, as modifiable through perceptual reappraisal. For example, if someone crashes into an individual in the supermarket, he is likely to perceive the incident as accidental and experience a low state of frustration. In contrast, if the same person bumps into the same individual on the sidewalk, the individual is more likely to become upset.[1]

The focus of intervention at the level of frustration tolerance is seen as being directed at two factors: the ability to withstand or absorb unpleasant feelings or emotions, and the perception or belief in one's capacity to endure emotional stress.

The third level of reaction in the hypothesized frustration process, that of coping behavior, seems to us to require a teaching focus which promotes a cognitive awareness of constructive alternatives and provides positive reinforcement following the display of constructive behavior.

The curriculum units in this area of managing frustration correspond to this theoretical model of the frustration process. Unit 1, Accepting Feelings of Frustration, relates to teaching, which essentially focuses on the frustration state level (Level 1). Unit 2, Building Coping Resources, corresponds to Level 3 of the process. Unit 3, Tolerating Frustration, relates to Level 2 of the frustration process. Our experience has shown that the unit on building coping resources should be taught *before* the unit on tolerating frustration, since children are better able to endure frustration when they are aware of their own coping resources. Given this sense of personal options for coping, children are equipped to handle the many types of frustration represented in Unit 3.

We are convinced that helpful ways of managing frustration can be taught in the classroom. It has become clear to us, however, that teachers are uncomfortable with the notion of intentionally creating experiences of frustration in the classroom in order to promote growth, even if such experience takes place under carefully regulated conditions. Educators seem to be especially leary of promoting discomfort in children, even when such actions are very likely to build the strens and resources necessary for effective coping with life's difficulties.

There is evidence to suggest that people are not nearly as vulnerable to frustration as we might think. Epstein (1967) and Fenz and

[1]Here we apply Feshbach's (1970) reasoning that "negative discrepancies from expected behaviors (i.e., sidewalk courtesy) and their consequences correspond to goal interferences or sources of frustration" (p. 202).

Epstein (1967), for example, have found through repeated studies of parachutists and pilots that experienced risk takers have learned to master anxiety by exposing themselves to moderate levels of stress *prior* to being called upon for action. Epstein (1967) reports that "anxiety is mastered and turned to adaptive advantage, providing an early warning signal at a low level of arousal" (p. 47). Thus, through a form of practice with moderate stress situations, risk takers learn to inhibit drastic defenses and acquire confidence in their resources for coping with stress.

Several investigators have even reported that people are attracted to other people, things, or causes for which they have suffered moderately (Aronson, 1961; Aronson and Mills, 1959; Gerard and Mathewson, 1966).

Much of the literature on psychotherapy, counseling, and sensitivity training emphasizes the importance of learning to acknowledge and deal in a straightforward manner with difficult and frustrating experiences (see Burton, 1969; Holt, 1972; Thorne, 1968; Tyler, 1969). Bach and Wyden (1969) and Satir (1967) lay down ground rules within which healthy fighting can take place between couples. A few studies even suggest that adaptive responses to frustrating circumstances can be taught to clients with emotional problems (Giebink, Stover, and Fahl, 1968; Winter, Griffith, and Kolb, 1968). Montagu (1966) sums up our position when he says that a major role of education is to "build internal controls in human beings so that they can withstand external pressures and maintain internal equilibrium" (p. 121).

Unfortunately, little educational effort has been made to help children learn to overcome rage or helplessness, the more primitive and automatic reactions to frustration. In fact, there seems to have been a decided aversion to dealing with stress or unpleasant emotions in school settings, as if stress was an illegitimate subject for teaching or learning.[2] Since hostility or withdrawal are the adult derivatives of rage or helplessness, it is not surprising to see that these are the major patterns of response in emotionally troubled

---

[2]Bower (1964) sought to counter this avoidance of dealing with unpleasant experiences in the classroom by focusing attention on the necessity for teaching students to cope more adequately with stress. He introduced the concept of "stress-immunity building programs" and attempted to show how normal developmental stresses could be integrated affirmatively into the school curriculum. Despite this effort and the increasing recognition that learning to cope with painful experiences (frustration, conflict, stress, crisis) is a critical developmental task for all people (see Caplan, 1965; Torrance, 1965; Wolff, 1969), public school education continues to shy away from facing negative affect in the classroom. As Clarizio (1969) puts it, "Deeply imbedded in our educational system is the philosophy that students should not have to face stressful situations" (p. 344).

youngsters. If hostile and withdrawing reactions to frustration are to be replaced by more constructive behaviors in these children, then experiences of, attitudes toward, and alternatives for coping with frustration must be accepted in the classroom as appropriate educational material.

One notable exception to the general lack of educational concern for teaching management of frustration is the recent publication from the Educational Research Council of America, *A Curriculum to Help Students Deal with Frustration and Aggression* (1972). Developed for application at elementary, junior, and senior high levels, this curriculum contains units on student protest, vandalism, and violence for the junior high level and covers a wide range of human emotional experiences at elementary and at senior high schools.

Rationale

Frustration of one's personal wishes, goals, or needs is an inexorable and critical life experience; moreover, frustration presents a powerful opportunity for toughening the fibre of individual character and learning to master inevitable emotional pain and disappointment. Unfortunately, the role of frustration in the socialization process has not been developed for controlled, positive, educational, and psychological application. Instead, there has been a tenuous, mistrustful, and sometimes explosive response to the negative feelings which often accompany children's frustrations.

The alternative to haphazard, misguided induction of frustration is a planned, regulated growth-facilitating approach. Children can and should be taught to view frustration as a natural and acceptable event, one which is not personally damaging or hurtful, but, rather, one which can enhance the individual's capacities for effectively enduring and coping with difficulties which are inherent in human growth and motivation.

TEACHING UNITS AND GOALS

This chapter contains three main units: Accepting Feelings of Frustration, Building Coping Resources, and Tolerating Frustration. Taken together, the units represent a process for managing frustration which consists of developing new perceptions, maintaining possibilities for success and self-satisfaction, and increasing capacity for experiencing frustration.

Unit 1: Accepting Feelings of Frustration

Goals: To help children acknowledge and accept feelings of frustration as normal, unavoidable events; to help children perceive that the feelings of frustration they experience are not caused by their own badness or inadequacy.

Unit 2: Building Coping Resources

Goals: To strengthen the children's resources for coping effectively with frustration experiences; to develop techniques and behaviors which maintain possibilities for success and positive regard for the self.

Unit 3: Tolerating Frustration

Goals: To increase children's capacity to endure upsetting or disappointing experiences; to strengthen children's belief in their ability to absorb disappointing life events.

Three sub-units are included: *experiencing obstacles*, which concentrates on providing controlled exposure to a variety of real-life obstacles to reaching one's goal; *experiencing conflicts*, which emphasizes the reality of conflicting and competing response requirements; *experiencing disappointments*, which highlights common dissatisfactions resulting from lack of reward or goal attainment.

UNIT 1. ACCEPTING FEELINGS OF FRUSTRATION

Goals: To help children acknowledge and accept feelings of frustration as normal, unavoidable events; to help children perceive that the feelings of frustration they experience are not caused by their own badness or inadequacy.

General Comments

Basic to the purpose of this unit is the assumption that frustration is a natural consequence of social interaction and that, therefore, it needs to be faced with objectivity and understanding. Despite the unpleasant feelings associated with frustration, we maintain that children can develop comfort and self-acceptance in relation to frustrating events. The crucial point in achieving tolerance for frustration involves the true *acceptance* of feelings of being upset in oneself. Acceptance of personal upset develops from two interrelated processes—formation of a cognitive understanding that goal-thwarting is a necessary part of life and formation of an experiential baseline or threshold for sensing unpleasant emotions.

To achieve such an acceptance requires a realization that frustration is not a function of personal badness, does not reflect on one's worth, and cannot be avoided in facing life as it is. We believe that a child is poorly served if he is taught that frustration can be escaped by denial, overindulgence, or flight into fantasy or manufactured pleasure states.

It should be evident that wherever differences in hopes and desires continue to exist between people, no one can expect to have all of his wants met. Unfortunately, to date, our primary strategy for reducing interpersonal frustration has been through avoidance or violence. More recently, however, our youth have been demanding love and compassion as an alternative means of avoiding frustration. In our opinion, neither of these approaches provides the bases for dealing constructively with our human differences. In our view, *frustration is the child of human differences* and can be extinguished only by the elimination of such differences. As we highly value these human differences, we must also prize the frustration that accompanies them. *Thus, the answer to living with frustration has to lie in our learning to accept frustration as a healthy and desirable part of our humanness.*

To teach acceptance of frustration necessitates the arousal of feelings of frustration in the presence of unpleasant affect. The following guidelines *must* be kept in mind in inducing frustration: Frustration induction should be attempted only after a positive relationship has been established in the classroom between teacher and pupils. The degree of frustration should be modulated to assure that initial inductions are mild and are followed by movement to moderate inductions. Severe frustration should not be induced, although it should be dealt with spontaneously when stressful incidents occur within the everyday classroom or school experience. Frustration induction must always be followed by clarification and closure procedures. That is, the teacher should be sure the children understand the meaning and purpose of the frustrating activity before moving on to other things.

It is important to recognize that degree of frustration can be modulated by attending to the following mediating variables:

1. *Group versus Individual Targets.* Focusing frustration on group or sub-group needs is less intense than focusing the frustration on specific individuals.
2. *Impersonal versus Personal Sources.* Frustration resulting from external events (e.g., closed doors, rainy days, flat tires) is less intense than that instigated directly by another person.
3. *Group versus Individual Sources.* Frustration by a unified group is more intense than by an individual (if all other variables are equal).
4. *Basic versus Incidental Goals.* Frustration is more intense when basic or important goals are upset than when relatively superficial goals are involved (e.g., desire to gain respect from another as opposed to the desire to get the best seat at the ballgame).
5. *Real-Life versus Simulated Induction.* Frustration arising from genuine, realistic events is more intense than that introduced in practice, play, theatrics, or prepared learning exercises.

As a general rule, it is best to induce mild frustration at the outset and gradually increase to moderate levels as the class demonstrates its capacity to accept lower level frustrations.

Basic Acceptance Tasks

Task 1: Sharing Group Frustration

Ask for four or five children who want to try a new kind of activity. Bring them together in a small group, with the rest of the class observing. The first objective of the activity is to establish the conditions for the feeling of frustration to be induced. This requires that you introduce a goal that the children are eager to achieve. The goal could be satisfying in itself (e.g., when asked what they might like to do, the children might agree that having a race would be fun) or desired because of a reward to follow successful completion of some other task (e.g., each team member gets a star, a free period, some money or some candy if the team reaches the goal). The initial factor is that the children truly *want* to attain the goal or complete the task. The number or range of goals that would meet this condition is limitless.

The second step in inducing frustration is to interfere with fulfillment of the goal without giving the children any explanation or reassurance. Thus, after the children begin their efforts to get to the goal, you must see to it that the task cannot be finished.

Some possible small group tasks might be:

1. A relay race to the blackboard, with each child taking turns writing his first name and then going up for a second time to write his last name. Frustration may be induced by removing the chalk, blocking the board with physical obstacles, or announcing that time is up (a temporal obstacle).

2. Passing a message from one person to another by whispering. The goal is for the last member to accurately announce the message as it had been originally presented. Thus, the teacher might show the rest of the class the message to be passed along (e.g., "The tomatoes are growing in the garden"; "The team plays football tonight"), and then whisper it to the first team member. Frustration is induced by talking aloud to the class or the team members while they are trying to remember the exact message (communication obstacle).

3. Ask the members to deal out an equal number of cards from a deck of playing cards, and then see how quickly they can trade cards so that each person gets four of one kind. Team members are told that if they can finish in three minutes they will receive a reward (e.g., keep the cards, coca cola, free play). Frustration is induced by arbitrarily indicating time is up before the deadline (temporal obstacle), or by changing the rules so that certain suites that children are working with cannot be used (general obstacle), or by not having a sufficient number of cards for each child to get four of a kind (physical obstacle).

Following the induction of frustration in the small group, indicate to the rest of the class that the team did not reach their goal. Then inquire as to how the teammates' classmates felt about what happened. For example, you might ask, "Can someone tell us how he felt when the chalk was missing?" "What did you think when the time was up?" "Was anybody mad about what happened? . . . Anybody sad? . . . Who thought the game was unfair?"

Questioning the observing classmates first provides a peer group base of support and identification for feelings aroused in team members. The children directly frustrated can begin to see that they are not alone in their feelings and that these feelings can be acknowledged publicly without fear of reprisal or humiliation. Following the "group support" period of questioning, the directly frustrated team members should be given an opportunity to express their reactions to the game.

During these periods of questioning for and expression of children's feelings regarding frustration, *several important points can be made:*

1. The planned experience was upsetting, uncomfortable, and frustrating.
2. Different feelings were aroused (e.g., anger, disappointment, fear, distrust) in different children.
3. Upset could not be avoided by anyone; it is impossible to always get what you want.
4. Frustration was unrelated to fault or wrong doing; it is possible to feel bad without being bad.
5. Children share similar feelings of upset.

In all likelihood it will not be feasible to carry out such a full discussion with primary-grade youngsters. Be ready to close the activity with a quick summary, such as:

1. "Today we talked about feelings of frustration—the way we feel when we don't get what we want or hope for or thought we'd get."
2. "We could see that everybody gets these feelings."
3. "We can talk about these things, and we will do more another time."
4. "These upset feelings are OK to have; you and all other people (grownups too) will get them a lot. They are part of life and have to be. We can learn about them in school, just like we do other things."

This activity should be followed up, at suitable times, with brief discussions about other things that frustrate children. Ask questions like: "Who can think of other things that seem unfair in school?" "Are there other things you wish you could do or get in school?" "Was anybody disappointed about anything this week?" Keep focus on expression of feelings relating to frustrations. *Do not explain, criticize, judge, or solve any problems mentioned.* The purpose is to develop an awareness that all children experience frustration and have normal and necessary feelings to such frustration.

Sharing Personal Frustrations

Ask the children to think of a time in school when there was something they wanted to do but could not, a time when their wish or hope was blocked. Indicate that they could think of things that happened anywhere in or near school (e.g., classroom, halls, playground, lunch room, bus).

After each child has had a chance to tell his partner about a frustration in school, announce that the class can now make a *School Frustration ("Bug") List.* Using the blackboard, draw five columns to record the class' frustrations in terms of goal (*"What I wanted"*), blocking (*"What happened"*), source (*"Who did it"*), location (*"Where it happened"*), and feelings (*"How I felt"*).

Calling on children around the room in turn, ask each child to tell about his partner's frustration. Summarize the situation under the appropriate columns on the board for all to see and hear. The summary ultimately should reflect a wide range of school-based frustrations affecting numerous personal goals, induced by various sources, and arousing some common feelings. It is likely that the use of partners will not be effective for the first and second graders, in which case each child should relate his own incident.

While the "School Bug List" can be used for several purposes (such as exploration of alternative behaviors and differences in goals and reactions), the primary purpose here is to foster a general acceptance of feelings of frustration. The emphasis thus is on acknowledging, describing, and identifying typical experiences of frustration in a school environment. It is not our desire to seek elimination of frustration—a futile and self-defeating effort, as we see it—but, rather, to strengthen our capacity to live with frustration and to prevent reactions of guilt and self-blame which do more damage than the original goal-thwarting.

UNIT 2. BUILDING COPING RESOURCES

Goals: To strengthen the children's resources for coping effectively with frustration experiences; to develop techniques and behaviors which maintain possibilities for success and positive regard for self.

Modifying Goal-Setting Behavior

Task 1: Flexible Goal-Setting

Role play or describe situations in which children want a particular goal but do not achieve it. Draw examples from academic, social, athletic, and artistic spheres. For example, Helen really wants to spell all her words correctly; Tim wants to be invited to the party with the older boys; Charley wants to play on the first team; Denise wants to paint the zoo scene just the way it looks. Indicate how the child does not achieve his goal in the desired way (e.g., Helen makes two errors out of ten words; Tim is not invited to the party, although some kids his age do come by to play; Charley has to stay on the sidelines as a substitute; Denise cannot draw the animals with the right shapes.

Then help the class to *re-focus* their thinking from what the children do *not* accomplish to possible goals that *are* accomplished. For example, Helen wants to show that she can learn to spell words; Tim wants to know that other boys like him; Charley wants to play on a real football team; Denise wants to draw things that she enjoys seeing. Several points can be made: (1) People can adjust their goals at such a height that they can reach them; (2) Just because an ultimate goal is not achieved does not mean that other important goals are lost; (3) People have the *power* to revise or re-define their goals so that progress, effort, and accomplishment can be recognized.

Task 2: Finding Alternative Routes

Role play or describe situations where children want a particular end-result but are unsuccessful in achieving it (e.g., wanting father to play ball, wanting attention from the teacher, wanting to be liked by others). Illustrate a specific way in which the child goes about trying to reach his goal (e.g., telling his father how other boys play with their fathers, shouting out in class, giving candy and money to peers). Then encourage class to express ideas about other ways that these goals might have been reached (e.g., asking his father if he would play catch later, offering to do some job for the teacher, showing interest in other kids' ideas and activities). The point to be made and practiced is that there are often several ways to get to a goal, and we cannot be sure which (if any) will work unless we try new ones.

Task 3: Revising Goals

Role play situations in which a child must initiate some alternative action on his own because he has been excluded, expelled, or refused. For example, in the situation where a child did not receive an invitation to a party, he could invite a friend to his house or arrange to visit a friend. Offer examples in which children did something entirely different from that which they had initially desired and yet felt satisfied after shifting. Ask the class for examples of other things they could do which might make them happy in such situations as: being unable to play outside on a rainy day, finding that someone else has their favorite toy, not being picked for a team or class play, etc.

Task 4: Reducing Own Behavior Goal Conflicts

Role play situations in which the child is seeking to accomplish two goals at the same time which require incompatible behaviors (e.g., wanting to gain approval from the teacher yet also wanting to be accepted by the "tougher" children who scoff at schoolwork). Show how these two goals may be incompatible by offering some illustrations of behavior which might relate to each goal.

To Gain Peer Acceptance	*To Gain Teacher Approval*
Talk and joke with select peers	Pay attention in class
Participate in peer activities	Complete homework
Occupy self with peer distractions	Follow directions

Ask children to give other examples of opposing behaviors. Show how a person can be "caught" or "trapped" in the middle by two motivating forces, using a simple diagram which might be similar to the following:

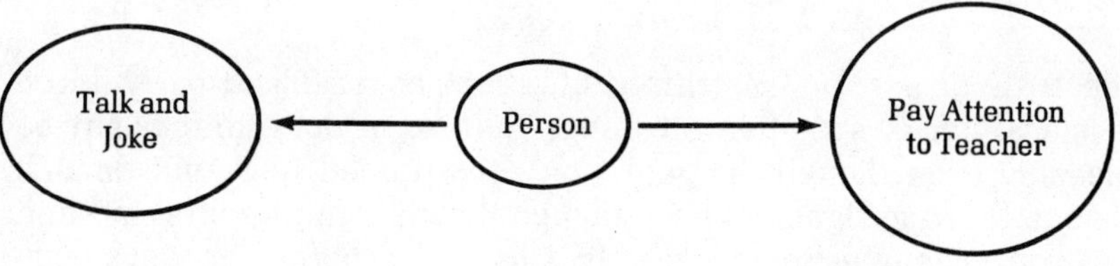

Figure 9

Talk briefly about other times when children felt "caught" in such situations. Then ask the children what they can do to get out of such "traps." Through discussion, bring out that there are at least three alternatives available to them in such a situation:

1. *Reduce the importance of one of the goals* (*"Crossing One Out"*). In talking about this alternative, help the students to understand that this is hard to do because people have many important needs. Emphasize, however, that need-satisfaction can be subject to personal choice and values.
2. *Place clear time or space limits around goal-related behavior* (*"Can't do everything at once"*). Help children see that both goals may be satisfied—but not at the same time and place. Illustrate times and places when children may talk and joke in school as well as pay attention to teacher. Emphasize that all children can put some limits around their own behaviors in order to reduce conflicts.
3. *Let others know about the conflict* (*"I'm mixed up about what to do"*). Provide examples of how one could express the feeling of being caught in the middle (e.g., "I want to have fun, but I also want to do my work." "I want to help you, but my friends want me to play with them.") Indicate that this alternative allows the other person(s) to suggest a way out, or, at least, it enables the other to understand the reason for a decision to restrict efforts toward their goal.

The point should be made that all of these alternatives can be employed in reducing one's own behavior conflicts. The advantages and disadvantages of each can be discussed later to increase the lesson's meaningfulness.

Identifying Positives

Task 1: Things I Did Do

Illustrate or ask for frustrating situations experienced by children in class. Focus attention on things that were done that might be pleasing even though the goal was not attained (e.g., not enough time to finish assignment even though the child did understand and answer some questions correctly. Chart of progress or work completed can be developed for visual reinforcement.).

Task 2: The Rest of Me Is OK

When frustration reflects weakness in ability or a situation where change is not possible (e.g., the child has poor motor coordination or buck teeth), ask the children to identify things they can accomplish in other areas. List several good points each child can feel and indicate that other parts of our life need not be dissatisfying because of frustration in one part.

Task 3: Building Expectations for Success

Have the children repeat tasks which involved earlier failure or mistakes, in order to demonstrate that improvement comes with practice. In addition, provide for repeated attempts on tasks which were structured to induce failure (not enough time allowed for excessive requirements for success). Allow ample time to work on previously incompleted tasks. Then discuss success as it relates to standards of difficulty.

Task 4: Success as Self-Improvement

Give a child something to do, such as a picture puzzle, and establish a time limit in which he is to complete it. Allow him to assemble it many times, thereby improving his time and his assembly skills. Emphasize and provide real-life examples of improvement with time and effort.

Task 5: I Did My Best and I Like It

Role play situations in which a child tries to accomplish something (e.g., write a poem, draw a picture, build a model), and someone else makes fun of it or makes disparaging remarks. Instruct the criticized child to respond with: "I did my best and I like it" or some other self-valuing statement. Use a variety of work efforts to be faulted, and allow children to play and reverse roles of the critical person.

UNIT 3. TOLERATING FRUSTRATION

Goals: To increase children's capacity to endure upsetting or disappointing experiences; to strengthen children's belief in their ability to absorb disappointing life events.

All frustration-induction activities in this unit should be followed by discussion of examples in real life and ways of coping with such frustrations. In addition, it is very important to indicate the purpose of the activities beforehand (e.g., "to build our courage") and to explain one's role as frustrator (e.g., "to make it seem real," "to show how to handle some hard parts in life," "to lead these teaching games"). Furthermore, in selecting tasks from this unit, it is important to remember that they be employed as a means of reinforcing the positive coping strategies presented in Unit 2, as well as a means of desensitization to a broad range of obstacles, conflicts, and disappointments.

Experiencing Obstacles

A common cause of frustration is the blocking of progress toward a particular goal by an obstacle. The obstacle may be *physical* (e.g., a wall, a person in the way, a car in front), *temporal* (e.g., time running out before the task can be finished), *interpersonal* (e.g., another person's not being interested in what you are saying), or *cognitive* (e.g., a task too complicated to be understood or completed). The exercises in the following sections are designed to create mild frustration through exposure to a variety of real-life obstacles which might be placed in one's way. The frustration exercises are meant to illustrate natural and predictable barriers to goal satisfaction. As a child comes to recognize that such barriers are normal and continuous in life and that concomitant feelings of frustration are also normal and continuous, his tolerance for frustrating experiences becomes greater.

Physical Obstacles

Task 1: Simple Obstacles Game

Present games or situations which offer clear goals and a series of obstacles to reaching these goals. Commercial games like "Candyland" or "Chutes and Ladders," in which progress toward a goal may be set back as a result of an "unlucky" pick or spin are useful. Create a variety of obstacle courses by following this simple pattern.

Task 2: Obstructing Actions

Indicate a series of steps to achieve a goal. For example, pick up a ball, toss it in the basket, crawl under a chair, and then return to a starting point. Introduce different kinds of obstructions along the way (e.g., somebody trying to kick the ball, covering the basket with a box, and someone sitting on the chair).

Task 3: Increasing Physical Demands

Set up a simple obstacle course in the classroom or on the playground. State conditions on how the course is to be run (e.g., forward). During the running of the course, change the physical requirements by stating that the remainder of the course is to be run on one leg or backwards. Vary the demands for goal accomplishment by changing the rules in mid-performance or changing the position of the goal to require more physical effort in order to overcome the obstacles.

Temporal Obstacles

Task 1: Reducing Time Limits

Gradually increase time pressures in performance situations. For example, select a variety of task areas (e.g., assembling puzzles, writing a story on paper, catching a ball, building block designs, finding objects removed from a collection of objects). Then progressively introduce or increase stress by shortening time allowed for completion of the assigned tasks.

Task 2: Lengthening the Task Sequence

Gradually increase task pressure by increasing the complexity of a task. For example, to increase complexity for the tasks mentioned in the preceding exercise, you might offer puzzles with more pieces within the same time limit, roll balls at a faster and faster pace, add more blocks within the same time limit, or remove more and more objects from the box.

Task 3: Obstructing Speed

Program a sequence of actions for a child. Allow him to perform the actions and record his time on the chalkboard. For example, the child's program might demand that he take the pencil from the desk, pick up the red book from the floor, put both in the cardboard box, and then put the box on the green chair. On the next trial, state that if he completes the task in the same time period, he will earn a reward. Following this message, introduce obstructions such as: scotch tape the pencil to the desk, put the red book at the other side of the room with several books on top of it, turn the box over with a trash basket on it, and move the green chair to another place.

Interpersonal (Communication) Obstacles

Task 1: Inattention Patterns

Ask the child to tell about some interesting thing he has done. As he tells his story, look away, walk around the room, yawn, talk to another person, or show general inattention to the story he is re ating.

Task 2: Interference Patterns

Ask a child to relate an interesting experience he has had. As he does so, interfere at one point by starting to tell a similar incident you have experienced. Interfere to such an extent that he cannot relate the remainder of his experience.

Task 3: Forcing Patterns

Ask a child to tell about an interesting trip that he has taken to the beach, a toy store, or other enjoyable location. After he has started his story, extract the story from him by using a series of questions, thus taking the initiative and forcing him to tell the story in the manner you dictate.

Task 4: Exit Patterns

Ask a child a question which will require use of considerable detail to answer, but one which is on his grade level and within his knowledge. When he is partially finished answering, get up and walk out of the room.

Task 5: Provocative Questioning

Ask the child to relate any kind of experience he has had. Whenever applicable, interrupt his story with the question: "Why?" Here the word "why" is meant to disrupt and provoke rather than to enhance communication.

Task 6: Derogatory Questioning

As a child tells a story about some experience he is proud of, interject derogatory questioning, such as: "How could you do that?" "Are you really that good?" "Do you expect me to believe that?"

Cognitive Obstacles

Task 1: Increasing Task Complexity

Ask a child to assemble a rather simple picture puzzle, establishing a reasonable time limit so the puzzle can be completely assembled. Using the same limit, introduce puzzles that are increasingly more difficult, until you reach the point where their completion is unattainable within the time limitations.

Task 2: Overwhelming Words

Direct a child to do something which requires additional explanation before he can proceed with the task. In explaining how the task is to be completed, use words or phrases that are beyond his comprehension.

Experiencing Conflicts

The purpose of the following tasks is to increase acceptance of conflicting and competing response requirements.

Teacher-Induced Conflicts

Task 1: Competing Work Tasks

Deliberately introduce conflicting directives or statements requiring opposing response modes. For example, tell the children to copy the sentence from the board before they do anything else. After the children have started copying the sentence, announce that everyone must clear their desk immediately and get ready for recess.

Task 2: Behavior Dilemmas

Create a situation where opposing behaviors appear desirable. For example, children are first told that working silently is important. Then stimulate talking by asking a child what he is doing and carrying on a conversation with that child.

Peer-Induced Conflicts

Task 1: Friendship Dilemmas

Role play a situation in a peer group where conflicting requests are made upon the child. For example, a child is playing baseball with his peers. Other friends of his come along and say, "Come to the store with us. We're getting some ice cream."

Task 2: Identification Dilemmas

Role play situations where a child is confronted by alternative values of two or more peer reference groups. For example, a youngster interested in athletics is invited after school for a neighborhood ball game at the same time that his debating club is holding a big event.

Self-Other-Induced Conflicts

Task 1: Resisting Pressure Situations

Role play a situation where a child is doing something he wants to do but which is in conflict with the influence of others. For example, a child might be trying to read a book, while his peers are noisily playing a game of kickball outside.

Experiencing Disappointments

The following exercises focus on increasing acceptance of common disappointments resulting from lack of reward or goal satisfaction.

Task 1: Delayed Reward

Outline several things a child must do to receive a reward. Just before the child completes the tasks, postpone the activity or remove or deplete the reward. At a later time, allow the child to complete the tasks with the reward being available. This period of delay can be lengthened progressively over a period of time.

Task 2: Interrupting Task Completion

Divide a small group or class into two reading sections. The material can be an interesting short story on the children's level. State the amount of time to be allotted for completion of the reading. When half the time has expired and each group is approximately halfway through the story, switch the stories from one group to another. After a discussion of the feelings aroused and ways the children coped with these feelings, allow both sections to finish reading the stories.

Task 3: Broken Promises

Announce to the class that for the next ten minutes the class will play "Simon Says." After five minutes have elapsed, announce that you had forgotten that the class had not completed their arithmetic, and that, therefore it is necessary for them to stop the game and get to work. Discuss examples of broken promises in everyday experiences at school, work, and home.

SUMMARY

Like death and taxes, frustration is inevitable. Despite this fact, little has been done to prepare children to accept and deal effectively with everyday frustration. We have sought to provide in this chapter a basis for controlled, systematic management of frustration. To this end, we have presented a set of teaching tasks which should better equip children to accept feelings of frustration; cope more successfully with frustration; and handle obstacles, conflicts, and disappointments. We assert that planned, psychoeducationally insightful learning tasks can substantially build strength in meeting adversity as well as establish a basic belief in one's ability to withstand pressure.

It should be noted, however, that tasks involving frustration must be used in a context of group discussion and clear understanding of purposes. Students should have the sense that the teacher is introducing learning experiences in a planned, controlled, and helpful manner. A role-playing atmosphere can best assure positive impact for the learner.

For tasks in this chapter to have relevance and purpose to the child, however, the teacher must continually attempt to relate them to real-life situations and the environment in which the child lives. The teacher should also clearly state the importance of these tasks for learning, mastery, and self-growth.

A summary of the curriculum units and tasks for the managing frustration area is presented in Table 11.

Table 11: *Summary of Curriculum Units and Tasks in the Curriculum Area: Managing Frustration*

Units	*Tasks*
Accepting Feelings of Frustration	1. Sharing Group Frustration 2. Sharing Personal Frustrations
Building Coping Resources	*Modifying Goal-Setting Behavior* 1. Flexible Goal-Setting 2. Finding Alternative Routes 3. Revising Goals 4. Reducing Own Behavior Conflicts *Identifying Positives* 1. Things I Did Do 2. The Rest of Me Is OK 3. Building Expectations for Success 4. Success as Self-Improvement 5. I Did My Best and I Like It
Experiencing Obstacles	*Physical Obstacles* 1. Simple Obstacle Games 2. Obstructing Actions 3. Increasing Physical Demands *Temporal Obstacles* 1. Reducing Time Limits 2. Lengthening the Task Sequence 3. Obstructing Speed *Interpersonal (Communication) Obstacles* 1. Inattention Patterns 2. Interference Patterns 3. Forcing Patterns 4. Exit Patterns 5. Provocative Questioning 6. Derogatory Questioning

	Cognitive Obstacles 1. Increasing Task Complexity 2. Overwhelming Words
Experiencing Conflicts	*Teacher-Induced Conflicts* 1. Competing Work Tasks 2. Behavior Dilemmas *Peer-Induced Conflicts* 1. Friendship Dilemmas 2. Identification Dilemmas *Self-Other-Induced Conflicts* 1. Resisting Pressure Situations
Experiencing Disappointments	1. Delayed Reward 2. Interrupting Task Completion 3. Broken Promises

REFERENCES

Aronson, E. "The Effect of Effort on the Attractiveness of Rewarded and Unrewarded Stimuli." *Journal of Abnormal and Social Psychology* 63 (1961): 375–80.

Aronson, E., and Mills, J. "The Effect of Severity of Initiation on Liking for a Group." *Journal of Abnormal and Social Psychology* 59 (1959): 177–81.

Bach, G., and Wyden, P. "Marital Fighting: A Guide to Love." In *Handbook of Marriage Counseling*, edited by B. Ard and C. Ard, pp. 313–21. Palo Alto, California: Science and Behavior Press, 1969.

Bower, E. M. "The Modification, Mediation, and Utilization of Stress during the School Years." *American Journal of Orthopsychiatry* 34 (1964): 667–74.

Burton, A., editor. *Encounter: The Theory and Practice of Encounter Groups*. San Francisco: Jossey-Bass, 1969.

Caplan, G. "Opportunities for School Psychologists in the Primary Prevention of Mental Disorders in Children." In *The Protection and Promotion of Mental Health in Schools,* edited by N. M. Lambert, pp. 9–22. Bethesda, Maryland: National Institute of Mental Health, 1965.

Clarizio, H. F. *Mental Health and the Educative Process.* Chicago: Rand McNally, 1969.

Educational Research Council of America. *A Curriculum to Help Students Deal with Frustration and Aggression.* Cleveland, Ohio: Educational Research Council, 1972.

Epstein, S. "Toward a Unified Theory of Anxiety." In *Progress in Experimental Personality Research,* edited by B. Maher, pp. 1–89. New York: Academic Press, 1967.

Fenz, W., and Epstein, S. "Gradients of Psychological Arousal of Experienced and Novice Parachutists as a Function of an Approaching Jump." *Psychosomatic Medicine* 29 (1967): 33–51.

Feshbach, S. "Aggression." In *Carmichael's Manual of Child Psychology,* Vol. 2, 3rd ed., edited by P. Mussen, pp. 159–259. New York: Wiley, 1970.

Gerard, H., and Mathewson, G. "The Effects of Severity of Initiation on Liking for a Group: A Replication." *Journal of Experimental Social Psychology* 2 (1966): 278–87.

Giebink, J.; Stover, D.; and Fahl, M. "Teaching Adaptive Responses to Frustration to Emotionally Disturbed Boys." *Journal of Consulting and Clinical Psychology* 32 (1968): 366–68.

Hollister, W. G. "The Concept of 'Strens' in Preventive Interventions and Ego-Strength Building in the Schools." In *The Protection and Promotion of Mental Health in Schools,* edited by N. Lambert, pp. 30–35. Bethesda, Maryland: U.S. Department of Health, Education, and Welfare Monograph Number 5, 1965.

Holt, R. R. *New Horizon for Psychotherapy.* New York: Basic Books, 1972.

Iglitzin, L.B. "Violence and American Democracy." *Journal of Social Issues* 26 (1970): 165–86.

Montagu, A. *On Being Human.* New York: Hawthorne, 1966.

Murphy, L. *The Widening World of Childhood: Paths toward Mastery.* New York: Basic Books, 1962.

Sanford, N., and Comstock, C. *Sanctions for Evil: Sources of Social Destructiveness.* San Francisco: Jossey-Bass, 1971.

Satir, V. *Conjoint Family Therapy.* Palo Alto, California: Science and Behavior Press, 1967.

Thorne, F. C. *Psychological Case Handling.* Brandon, Vermont: Clinical Psychology Publishing, 1968.

Toch, H. *Violent Men.* Chicago: Aldine, 1969.

Torrance, E. P. *Mental Health and Constructive Behavior*. Belmont, California: Wadsworth, 1968.

Trieschman, A. E. "Temper Tantrums." *Today's Education* 58 (1969): 33–36.

Tyler, L. *The Work of the Counselor*. New York: Appleton-Century-Crofts, 1969.

Winter, S.; Griffith, J.; and Kolb, D. "Capacity for Self-Direction." *Journal of Consulting and Clinical Psychology* 32 (1968): 35–41.

Wolff, S. *Children under Stress*. London: Penguin Press, 1969.

Yates, A. *Frustration and Conflict*. New York: Wiley, 1962.

ADDITIONAL RESOURCES

Aspy, D. *Toward a Technology for Humanizing Education*. Chicago: Research Press, 1972.

Bessell, H., and Palomares, U. *Methods in Human Development*. San Diego, California: Human Development Training Institute, 1970.

Lederman, J. *Anger and the Rocking Chair: Gestalt Awareness with Children*. New York: McGraw-Hill, 1967.

Wrenn, G., and Schwarzock, S. *The Coping with Books*. Circle Pines, Minnesota: American Guidance Service, 1970.

12

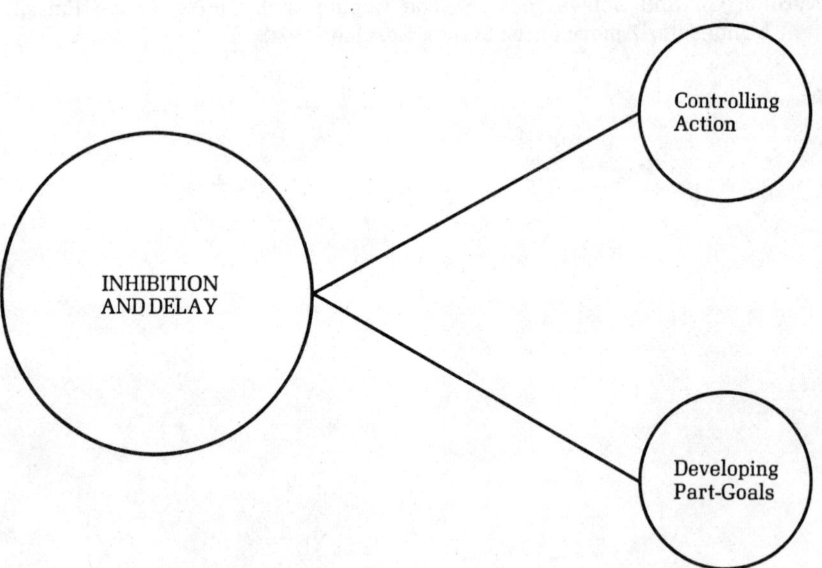
INHIBITION
AND DELAY
Controlling
Action
Developing
Part-Goals

Curriculum Area: Inhibition and Delay

INTRODUCTION TO INHIBITION AND DELAY

Inhibition or delay can be described as the act of restraining strong action tendencies from immediate release. As a result, a certain behavior may be postponed until a later time, channelled into a related but different form of expression, or replaced by new behavior. Without the capacity to inhibit or delay impulses to action, volitional control is impossible, and action becomes subject to primitive, unsocialized urges; therefore, all children must learn to regulate their powerful action tendencies if they are to gain even the most rudimentary social acceptance or school success.

Inhibition is not an inherent attribute but, rather, a self-regulation that develops with neurological maturation and social experience (see Dykman, Ackerman, Clements, and Peters, 1971). Many youngsters, therefore, are handicapped in developing inhibition because they have maturational lags or weaknesses, or erratic social experiences which result in faulty inhibitory controls. Fortunately, inhibition and delay functions can be improved through prescribed learning activities and practice. In addition, latent capacities for inhibition and delay can be strengthened by promoting the child's awareness and confidence in his ability to exercise control over his own impulses.

Research on choice of delayed versus immediate reinforcement indicates that children need immediate reinforcement only to the extent that they have not been reinforced previously for acts of delayed gratification (Mischel, 1966). The disposition to accept delayed external reinforcement appears to be related positively to ability to resist temptation (i.e., inhibition of impulses to action) (Burton, Maccoby, and Allinsmith, 1961; Mischel and Gilligan, 1964). In addition, there is evidence that experiences of success at a task increase the likelihood of accepting delayed reinforcement as an outcome of task completion, providing the expectancy is for behavior-contingent reinforcement (Aronfreed, 1968; Metzner, 1963; Mischel and Staub, 1965).

Several investigators have successfully applied behavior modification principles to disruptive, hyperactive, and/or over-aggressive school children (Home, de Baca, Devine, Steinhorst, and Richert, 1963; O'Leary and Becker, 1967; Thomas, Becker, and Armstrong, 1968). Thus, it appears that many youngsters are capable of curbing impulsivity when they are provided with clear discriminating stimuli and with rewards for better control. In one study (Home, et al., 1963), breaks for noise and movement were made contingent upon calm, purposeful participation in activities (i.e., the Premack Principle), with the result that behavior became more settled and regulated.

This research strongly suggests two conclusions: inclination or capacity to delay or inhibit gratification can be *increased* by new learning experiences in which positive reinforcement is obviously contingent upon the act of impulse inhibition, and confidence in one's own ability to influence and receive positive reinforcement at a later time can be *strengthened* by creating actual experiences which provide evidence that one's own ability to control action can increase the probability of a successful outcome.

The present structure for teaching activities designed to improve inhibition and delay skills incorporates both of these research suggestions. For all tasks presented in this chapter, positive reinforcement (e.g., praise, points, recognition) is consistently given for controlling action, and controlled action is clearly related to more general prospects for success.

Robins and Robins (1968) and Kallan (1972) have found that hyperactive children can be helped to slow down when they are provided with an external rhythm against which to pace themselves. For example, Kallan used a metronome to create a situation in which the child's naturally hard-driven pace had to be controlled to match the rhythm of the metronome. Gradually, the child was able to achieve efficiently at a slower pace with the metronome; with continued practice, he began to regulate his actions independently. Kephart (1971) and Cratty (1967) have reported similar results with other methods of rhythmic matching (e.g., trampoline bounces in tandem).

Thus, there appear to be several lines along which to work toward improving inhibition and delay skills. Gain in ability to delay action tendencies toward inappropriate, irrelevant behavior should greatly enhance a child's chances for successful goal achievement. In addition, postponement of immediate gratification in order to achieve the satisfaction of goal accomplishment should contribute to an improved self-image and a feeling of confidence in one's ability to master difficult tasks.

Rationale

Many students attempt to satisfy their needs or desires through immediate, hasty, unchecked actions. For these students, impulses rush from arousal to overt expression, often with distressing consequences for the child and those around him. Requirements for following rules, regulating behavior to social norms, and respecting the rights and property of others often go unheeded. The occurrence of such behavior generates a snowballing cycle of punishment and rejection, at the end of which lies a tragedy of deviancy, destructiveness, and social waste. Prevention of this type of misbehavior-rejection process is contingent upon a child's appreciation and capacity for the inhibition and delay of impulses. Assuring inhibition and delay skills as a basic part of a child's behavioral repertiore should immensely enhance long-term prospects for personal and social success.

TEACHING UNITS AND GOALS

This chapter has been divided into two units: controlling action and developing part-goals.

Unit 1. Controlling Action

Goals: To increase a child's capacity to delay or inhibit impulses toward immediate expression; to strengthen possibilities for checking action tendencies until they become more appropriate for success.

Unit 2. Developing Part-Goals

Goal: To build an appreciation for partial success and future gratification.

UNIT 1. CONTROLLING ACTION

Goals: To increase a child's capacity to delay or inhibit impulses toward immediate expression; to strengthen possibilities for checking action tendencies until they become more appropriate for success.

Task 1: Silence Training

Develop the child's ability to maintain silence for varying lengths of time under varying conditions. Begin by requesting silence for short periods, gradually stretching the period to a minute or more. Introduce noises, visual objects or events, announcements, facial expressions, and other deliberate actions to provoke or distract. A teacher may provide meaningful incentives by offering points toward a prize or privilege or an immediate reward like candy or gum.

Task 2: Red Light

This game lends itself well to a recess period and involves "runners" and a "traffic light." One pupil is chosen to be the traffic light; he turns his back to the runners who are located at a starting point (about 100 feet from the light) and covering his eyes, counts "1,2,3,4; red light"; he then turns around and tries to spot anyone who is still moving; moving players must return to the starting line. Runners try to reach the light without getting caught in motion; the first one to reach the light tags the light and runs back to the starting line. The student serving as traffic light then tries to tag one of the runners before he returns to starting line; if the "traffic light" player succeeds, the player tagged then becomes the "traffic light." Score a point or praise the runner who makes a tag and returns safely.

Task 3: Body Sculpture

Designate one person to act as the "sculptor." His job is to shape another person into any pose or position, with the "model" allowing the sculptor to place his arms, legs, head, and trunk into position. The sculptor may be directed to try to sculpt such things as a fighting pose, a playing pose, a dancing pose, a sports pose, etc. Other children can try to guess the pose the model portrays, as they would in charades. The length of time for holding the pose can be varied depending upon its difficulty and the child's ability. The children can be assigned a partner and can alternate being "sculptor" and "model," thereby giving every child a chance to play both roles.

Task 4: Controlled Starts

Practice stops and starts as they will occur in racing, hockey, football, etc. (e.g., "Ready, on your mark, get set, go" as is done in racing; hitting a puck when dropped on the ice in hockey; not jumping "offside" in football; going up for a tip off in basketball). Build in a minor penalty if the person moves before the proper signal is given. For instance, in a "ready-set-go" game, if a child starts before "go" is said, he must take one step backward. The purpose of the game is to avoid taking steps backwards, while trying to run on signal (i.e., "go"). Interest and challenge may be increased by use of deceptive rhythms or gestures to promote false starts.

Task 5: Steal the "Bacon"

Choose teams; then assign the same individual numbers to members of both teams. With each team in back of its baseline, place an old rag in the center between the teams. As numbers are called, players advance and try to steal the "bacon" (the rag) without being tagged with it in their possession by a member of the other team. The first team to get the "bacon" over its line wins a point. If a player is tagged with the "bacon" in his possession, it is brought back to the center and the game starts again with new players. If the "bacon" is taken over a baseline without the person's being tagged, a point is scored.

Task 6: Music Inhibition

Establish a regular beat, using a metronome or tapping with a drumstick or pencil. The pupil's task is to regulate his free-form movement to every other beat or to half-beats. The task may be varied by asking pupils to regulate their foot tapping to the pace of pencil tapping in such a way that they are sure to include numerous pauses and changing tempos.

Task 7: Inhibition of Spontaneous Movement Impulse

With the use of a tape recorder, record a series of songs with different tempos (slow and fast). Allow the children to move in free form—except that when the music is fast, they must move slowly and when the music is slow, they must move fast. Each tempo can last one to two minutes before being changed. The purpose is to inhibit the natural rhythm movement.

Task 8: Pump Handle Game

Pair the children off within the class. Allow each pair to face each other as they clasp hands, with one child designated "A" and the other "B." At a signal from the teacher, "A" is told to start pumping. "A" descends to a squatting position and then slowly rises to a position of standing tall. "B," meanwhile, moves in the opposite direction. As the children's hands are clasped, their arms should be fully extended from the body. As the pairs move up and down, the arms should resemble the pump-handle and the point where the hands are clasped should resemble the fulcrum. If "A" or "B" moves in the same direction as his partner, then they both must sit down. The last pair standing is the winning team.

Task 9: "Do It" Game

The class forms a circle with the teacher who serves as a model. The teacher makes a move as he verbalizes what he is doing. At the words "do it," the children make the same move. For example, the teacher says and demonstrates, "Put your right foot in and take your right foot out" (in and out of the circle). Hesitate. "Do it." "Put your hands on your hips, turn all the way around." Hesitate. "Do it." If anyone moves when the teacher moves, he must sit down. The last person standing wins the game. Difficulty may be increased by requiring several sequential moves on one command of "Do it." Let children know that they should wait for a signal even though they might not remember all the moves in a sequence.

Task 10: "Magic Word" Game

The class is divided into two teams of equal membership, and each team lines up. An eraser is placed on the chalkboard some distance in front of each team. The magic word for the first team is "the"; the magic word for the second team is "and." Read a story to the children that has an equal number of "the's" and "and's" in it, or you may wish to construct sentences that have an equal share of "the's" and "and's" in them. For example, sentences could include:

The dog and cat got in a fight.

Stay after school and read the book.

We are going to the zoo and can see lions there.

Tell me about the story and draw a picture about it.

When the first person on each team hears his magic word, he goes to the chalkboard, gets the eraser, gives it to the next person in his line, and goes to the end of the line. The second person in the row, upon hearing the next magic word, takes the eraser to the chalkboard and then goes to the end of the line. If anyone starts to the chalkboard upon hearing the other team's word or a word that sounds like but is not his magic word, he does not earn a point for his team. Or if a player is drawn over the line "offside" by movement of the other team, he does not earn a point. Other team members in the row should not be allowed to help the person whose turn it is. On second or third readings, the sentence could be reworded to increase difficulty. A team member who fails to hear his magic word does not earn a point, while successful members earn a point following each turn. After a sufficient length of time, the team having the most points wins.

Difficulty may be further increased by more rapid reading of the sentences, and variation could include lists of rhyming words. For example, one team could have magic words rhyming with "sad," while the other team has words that rhyme with "ball." The verbalizations of the teacher might go as follows: "pin, tin, bin, call, sat, bat, cat, bad, sin, mad, cry, try, fall, pry, pit, sit, bit, tack, dad, etc."

Task 11: Stay Put

The class is divided into five or six equal rows. All children stand beside their own desks. When the teacher says, "Now go," the first child in each row goes to the chalkboard and writes "AB" and returns to his seat. The second child in each line waits until the teacher says, "Now go," or "Stay put." If a child moves toward the chalkboard when the teacher says, "Stay put," he or she must forfeit his turn. The goal is to have each child put two letters of the alphabet on the chalkboard in sequential order. At the end of a certain period of time, the line having the most letters on the chalkboard wins. To make the game longer, the alphabet can be written several times by each line. Difficulty may be increased by calling out "Stay put" several times in rapid succession or raising and lowering your voice with accompanying hand movements. The children should remember that no benefits accrue from writing fast and returning to the seat. Additional rules could include a child's having to miss a turn either because he couldn't write the letters or because he wrote the wrong letters.

Task 12: Even Number Move

The class members stand next to their desks while playing this game. Count and make a series of moves on each number which the children imitate on all even numbers. For example, count, "one," and put both arms above your head; "two," and put both arms at your sides. On the count of "two," the children should put their arms at their sides and hold that position until you count, "three," and demonstrate a new move; then, on "four" and another move, the children copy your actions once again. In other words, the children copy only the even numbered moves. Anyone caught moving on an odd number is out of the game. The last person standing wins. Difficulty may be increased by going at a faster pace or using numbers ending in zero as numbers to which the children move while you count by fives. The game can be made easier by placing numbers on a chalkboard marked for even cues (signals).

Task 13: Click, Click, Don't Move

The children may stand next to their desks while playing this game. The model announces some move that is to be performed, as in the "Simon Says" game. No one is to move until they hear three clicks from the model. For example, the model might say, "Put your hands on your head." (The model demonstrates.) "Click, click, [delay] click." "Put your hands on your hips."

If anyone moves before three clicks are given, he is out of the game. The third click may be delayed for some time or not given at all—in which case the model simply announces the next move. Again, the last person standing wins the game. You may act as a model to start the game, but the models should soon be children.

Extremely inhibited, over-controlled children are apt not to move in this game or other games where quick action is required. To help them gain confidence in taking action, it is important to structure the activity so that speed of movement is reinforced. For example, in the "Click, Click, Don't Move" game, instructions can be varied so the children are required to complete the action *before* the model finishes saying, "Click, click, click." The teacher as model can regulate the speed of saying "click" to assure that the slow-moving children can succeed—or at least be very close to succeeding. Gradually, the pace can be quickened to promote increased willingness to release actions.

UNIT 2. DEVELOPING PART-GOALS

Goal: To build an appreciation for partial success and future gratification.

Task 1: Question-and-Answer Games

Use word games like "Twenty Questions," "Ghost," "Geography," etc. for this task. For example, a child might try to guess a person, place, or thing by asking a series of questions to be answered "yes" or "no"; a child might try to fill in the blanks for a four- or five-letter word or a famous name, etc., guessing letters as he goes until a figure is "hung"; two players alternately might give letters until a word or name is formed, with the object being to avoid naming the letter which ends the word.

Task 2: Planning to Teach

Give students the task of planning a way to teach other students how to do things, such as playing basketball, buying something in a store, making a long distance phone call, driving a car, climbing a rope, etc. Use role-playing to emphasize reality and present learner problems as the teaching unfolds (e.g., learner cannot play basketball because he doesn't know how to pass the ball).

Task 3: Jigsaw Puzzles

Provide cardboard or posterboard models of simple shapes (e.g., circle, square, triangle, etc.). Along with the model, provide cut-up pieces which can be put together to form the shape of the model. Start with a small number of pieces (three–five) and gradually increase difficulty by cutting more pieces and more complicated shapes. Demonstrate how the model can be cut up and reassembled.

Vary the degree of difficulty by introducing irrelevant pieces, providing cues to selecting the relevant pieces by color coding or marking with identifying shapes or patterns. Gradually add additional challenge by using pictures or scenes and repeating the process of cutting a model into its parts. At more advanced levels, request that the children try to assemble puzzles without having a model against which to match their work.

It is helpful to reinforce the concept of partial success by structuring the tasks so that the pupils complete the puzzles over several daily periods. In this case, it will be necessary to have a means of carefully storing a partially completed puzzle, perhaps by providing gift boxes which can be stacked neatly on a shelf.

Task 4: Sorting Objects by Function

Select common whole-objects or entities which have clear and well-known parts (e.g., a person's arms, legs, head, body, feet; the roof, door, windows, walls, or furniture of a house; the tires, steering wheel, engine, roof, and fenders of a car; the brushes, paint, easel, paper, or water cup of a paint set). Ask the children to try to find the parts that go together.

Vary the difficulty of the game by altering the complexity of the whole-object, its number of parts, or by revealing or withholding the nature of the whole-object to be identified. Add interest by asking pupils to select their own whole-objects and find and cut part-objects from old magazines.

Teams can be formed, with members trying to sort objects selected by other teams which are new to them. Different teams can be provided with a designated set of objects and given a specified length of time to sort them. Or teams can be assigned certain whole-objects, with parts scattered around the room and members trying to locate those parts which are included in their team's whole-object.

The game also can be used individually, with each child being given a whole-object of his own to compose. If used with the small-group format, this activity helps to create a sense of constructive participation in a team effort, thereby illustrating how individuals partially contribute to a team's success.

Task 5: Object Recall Game

Place a large number of common small objects on a desk or table (e.g., an eraser, pencil, paper-clip, chalk, thumb-tack, ruler, pad, crayon, pen, penny, rubberband, key, scissors, book, etc.). Divide the table (with string, a chalk mark, or scotch tape) into four or five numbered sections. Place the objects inconspicuously so they are divided equally into the marked sections. Inform the pupils that they will be playing a memory game and that each row or group of pupils will be given a chance to file by the table in order to inspect the objects set out. The task will be for a small group (four–five) to remember as many of the objects as they can and to draw or write the ones they remember on their papers when they return to their seats. Keep the line moving so that each child has about ten seconds to look at the objects. At this point, say nothing about the sections.

Following this phase, collect the papers—one group at a time—adding the correctly remembered number of separate objects for each group and marking the number on the board. Indicate how many objects there were in all and then ask if anyone can think of a way that his group might have been able to remember more than they did. Ask if anyone noticed the numbers on the table. Lead the children to suggest that each child could have remembered the objects in just one section, with each member of the group taking a different numbered section. Repeat the recall task using this format and then tabulate the results from each group.

This game should help the children to see that some tasks, because of their difficulty, can only be achieved partially by individuals, that there are alternatives to solving a problem—a major one being to divide the labor, and that individual efforts can contribute significantly to the success of a team effort.

ADDITIONAL SUGGESTIONS

Teaching children to inhibit their movement and to delay, postpone, or put off gratification until it is more appropriate for action has many of the elements of teaching self-discipline. For example, all athletes undergo rigid training in inhibiting body movements and delaying maneuvers in an effort to discipline the body for rigorous controlled action. To be ready to spring forward at the crack of a gun necessitates control over one's thoughts as well as body. The more one is in control, the more assurance there is of at least completing the first step toward goal achievement.

Children, with their great abundance of energy, their drive to be first in line or first chosen, their eagerness to experience something new and exciting, often give no thought to the controlled, delayed movement necessary to ensure success in reaching a desired goal. Many good examples of failure in sports due to insufficient delay are available and should be pointed out to children (e.g., a batter swinging too early at a change-up pitch from the pitcher; a football player jumping offside before the ball is snapped; a relay runner moving before he has a firm grip on the baton; a basketball player trying to shoot when he is off balance, and many more). Teachers can take these examples of failures and make good discussion sessions on how they could have been successes.

In particular, teachers should encourage children to talk to themselves while regulating their actions. For example, it helps to be thinking, or even whispering, phrases like: "wait a little bit longer," "hold it," "not so fast," "slow down," "stay ready," etc. The use of such self-mediated verbal cues is very helpful in modifying impulsivity and in developing additional resources (i.e., thinking, reflecting, verbalizing) for purposeful action (Luria, 1961; Meichenbaum, 1971; Meichenbaum and Goodman, 1969).

SUMMARY

To insure an adequate degree of socialization, it is necessary that a child be capable of postponing or delaying immediate gratification of impulses until more appropriate times for action. Abrupt reactions to emotionally arousing situations often brings the child the opposite of his desired goal. Without the safeguards of delay and inhibition, the child's behavior is similar to a snowball rolling down a hill—it gathers force and momentum as it plunges forward on a course of self-destruction. Overtly explosive, destructive acts result in harsh punishment and rejection as well as in long-term failure to achieve personal gratification.

As they were presented in this chapter, those tasks listed under "Controlling Action" were specifically designed to teach children to inhibit action that is clearly inappropriate in a given situation. "Developing Part-Goals" becomes a method for learning to plan action leading to ultimate success carefully, while deriving self-satisfaction from steady progress toward an objective, whether as an individual or as a contributing member of a group.

For tasks in this chapter to have relevance and purpose to the child, however, the teacher must continually attempt to relate them to real-life situations and the environment in which the child lives. The teacher also should clearly state the importance of these tasks for learning, mastery, and self-growth.

Table 12 presents the curriculum content for the Inhibition and Delay area.

Table 12: *Summary of the Curriculum Units and Tasks in the Curriculum Area: Inhibition and Delay*

Units	*Tasks*
Controlling Actions	1. Silence Training 2. Red Light 3. Body Sculpture 4. Controlled Starts 5. Steal the "Bacon" 6. Music Inhibition 7. Inhibition of Spontaneous Movement Impulse

Table 12 (continued)

	8. Pump Handle Game 9. "Do It" Game 10. "Magic Word" Game 11. Stay Put 12. Even Number Move 13. Click, Click, Don't Move
Developing Part-Goals	1. Question-and-Answer Game 2. Planning to Teach 3. Jigsaw Puzzles 4. Sorting Objects by Function 5. Object Recall Game

REFERENCES

Aronfreed, J. *Conduct and Conscience: The Socialization of Internalized Control over Behavior*. New York: Academic Press, 1968.

Burton, R.; Maccoby, E.; and Allinsmith, W. "Antecedents of Resistance to Temptation in Four-Year-Old Children." *Child Development* 32 (1961): 689–710.

Cratty, B. *Social Dimensions of Physical Activity*. Englewood Cliffs, New Jersey: Prentice-Hall, 1967.

Dykman, R.; Ackerman, P.; Clements, S.; and Peters, J. "Specific Learning Disabilities: An Attentional Deficit Syndrome." In *Progress in Learning Disabilities*, edited by H. R. Myklebust, pp. 56–93. New York: Grune & Stratton, 1971.

Home, L.; de Baca, P.; Devine, J.; Steinhorst, R.; and Richert, E. "Use of the Premack Principle in Controlling the Behavior of Nursery School Children." *Journal of Experimental Analysis of Behavior* 6 (1963): 544.

Kallan, C. "Rhythm and Sequencing in an Intersensory Approach to Learning Disability." *Journal of Learning Disabilities* 5 (1972): 68–74.

Kephart, N. C. *The Slow Learner in the Classroom*, 2d ed. Columbus, Ohio: Charles E. Merrill Publishing Co., 1971.

Luria, A. *The Role of Speech in the Regulation of Normal and Abnormal Behavior*. New York: Liveright, 1961.

Meichembaum, D. H. *The Nature and Modification of Impulsive Children: Training Impulsive Children to Talk to Themselves*. Research Report

Number 23. Waterloo: University of Waterloo Department of Psychology, 1971.

Meichembaum, D. H., and Goodman, J. "Reflection-Impulsivity and Verbal Control of Motor Behavior." *Child Development* 40 (1969): 785–97.

Metzner, R. "Effects of Work Requirements in Two Types of Delay of Gratification Situations." *Child Development* 34 (1963): 809–16.

Mischel, W. "Theory and Research on the Antecedents of Self-Imposed Delay of Reward." In *Progress in Experimental Personality Research*, Vol. 3, edited by B. A. Maher, pp. 85–132. New York: Academic Press, 1966.

Mischel, W., and Gilligan, C. "Delay of Gratification, Motivation for the Prohibited Gratification, and Responses to Temptation." *Journal of Abnormal and Social Psychology* 69 (1964): 411–17.

Mischel, W., and Staub, E. "The Effects of Expectancy on Working and Waiting for Larger Rewards." *Journal of Personality and Social Psychology* 2 (1965): 625–33.

O'Leary, K., and Becker, W. "Behavior Modification of an Adjustment Class: A Token Reinforcement Program." *Exceptional Children* 33 (1967): 637–42.

Robins, F., and Robins, J. *Educational Rhythmics for Mentally and Physically Handicapped Children*. New York: Association Press, 1968.

Thomas, D.; Becker, W.; and Armstrong, M. "Production and Elimination of Disruptive Classroom Behavior by Systematically Varying Teacher's Behavior." *Journal of Applied Behavioral Analysis* 1 (1968): 35–45.

ADDITIONAL RESOURCES

Gnagey, W. *The Psychology of Discipline in the Classroom*. New York: Macmillan, 1968.

Hewett, F. *The Emotionally Disturbed Child in the Classroom*. Boston: Allyn & Bacon, 1968.

Johnson, D., and Myklebust, H. *Learning Disabilities: Educational Principles and Practices*. New York: Grune & Stratton, 1967.

Leacock, E. B. *Teaching and Learning in the City Schools*. New York: Basic Books, 1969.

Smilansky, S. *The Effects of Sociodramatic Play on Disadvantaged Preschool Children*. New York: Wiley, 1968.

Valett, R. *Effective Teaching: A Guide to Diagnostic-Teaching Task Analysis*. Belmont, California: Fearon, 1970.

13

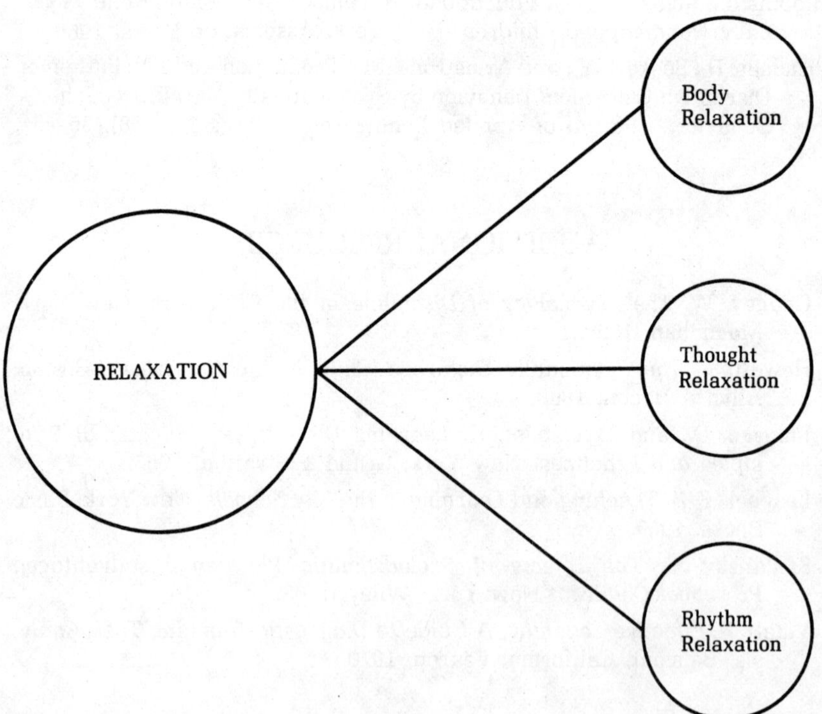
RELAXATION
Body Relaxation
Thought Relaxation
Rhythm Relaxation

Curriculum Area: Relaxation

INTRODUCTION TO RELAXATION

Given such demands made on each of us every day by our accelerating society, the unceasingly high decibel level, the threat of an increasingly polluted environment, and the multitude of complex, emotionally tense relationships, it is no wonder that we search desperately for ways to relax. It appears that as our technology becomes more efficient and pressurized, the need for a change of pace also becomes more critical. The frequency of crimes against persons, the increasing divorce rate, the extent of drug and alcohol addiction, and the wanton, reckless destruction of public property tear at our nerves and threaten our piece of mind, for the impact of these social conditions on the person can be devastating. Since there is no pure society to which we can retreat in order to escape these tensions, we are becoming increasingly aware that people must learn techniques for bringing about more relaxed internal conditions.

As London (1972) points out in a review of the status of behavior modification, developments are shifting from a concern about theory and principles to an application of techniques which can work *for* man. London notes the proliferation as well as the prospects of a number of new techniques for reducing tension and anxiety, including on-line computers to implement anxiety desensitization procedures (Lang, 1969); self-directed alteration of blood pressure, heartbeats, or brain states through biofeedback systems (see Barber, DiCara, Kamiya, Miller, Shapiro, and Stoyva, 1971); and machines to induce hypnosis and deep relaxation states (Wolpin, 1969).

Lazarus (1971a), in his book *Behavior Therapy and Beyond*, presents a wide range of strategies for reducing human tensions—from imagery exercises to differential relaxation to covert sensitization for aversive imaging. Lazarus is probably the first of the "behavior integrationists"; he is not self-conscious about employing the techniques he needs for a specific purpose—regardless of whose theoretical territory might be involved. Thus, Lazarus (1971) states, "Durability of therapeutic outcome often seems to be in direct proportion to the amount of effort expended during the treatment process and the range of procedures employed" (p. 194).

For the purposes of this curriculum, we need not review the entire spectrum of approaches for inducing a state of relaxation; it is sufficient to say that there are a great many. We are impressed, however, by the apparent effectiveness and availability of some rather precise techniques for reducing tension states (Jacobson, 1964; Nawas, Fishman and Pucel, 1970; Wolpe, 1958; Wolpe and Lazarus, 1966).

In constructing the exercises in the curriculum units of this chapter, we have attempted to translate some of the more clinical procedures for inducing relaxation into simple and innocuous activities which can help children to relax in the classroom. We usually have found the suggested tasks to be enjoyable, unthreatening, and able to be presented comfortably by the classroom teacher.

The ability to relax is not just a physical attribute or psychic state which only a few strong, well-adjusted people possess; it is a skill which can be acquired and practiced by most children. To successfully teach pupils to acquire this skill, establish calm and quiet conditions in the classroom prior to any attempted task involvement. In teaching relaxation, strive to create an atmosphere that is soft, free of distraction, and unhurried, even though this may mean a considerable change from the usual pace of classroom or learning center activities, where creative noise and movement abound. Gentle, calming background music often is helpful in producing this desired climate.

Keep in mind that it is important to establish a state of mental as well as physical relaxation. To do this, introduce tasks in a pleasant, easy voice. Since keen concentration and freedom from self-consciousness is needed, you should take time to bring the group to such a state before initiating tasks. Some brief warm-up or readiness activities may be used to set the mood for the exercises. For example, instruct the children to close their eyes, rest their heads on their desks, think about something slow and gentle, concentrate on the soft music, or count from one to ten to themselves as slowly as they can.

Rationale

Flexible behavior control is partially a function of a person's ability to maintain or achieve a state of relative calm, even while he is being stimulated by inner impulses. There is considerable evidence that an optimal range of drive or impulse arousal exists for each individual and that beyond this range effective performance suffers. In allowing for individual differences in handling pressure, it is important to give evidence of a personal belief and capability for reducing tension to a comfortable level. A child equipped with usable techniques for physical and mental relaxation is not likely to spill over with diffuse, poorly regulated behavior outbursts.

TEACHING UNITS AND GOALS

This chapter has been divided into three units: body relaxation, thought relaxation, and movement relaxation. Each unit is designed to help establish a state of mental and physical calm.

Unit 1. Body Relaxation

Goal: To teach children to relax one part of the body at a time, allowing tension to flow out of a limb or part while holding other parts in a readiness stage.

Unit 2. Thought Relaxation

Goal: To develop skills in using self-suggestion and imagination to induce a state of mental relaxation.

Unit 3. Movement Relaxation

Goal: To teach children to release tension through natural, rhythmical body movement.

UNIT 1. BODY RELAXATION

Goal: To teach children to relax one part of the body at a time, allowing tension to flow out of a limb or part while holding other parts in a readiness stage.

Task 1: Arms and Head Relaxation

Establish a quiet atmosphere before giving directions in a soft voice. While the pupils are seated at their desks, ask them to stiffen their necks and tighten their jaws as tightly as possible. Have them hold the tightness for three to five seconds and then slowly let go and soften the neck muscles and the jaws. After the pupils have felt the tenseness drain out of the muscles as they slowly soften them once, have them tighten or harden the muscles only halfway and then slowly soften them again.

Task 2: Arms, Head, and Fingers Relaxation

Ask the pupils to stand and shake their arms, hands, and fingers at their sides. Pretend that the limbs are hanging from a "clothesline" at the shoulders and that you are trying to shake them out straight. Do this until a tinge of fatigue sets in and the relaxation will be more complete.

Task 3: Arms and Trunk Relaxation

While they are seated at their desks, have the pupils make a hard, straight arm and a tight fist, hold both for three to five seconds, and then slowly let go and soften or relax the muscles. Repeat the same procedure with the arms bent at the elbow. Instruct the children to push the shoulders as far back as they can and tighten them; also have them tighten the back and chest muscles, hold them for three to five seconds, and then slowly let go and soften. It may help if they allow one muscle at a time to soften until all muscles are completely relaxed. Holding one's breath will add to the feeling of tenseness and the subsequent feeling of softened relaxation.

Task 4: Body Limpness (The Rag Doll)

While they are seated at their desks, ask the pupils to inhale deeply until their chests are fully expanded and then exhale and flop their trunk forward at the waist. The chin touches the chest, and the arms dangle between the knees. If the fully expanded chest is held for three to five seconds, the limpness will be greater after exhaling. You might suggest to the children that they make their chests as big as possible. If you are working in reverse order, you might suggest they make as small a waist as possible and then as large a waist as possible.

Task 5: Arm Lifting

Ask the children to stand quietly beside their seats, with their eyes closed. Request that they inhale and exhale deeply, while allowing their arms to go limp at their sides. Then instruct the group to make a tight fist with both hands and rise gently on the toes. Then tell them to unsqueeze the fists and bring the heels to the floor. Have the group to repeat the fist squeezing and raising off toes exercise a few times, for about a minute each time. Then request that the students spread their fingers apart, with elbows straight, and slowly raise both arms from their sides to shoulder height. The arm lift should be done very slowly (at a rate of twenty to thirty seconds). Instruct the children to hold the arms out in the lift position for about ten seconds and then lower the arms slowly back to the sides. Tell the students to repeat the lift several times.

UNIT 2. THOUGHT RELAXATION

Goal: To develop skills in using self-suggestion and imagination to induce a state of mental relaxation.

Task 1: Pleasant Physical Sensations

The teacher suggests to the pupils that the pleasant physical sensations they are going to imagine should take place in an atmosphere that is calm, quiet, and secure. The pupils may demonstrate physically how they feel in each situation. Each pose may be held for fifteen to thirty seconds before proceeding to the next pose. While the children close their eyes, ask them to think of how they might feel in pleasant physical situations (e.g., going to sleep at night, listening to soft music, swimming in a cool lake, with someone gently rubbing his back, lying in the warm sun, sitting before a warm open fire, lying in a bathtub of hot water, taking off a pair of tight shoes, dangling the feet in a cool stream, walking barefoot in the cool green grass).

Task 2: Pleasant Fantasies

To fantasize is to make believe, and this is a situation which most children engage in every day. The following suggested fantasies are fun for the children to imagine as well as being likely to produce calm and relaxation. While the pupils are seated at their desks, ask them to make believe that they are experiencing the following: bouncing on a cloud, having the soft wind blowing in their faces, being an astronaut on a space walk, being the ripples in a stream, floating in the water, being a soaring bird, lying on a magic carpet, being a leaf falling gently to the ground. To gain the full effect of the suggestions, suggest some gentle in-seat movements such as swaying from side to side when blown by the wind or slowly reaching out on a space walk.

Task 3: Pleasant Memories

Ask the children to remember a very happy or enjoyable experience they have had, for recalling pleasant events promotes a feeling of well-being, comfort, and security. Allow the class a minute to think of something while you play relaxing music. Then ask for a volunteer to relate a pleasant experience, using his own words. Encourage the class to listen to the speaker without interrupting and to imagine that they are also having the experience. When the speaker finishes, introduce another period of quiet thought and then repeat the story telling with a second volunteer.

This activity should be done for short periods (e.g., five minutes), but it can be repeated on several occasions in order to give all the children an opportunity to share a pleasant memory. It can also become a catalyst for art and language activities and the selection of reading material and of social studies topics. For example, it might encourage the children in drawing, writing, or reading stories or in obtaining information about aspects of their pleasant memory (e.g., a trip to a farm, catching a fish, going to a party).

Task 4: Imaginary Tension-Relaxation Scenes

The room should be quiet and calm, with only the teacher speaking in order to promote the best possible concentration on the task requirements. The imagined position or scene can be demonstrated physically by the students, using the arms, head, and upper part of the body sprawled on the top of the desk. While they are seated at their desks, ask the students to imagine themselves lying on their desks as the following objects: a frozen towel, then a hanging wet towel; an angry dog, then a sleeping dog; a frozen ice cream bar, then a melted ice cream bar; a tightly tied book, then an open book; frozen water, then spilled warm water; a balloon about to burst, then a burst balloon; dried gravy on a large plate, then hot gravy on a large plate. Request that the children make their bodies feel like the scene they are imagining. Each pair of scenes should include a "tension-image" followed by a "relaxation-image."

Task 5: Active Relaxation Coping

Instruct children to imagine some scene or image that "worries them a little." Explain that as soon as they imagine something worrisome, they will begin to relax themselves by following the procedures used in Unit 1, Body Relaxation. Ask the students to lift their finger or hand when they have imagined a "worry scene", and then guide them in bringing about bodily relaxation. Encourage the students to use these relaxation techniques in other situations outside the classroom when they are experiencing real tension or anxiety.

UNIT 3. MOVEMENT RELAXATION

Goal: To help the child release tension through natural, rhythmical body movement.

Task 1: Directed Movement Regulation

Devise low-keyed, slow-moving exercises to the beat of music. Exercises may include hopping from one foot to another; touching hands to the head, chest, or hips; or one-half turns and full turns. The period should be programmed so the tempo gets slower and slower. You may also want to use slow waltzes which permit the pupils to use or create their own steps. The purpose is to establish a body rhythm that is slow but coordinated to music and to cultivate a feeling of physical freedom.

Task 2: Free Movement Regulation

Introduce a moderate beat on the piano or a musical instrument or record and ask the pupils to move freely in response to various musical sounds. Promote responses to a range of musical stimuli, such as long and short notes, high and low notes, soft and loud music, cool and warm music, sleepy and happy music. The purpose is to develop a comfort with open and graceful movement to music and a feeling of physical freedom. It may be helpful to ask certain pupils to demonstrate their movements to the class as a way of increasing ease and peer acceptance.

Task 3: Movement Interpretations

Establish a slow beat or tempo so that children may pretend and interpret the following images through natural, self-initiated movement:

You are a cork floating on a lake.

You are a stately tree swaying in the gentle wind.

You are a soft cloud floating across the sky.

You are the ripple circles in a lake getting larger and gentler

You are the snow gently falling to the ground.

You are the soft rain running down the window pane.

Encourage slow, graceful, free-flowing movement as you indicate what the class is to interpret.

ADDITIONAL SUGGESTIONS

This chapter provides some basic goals and activities for teaching relaxation. However, you should consult with the physical education instructor in the school for more extensive information about physical relaxation techniques.

The activities suggested in this chapter are intended to help the child slow down and feel less threatened by his environment. By employing the tasks presented in this chapter, you can promote an atmosphere that is quiet, non-threatening, and pleasant. But, more importantly, the child can learn techniques for reducing anxiety within himself as he practices these exercises. In particular, the body relaxation tasks lend themselves most readily for personal use during times of tension or strain. The technique of tensing and relaxing muscle groups enables the child to become aware of tense situations and use these sensations as cues for initiating relaxation procedures.

Recent evidence indicates that body relaxation techniques may be effectively combined with imagined or real situations that *produce* anxiety or tension (Cautela, 1966; Lang, 1969).

In fact, there is reason to believe that relaxation as an active coping technique cannot be developed fully unless skills are practiced in the presence of tension-producing thoughts or events (Goldfried, 1971). Task 5 of Unit 2 creates the conditions for optimizing the use of relaxation as a means of combatting tensions in reality. The teacher should also be alert to spontaneous situations in which children can be encouraged to actively employ relaxation techniques to reduce real tensions (e.g., when the child is on the verge of hitting or yelling back; before tests or other anxiety-producing events).

SUMMARY

Relaxation, like most other human functions, is not an inherent quality; rather, it is a skill that has to be learned, practiced, and mastered. The purpose of this chapter has been to teach students the skills which are necessary for reaching a state of relative calm—even when they are being stimulated by inner impulses. Techniques have been suggested by which students may achieve a more relaxed condition, through both physical and mental means, thus increasing their potential for directing energies effectively.

For tasks in this chapter to have relevance and purpose to the pupil, however, the teacher must continually attempt to relate them to real-life situations and the environment in which a pupil lives. The teacher should also clearly state the importance of these tasks for learning, mastery, and self-growth.

Table 13 summarizes the curriculum units and tasks comprising the Relaxation area.

Table 13: *A Summary of the Curriculum Units and Tasks in the Curriculum Area: Relaxation*

Units	*Tasks*
Body Relaxation	1. Arms and Head Relaxation 2. Arms, Head, and Fingers Relaxation 3. Arms and Trunk Relaxation 4. Body Limpness 5. Arm Lifting
Thought Relaxation	1. Pleasant Physical Sensations 2. Pleasant Fantasies 3. Pleasant Memories 4. Imaginary Tension-Relaxation Scenes 5. Active Relaxation Coping
Movement Relaxation	1. Directed Movement Regulation 2. Free Movement Regulation 3. Movement Interpretations

REFERENCES

Barber, T.; DiCara, L.; Kamiya, J.; Miller, N.; Shapiro, D.; and Stoyva, J., editors. *Biofeedback and Self-Control, 1970*. Chicago: Aldine-Atherton, 1971.

Cautela, J. R. "A Behavior Therapy Approach to Pervasive Anxiety." *Behavior Research and Therapy* 4 (1966): 99–109.

Goldfried, M. R. "Systematic Desensitization as Training in Self-Control." *Journal of Consulting and Clinical Psychology* 37 (1971): 228–34.

Jacobson, E. *Anxiety and Tension Control.* Philadelphia: J. B. Lippincott, 1964.

Lang, P. J. "The Mechanics of Desensitization and the Laboratory Study of Human Fears." In *Behavior Therapy: Assessment and Status,* edited by C. M. Franks, pp. 160–91. New York: McGraw-Hill, 1970.

Lazarus, A. A. *Behavior Therapy and Beyond.* New York: McGraw-Hill, 1971.

———. "Notes on Behavior Therapy, the Problem of Relapse, and Some Tentative Solutions." *Psychotherapy: Theory, Research, and Practice* 8 (1971): 192–94.

London, P. "The End of Ideology in Behavior Modification." *American Psychologist* 27 (1972): 913–20.

Nawas, M.; Fishman, S.; and Pucel, J. "A Standardized Desensitization Program Applicable to Group and Individual Treatments." *Behavior, Research, and Therapy* 8 (1970): 29–56.

Wolpe, J. *Psychotherapy by Reciprocal Inhibition.* Palo Alto, California: Stanford University Press, 1958.

Wolpe, J., and Lazarus, A. *Behavior Therapy Techniques.* London: Pergamon, 1966.

Wolpin, M. "Guided Imagining to Reduce Avoidance Behavior." *Psychotherapy: Theory, Research, and Practice* 6 (1969): 122–24.

ADDITIONAL RESOURCES

Gunther, B. *Sense Relaxation: Below Your Mind.* New York: Collier, 1968.

Jacobson, E. *You Must Relax.* New York: McGraw-Hill, 1957.

Rathbone, J. L. *Teach Yourself to Relax.* Englewood Cliffs, New Jersey: Prentice-Hall, 1957.

Steinhaus, A. *Teaching Neuromuscular Relaxation.* Chicago: George Williams College, 1964.

Schwartz, H. S. *The Art of Relaxation.* New York: Thomas Y. Crowell, 1954.

PART THREE

Further Consideration

14

Issues Pertaining to the Curriculum

TRANSFER OF SKILLS TO REAL LIFE

Transfer of learning has been a longstanding concern of educators and psychologists (Dewey, 1913; James, 1890; Thorndike, 1903). This concern has been evidenced in the many theories which have been advanced on how and when transfer takes place, the mechanisms which promote transfer from one context to another, and the teaching strategies for enhancing transfer.

The earliest approach to transfer of learning was the Faculty Psychology theory which emphasized the formal disciplining of mental faculties through regular practice in applying memory, reason, and judgment to a variety of meaningful tasks in the classroom (see Hilgard and Bower, 1966). The assumption was that, through practice, a mental process or skill could be developed, which could then be applied in other situations which required the use of that skill or function. For example, the theory states that a memory trained through learning vocabulary words or poetry would be better able to handle law cases or business details.

A different approach can be found in the theory of Identical Elements or Components which states that "a change in one function alters any other only insofar as the two functions have as factors identical elements." Thus, memory training could only be expected to transfer if the new situation had a clear equal relationship with the original learning situation. For example, if memory practice called for grouping numbers and the transfer situation involved grouping numbers or figures, then transfer might be expected. If, however, the new memory task involved recall of meaningful sentences, which is a different element of memory, then transfer would not be likely.

The theory of Generalization appears to have gained the most acceptance (Deese and Hulse, 1967; Ellis, 1965). This theory posits that original learning outcomes are more likely to have application or transfer value when principles or generalizations are made clear. The relationship of classroom learning to current or subsequent reality experience is stressed, so that similarities are developed between the original learning situation and possible transfer situations. For example, students may be taught that problem solving consists of gathering data, formulating and testing a hypothesis, and drawing a conclusion. Transfer of learning will not take place, however, unless the students are helped to see how this process relates to such problems as buying a car, choosing a career, or other relevant issues.

The curriculum model presented in this volume actually has incorporated each of these three transfer of training theories into its design. The Formal Discipline theory is applied by emphasizing repeated practice on a particular task before moving on to new units or tasks. The Identical Components theory is recognized by the construction of tasks with sufficient breadth to maximize the possibility that new situations will present some element which is consistent with prior elements. Thus, both of these applications are incorporated into the structure of tasks within curriculum units.

However, the theory of Generalization approach is not primarily built into the suggested tasks. Instead, the importance of generalization is explicitly stated in each curriculum area summary. Thus, each summary contains the statement: "For tasks in this chapter to have relevance and purpose to the pupil, however, the teacher must continually attempt to relate them to real-life situations and the environment in which the pupil lives. The teacher should also clearly state the importance of these tasks for learning, mastery, and self-growth."

By inserting this reminder, we hope you will include ideas, examples, and events which the pupils introduce from other life settings. For example, ask children what things they have done at home or in their neighborhood that remind them of activities they have done in the classroom (e.g., waiting for light before crossing street might remind them of inhibition and delay exercises; deciding not to hit his brother because his father would have punished him involves anticipating consequences). Or you may request that the pupils try classroom activities outside of the classroom and then follow up on your request by asking for reports on any try outs (e.g., body relaxation as done in class applies to being in crowds; stating "I feel . . ." type messages to friends or parents reflects appreciating feelings). Reaffirm the value of the skill involved by offering some ideas and examples of how that skill can be useful. As an example, one can readily see the value of mastering frustration pertinent to a difficult and demanding task.

CURRICULUM DEVELOPMENT AND RESEARCH

Development of the Self-Control Curriculum

The basic idea and structure for a self-control curriculum was generated in the spring of 1968, when the authors were associated with the Psychoeducational Institute of Hillcrest Children's Mental Health Center in Washington, D.C. Hillcrest Children's Center is a comprehensive diagnostic, psychoeducational, treatment facility for children with serious emotional problems. Previous work in the Hillcrest Therapeutic School with children with perceptual-movement dysfunctions had alerted us to the need for techniques for fostering impulse control. Following a period of careful observation of students in the Hillcrest School, it became apparent to us, however, that impulsivity was a far more general problem than was perceptual-movement dysfunction. We then began to search the literature for clues regarding the types of skills that promoted impulse control; simultaneously, we made detailed observations of disruptive behavior incidents in the classroom.

We were particularly impressed by the works of Cameron (1963), Kvaraceus (1966), Bandler (1967), and Pavenstedt (1967), all of which dealt with behavioral characteristics of inner-city, lower-class children. The studies conducted by these researchers converged in suggesting common behavioral weaknesses in aggressive and disruptive children. The weaknesses most often identified were limitations in postponement of gratification, tolerating frustration, perseverance, forethought, verbal or symbolic regulation, and delaying actions. These findings were noted, along with the data gathered from direct observations in the Hillcrest School (see Fagen and McDonald, 1969). By this time, we were beginning to see the need for an approach that could build skills which would mediate the control of impulses. From this position, we developed a skeleton curriculum incorporating skill areas which appeared naturalistically or empirically related to self-control.

Between September 1968 and June 1969, parts of the original curriculum were tried with children attending the Hillcrest School and the neighboring Harrison Public Elementary School in Washington, D.C. Children were selected for this pilot program on the basis of teacher ratings of impulsivity and brief observations of disruptive behavior in the classroom. At Hillcrest, the skeleton curriculum was presented to small groups of two or three children at fifth- and sixth-grade levels. At Harrison, the skeleton curriculum was applied to an entire second grade class of thirty-five youngsters and was used with two small groups at first- and second-grade levels.

Informal results at the end of the school year were very encouraging. Both principals and the classroom teachers involved felt that improvement had taken place in the children exposed to the curriculum tasks, although this was more true in some cases than in others. Many tasks were found to be unsuitable or unappealing, and tasks were added or revised based on staff comments and direct experience.

During the 1969–1970 school year the pilot program was modified to place the emphasis on teaching in elementary public school settings and to include more classes. Thus, the revised curriculum was taught to one second and one fourth grade in addition to a small group of disruptive second graders at the Harrison School. The program also was introduced to a class of nine children with learning disabilities and to an entire third grade at the Meyer Elementary School of the District of Columbia.

Instruction for these pilot programs was initiated by one of the authors, with the regular teacher observing or co-teaching.[1] Classroom teachers were encouraged to repeat activities demonstrated by the project staff as well as to initiate additional learning activities as suggested within a given curriculum unit.

Participating classroom teachers were later asked to evaluate specific tasks attempted with their children in relation to two

---

[1] Donald Stevens carried out the classroom instruction, with consultation and observation provided by Stanley Fagen and Nicholas Long.

dimensions: student response and teacher application. Using a five-point scale from excellent to poor, the teachers rated student response to a given task in terms of interest, acceptance, and challenge. Teacher application was rated in terms of ease, range, and utility. Spontaneous comments were also solicited to capture the teacher's general reactions and impressions.

The tabulation of teacher ratings of task value indicated that of the 177 tasks included in the 1969–1970 curriculum, 151 had been tried and evaluated by at least one teacher. Based on combined ratings for the various categories, and mean scores where more than one teacher rated a task, the following results were obtained: Excellent — 68 tasks; Very Good — 55 tasks; Good — 25 tasks; Fair — 3 tasks; Poor — 0 tasks. Considering the probable "halo effect" which existed around the program and associated tasks, we decided to eliminate tasks rated "Fair." Thus, judging from teacher evaluations, 148 of the 177 tasks in the first curriculum revision were presumed to be of at least moderate value. Twenty-six of the tasks were not rated, but it was not possible to ascertain the exact reasons for their absence. When asked if they were reluctant to rate a program negatively (i.e., "Poor"), teachers indicated that this was not the case, but that, rather, they did not regard any task as being poor. Since the twenty-six tasks not formally rated by teachers had previously been tried and accepted by the authors, it was decided to retain them in the curriculum.

Following the second pilot year, 1969–1970, we felt that the self-control curriculum had considerable potential for a positive impact on elementary school children in the classroom. Encouraged by the enthusiastic support of the staff and administration at Harrison and Meyer Schools, we prepared and submitted a proposal to the Eugene and Agnes Meyer Foundation of Washington, D.C. to conduct an initial research evaluation on the effectiveness of the self-control curriculum. This proposal was subsequently approved by the Meyer Foundation, and we were enabled to undertake the first controlled research investigation of the self-control curriculum.

Initial Research

With the support of the Meyer Foundation and under the direction of Dr. Burwell Vaden, an initial research investigation on the impact of the self-control curriculum was conducted during the period from 1970–1972. The purpose of this initial study was to determine the effectiveness of the self-control curriculum in relation to three aspects of pupil behavior: general school adjustment, academic achievement, and observable classroom behavior. This research investigation is described fully in Vaden's doctoral dissertation for the University of Virginia, *An Evaluation of a Psychoeducational Approach to the Concept of Self-Control* (1972).

During the period from November 1970 to September 1971, the project staff devoted its efforts to further revising and refining of the self-control curriculum preparing curriculum and instructional materials developing the research design, including arranging for appropriate experimental and control classes in the District of Columbia School System, obtaining data analysis services, planning statistical evaluation procedures, and selecting or developing necessary research instruments. The actual study was conducted from October 1971 to June 1972.

The study sample consisted of 159 second-grade children attending three Washington, D.C. elementary schools within the Model Schools Division.[2] One experimental and one control class were located in each of the three schools. Table 14 presents the experimental design of the self-control curriculum study. Members of the study group were primarily black children living in the lower socioeconomic area of the northwest section of the city.

Teachers of the experimental classes received instruction in the use of the self-control curriculum through weekly seminars conducted during the period from October 25, 1971 to May 8, 1972. In addition, teachers were provided with written instructional materials containing suggested tasks for developing specific self-control skills in the classroom. To regulate the effect of attention and expectation on study outcomes, teachers of the control classes were visited periodically throughout the treatment period and were assembled as a group approximately once every two months. Control teachers were not given curriculum instruction but were encouraged to discuss classroom problems in an atmosphere of support and understanding.

Data required for the purposes of this study were obtained by administering to all subjects the Psychoeducational Screening System for Identifying Resourceful, Marginal, and Vulnerable Pupils in Primary Grades; reading and math subtests of the California Achievement Test; and Task Attention Test.

---

[2]The Model Schools Division is an educational sub-system within the District of Columbia Public School System. Its purpose is to provide a concentration of new methods, techniques, and organization patterns and to facilitate efforts "to improve the self-image of the child so as to enable him to serve now and later as a change-agent in relation to his physical and political environment" (D.C. Public Schools, Model Schools Division), p. 1.

Table 14: *Experimental Design of the Self-Control Curriculum Study*

Population	*Pre-Test Data Oct. 1971*	*Treatment*	*Post-Test Data May 1972*
Three Experimental Second Grade Classes School A School B School C	Time 1	Self-Control Curriculum	Time 2
Three Control Second Grade Classes School A School B School C	Time 1	Intermittent Attention	Time 2

The Psychoeducational Screening System (Long, Fagen, and Stevens, 1971) was the primary criterion measure used in this study. This system is composed of the following four instruments: Pupil Assessment of Self in School (PASS); School Self-Control Behavior Inventory (SCBI); Patterns of Achievement (PA); and Significant Life events (SLE). Scores derived from these instruments were combined to arrive at one score which indicated the child's ability to cope with school tasks and to achieve success. Data was analyzed by applying Chi Square statistics.

In the past, the California Achievement Test (CAT) has been administered twice each year to all children attending the Washington, D.C. schools—in October and again the following April. The reading and math subtests of the 1970 edition of the CAT Level 1, Form A were administered in October 1971. Level 1, Form B was administered in April 1972. Test data were analyzed by means of analysis of covariance.

The Task Attention Test was employed as a post-test measure of distractability and persistence on a concentration task. The rationale for this instrument follows the research on moral conduct reported by Hartshorne and May (1930) and Grim, Kohlberg, and White (1964). Hartshorne and May defined self-control as persistence and nondistractability, while Grim, Kohlberg, and White emphasized the capacity to maintain focused, stable attention. The TAT consists of four mimeographed sheets containing a random order of digits or letters. The task is to cross out the pre-designated digit (or letter), while circling all other digits and letters, within a five-minute period. The number of correct responses given within the time limit constitutes the raw score; these scores were analyzed statistically by testing the significance of the difference between mean scores for experimental and control groups.

The analysis of data revealed that the *self-control program was significantly related to general school adjustment* (based on teacher ratings of learning progress, self-control skills, and self-concept as a learner) at the .01 level of confidence. However, the relationship between the self-control program and academic achievement was not found to be significant at the .05 level of confidence. There was a trend toward improvement in observable classroom behavior in the experimental groups, as measured by the Task Attention Test, although differences between experimental and control groups did not reach the .05 significance level.

The results of this initial study suggested some value to implementing the self-control curriculum in elementary schools. Given the limitations of a relatively brief period of teacher training and curriculum implementation for students, the tenuous reliability of the Task Attention Test Measure, the transience of the student population under study, teacher differences regarding administration of achievement tests, and the small sample size, the overall results appear to be quite promising.

Future Research Needs

Further research on the self-control curriculum is very much needed. While the initial study indicates that the curriculum facilitates school adjustment and tends to enhance task attention and concentration, the results are not nearly conclusive. Programmatic research is currently being planned to provide answers to several important questions.

1. Do the various skills comprising the concept of self-control contribute equally or differentially to changes in pupil behavior and adjustment? Measures of behavior for each curriculum skill area will have to be developed in order to determine skill increments.

2. To what extent are changes in pupil behavior and adjustment temporary or enduring? Longitudinal studies of children who have received instruction in self-control must be conducted.
3. Does instruction in the self-control curriculum promote gains in learner resourcefulness and coping skills which prevent subsequent maladjustment or behavior disruption? Initial data suggest that children receiving instruction in self-control skills become more resourceful, while those who have not participated in the program tend to increase in vulnerability.
4. What are the most effective patterns or modes of instruction for the self-control curriculum? Are in-service seminars indispensable or can the curriculum be successfully taught via videotape, programmed instruction, or textbook models? Research will have to be designed to study the comparative influence of one mode of instruction to another.
5. Can diagnostic-prescriptive and individualized programming strategies be incorporated into the self-control curriculum model? Diagnostic tools for assessing strengths and weaknesses have to be developed in such a way as to tie assessment closely to the objectives of instruction.
6. How do differences in teacher style and personality affect learner outcomes in the various curriculum areas? The teacher variable should be regulated experimentally to study different styles of teaching in relation to differential implementation of the curriculum.

PLANNING FOR INDIVIDUALIZED INSTRUCTION

In Chapter 5, we indicated that the self-control curriculum may be implemented flexibly with regard to time set aside for it and the pattern of grouping for instruction. We have stated the belief that the skills mediating self-control are vital for all youngsters and that, therefore, a teacher might very well elect to involve the entire class in the curriculum. At other times, however, the teacher may prefer to place the children in subgroups so that instruction can be more specifically tailored to identified weaknesses or needs.

To move toward a more *individualized or prescriptive* option for implementing the self-control curriculum, it is necessary to define the specific variables or behaviors that make up the larger skill areas. For example, to arrange a small group of learners who need instruction in sequencing and ordering, you would need to know what behaviors exemplify lack of mastery in the sequencing and ordering curriculum area.

One effective and economical means of assessing learner needs is through careful and directed observation of a child's in-class behavior. To aid the teacher in making these observations, we have developed an assessment instrument called the School Self-Control Behavior Inventory (SCBI) (Long, Fagen, and Stevens, 1971). In developing this inventory, we made a deliberate effort to establish clear school behavioral referents for self-control parameters. With the exception of relaxation, each of the eight self-control skill-clusters is manifested directly in the SCBI. By assessing individual limitations in self-control skills, you have a basis for planning experiences to strengthen capacity for self-control.

The School Self-Control Behavior Inventory contains eight items which we regard as components of self-control, with each item to be rated by the classroom teacher. To facilitate clarity and meaningfulness in rating, each item is identified with a list of behavioral statements specific to that aspect of self-control. Item ratings should be made *after* careful consideration of the related set of behavioral criteria for that item. This procedure is essential, since the rating scales have been constructed to reflect degree of agreement with stated behavioral criteria.

For example, in rating a child on Item 1, "Pays Attention to Teacher Direction or Instructions," it is first necessary to review the statements for evaluating concentration. The rater must then decide the extent to which the child in question displays concentration behavior.

Each rating scale represents a continuum of four points (ranging from "rarely does" to "almost always does") describing the extent to which a child's behavior is characteristic of a particular ability. It is important to check the *one* box which best describes the youngster in relation to that ability. Thus, if you feel the child sometimes does exhibit behavior indicative of concentration, you place a check under column B in Table 15.

If, on the other hand, your observations suggest that concentration is "almost always" evident, you should check under Column D.

Table 15: *Rating Scale*

A	*B*	*C*	*D*
Rarely Does (less than 20% of time)	Sometimes Does (less than 50% of time)	Usually Does (more than 50% of time)	Almost Always Does (more than 80% of time)

Self-Control Components

1. *Pays Attention to Teacher's Directions or Instructions (Selection).*

   Behavioral Examples:

   — Pays attention to teacher directions or instructions (e.g., listens and observes with care).

   — Can work intently on tasks (e.g., maintains span of attention and interest; makes steady progress toward completing tasks).

2. *Remembers Teacher's Directions or Instructions (Storage).*

   Behavioral Examples:

   — Can accurately recall or repeat verbal instructions given by teacher (or peers).

   — Can accurately perform behavior(s) after directions have been given (e.g., seems to know what is to be done; does not ask for instructions to be repeated).

3. *Organizes Self to Perform Assignments (Sequencing and Ordering).*

   Behavioral Examples:

   — Has the ability to organize himself for a task (e.g., material on desk arranged, pencil sharpened, a lack of clutter).

   — Can perform an action that requires several steps to be taken in order (e.g., folding paper to produce shapes).

- Does not become easily flustered, confused, or overwhelmed when he has to perform a series of actions to complete a task.
- Is able to find several ways of achieving a goal.

4. *Anticipates the Consequences of Own Behavior (Anticipating Consequences).*

   Behavioral Example:

   - Can verbalize what might happen if certain behavior occurs (e.g., can anticipate teacher's reaction if assignment is not completed; can anticipate peers' reaction to unacceptable social behavior; can explain to other children what might happen if certain actions are taken).

5. *Manages External Frustrations while Working on an Assignment (Managing Frustration).*

   Behavioral Examples:

   - Can accept obstacles placed in way (e.g., persists on task even when faced with outside interference; does not strike back or withdraw quickly when faced with difficulty).
   - Can accept disappointment (e.g., seems to understand and maintain control when not able to get own way; does not become overly distressed when let down by others).
   - Can continue working effectively even after interruption or interference (i.e., returns to drawing a picture after others have teased about it).

6. *Can Delay Actions even when Excited (Inhibition and Delay).*

   Behavioral Examples:

   - Able to inhibit actions, even when excited or eager to respond.
   - Can perform a task in part and set it aside for another time (e.g., able to complete projects requiring gradual progress rather than instant attainment).

— Can express movement, feeling, and action in moderation without extreme responses (e.g., laughing, not hysterics; noisiness, not chaos, etc.).

— Does not exhibit temper tantrums or aggressive outbursts.

7. *Expresses Feelings through Acceptable Words and Behavior (Appreciating Feelings).*

Behavioral Examples:

— Can use words to describe feelings (e.g., he looks sad, happy, angry, etc.).

— Can express own feelings in words (e.g., expresses feelings of loneliness, anger, happiness, etc.).

— Seeks help or substitute activities when strongly upset rather than displaying gross outbursts or marked withdrawal (e.g., calls for teacher; asks to change task or situation rather than blowing up).

— Is not hypersensitive.

8. *Thinks Positively about Self (Appreciating Feelings).*

Behavioral Examples:

— Shows pleasure at own efforts or accomplishments.

— Shows willingness to display work or interests to others.

— Is willing to volunteer to help others.

— Expresses liking and enjoyment of own behavior.

The teacher records the rating made on each self-control component in the Self-Control Behavior Inventory summary form (see page 257). This SCBI form can then serve as a simple reference for recalling the strengths or weaknesses of any pupil. Besides using the summary form to decide which children need help in certain areas, you can also use the form as a reminder to choose students with strength in a given area for assistants or leaders. This global, inspection-type approach to using the SCBI seems to have been very helpful to most teachers interested in the self-control curriculum.

You may want to use the SCBI as a basis for evaluating pupil progress or for comparing one class to another. For such purposes it is usually necessary to quantify data and arrive at composite scores.

Given these purposes, the rules for more formal scoring of the SCBI are the following:

1. Assign the following scoring values to ratings: Rarely Does = 0 points; Sometimes Does = 1 point; Usually Does = 2 points; Almost Always Does = 3 points.
2. Find the total number of points within columns B, C, and D and apply the above values for each item checked. For example, three items checked under Column B, "Sometimes Does," yields a column score of 3 points (3 items x 1 point). Two items checked under Column C, "Usually Does," yields a column score of 4 points (2 items x 2 points). Two items checked under Column D, "Almost Always Does," yields a column score of 6 points (2 items x 3 points).
3. Compute the total SCBI score by adding the sums of Columns B, C, and D and enter the score at bottom of Inventory.

REFERENCES

Bandler, L. S. "Family Functioning: A Psychosocial Perspective." In *The Drifters: Children of Disorganized Lower-Class Families,* edited by E. Pavenstedt, pp. 225–53. Boston: Little, Brown, 1967.

Cameron, N. *Personality Development and Psychopathology.* Boston: Houghton Mifflin, 1963.

Deese, J., and Hulse, S. *The Psychology of Learning.* New York: McGraw-Hill, 1967.

Dewey, J. *Interest and Effort in Education.* Boston: Houghton Mifflin, 1913.

District of Columbia Public Schools. "A Brochure Describing the Model Schools Program." Washington, D.C.: District of Columbia Public Schools, Model Schools Division, 1971.

Ellis, H. *The Transfer of Learning.* New York: Macmillan, 1965.

Fagen, S., and McDonald, P. "Behavior Disruption in the Classroom: Potential of Observation for Differential Evaluation and Program Planning." *Clinical Proceedings of Children's Hospital* 25 (1969): 215–26.

Name of Pupil ____________________
School ____________________
Grade ____________________

Teacher ____________________
Date ____________________
County ____________________

	A Rarely Does 0	B Sometimes Does 1	C Usually Does 2	D Almost Always Does 3
1. Pays attention to teacher's directions or instructions.				
2. Remembers teacher's directions or instructions.				
3. Organizes self to perform assignments.				
4. Anticipates the consequences of own behavior.				
5. Manages external frustration while working on an assignment.				
6. Can delay actions even when excited.				
7. Expresses feelings through acceptable words and behavior.				
8. Thinks positively about self.				
Column Score	X			

Scoring Values:

Rarely Does - 0 points
Sometimes Does - 1 point
Usually Does - 2 points
Almost Always Does - 3 points

*Total SCBI Score - ____________________

Self-Control Behavior Inventory [SCBI]

Grim, P.; Kohlberg, L.; and White, S. "Some Relationships between Conscience and Attentional Processes." Unpublished paper, 1964. Cited by Kohlberg, L. in "Development of Moral Character and Moral Ideology." In *Review of Child Development Research*, Vol. 1, edited by M. L. Hoffman and L. W. Hoffman, pp. 383–431. New York: Russell Sage Foundation, 1964.

Hartshorne, H., and May, M. *Studies in Self-Control. Volume 3: Studies in the Nature of Character*. New York: Macmillan, 1930.

Hilgard, E., and Bower, G. *Theories of Learning*. New York: Appleton-Century-Crofts, 1966.

James, W. *Principles of Psychology*. New York: Holt, 1890.

Kvaraceus, W. C. *Anxious Youth: Dynamics of Delinquency*. Columbus, Ohio: Charles E. Merrill Publishing Co., 1967.

Long, N.; Fagen, S.; and Stevens, D. *A Psychoeducational Screening System for Identifying Resourceful, Marginal, and Vulnerable Pupils in the Primary Grades*. Washington, D.C.: Psychoeducational Resources, 1971.

Pavenstedt, E., editor. *The Drifters: Children of Disorganized Lower-Class Families*. Boston: Little, Brown, 1967.

Thorndike, E. L. *Educational Psychology*. New York: Lemcke and Beuchner, 1903.

Vaden, T. B., with Long, N.; Stevens, D.; and Fagen, S. *An Evaluation of a Psychoeducational Approach to the Concept of Self-Control*. Washington, D.C.: Psychoeducational Institute, Hillcrest Children's Mental Health Center, 1972. Submitted in partial fulfillment for the Doctoral Degree, University of Virginia, 1972.

15

Closing Remarks

This book has attempted to illustrate how a psychoeducational approach to instruction can allow for the parallel development of a child's cognitive and affective needs. We have proposed that a child cannot be expected to fulfill educational task requirements unless he has acquired an identifiable set of skills which promote self-control (i.e., a flexible and regulated choice of behavior). We have also maintained that optimal self-control requires skill development in management of both emotional and cognitive processes.

As pupils are helped to gain skill in areas contributing to self-control, negative, disruptive behaviors will decrease. By attending to the eight skill clusters set forth in this self-control curriculum, you, as the classroom teacher, have a framework for identifying and strengthening pupil weaknesses which hinder a favorable school adjustment. The self-control curriculum offers an alternative to referral of a disruptive student for psychological treatment or to the perpetuating cycles of nonachievement, failure, and avoidance which are all too common. A teacher who is well versed in the skills and subskills (i.e., curriculum areas and units) of self-control can intervene early in the development of behavior problems by specifying an area of weaknesses and then selecting appropriate learning tasks to facilitate skill enhancement in that area.

Furthermore, we believe the self-control curriculum can be an important element in the development of *a school program of primary prevention in mental health.* In the past, much professional time and skill has been mobilized for mental health "repair" services, including individual, group, and family psychotherapy; crisis intervention; and counseling or interviewing around behavior and adjustment problems. While these services are often essential, there is a growing commitment to the concept and thrust of primary prevention of mental illness in public school settings (see Joint Commission on Mental Health of Children, 1970; Lambert, 1965; Lawrence, 1971; Long, 1972; Sarason, Levine, Goldenberg, Cherlin and Bennett, 1966).

In moving toward the development and organization of any primary prevention program, the following conditions must be kept in mind:

1. It should be available to all children.
2. It should begin as early as possible in the child's development.
3. It should focus on the concept of health rather than illness or pathology.
4. It should be educationally focused.
5. It should emphasize normal adult-peer-self interactions.
6. It should be functional to the teacher.
7. It should be intrinsically pleasant and satisfying to children.
8. It should be inexpensive enough to be applied on a mass basis.
9. It should increase or strengthen skills for effectively coping with the stresses of living.

The self-control curriculum appears to meet all of the above conditions, but we do not claim to have created a comprehensive prevention program. We do believe, however, that this curriculum provides the average elementary school teacher with a direct and realistic means of enabling pupils to strengthen their coping skills. While the goal of providing the elementary teacher with a curriculum that can help to *prevent* behavior and learning problems is ambitious, we are convinced that educators are ready to implement innovative strategies in the classroom. In a sense, we view the self-control curriculum as being similar to the proverb that a journey of a thousand miles begins with one step. Thus, the self-control curriculum is a beginning attempt to convert the stumbling blocks of life into stepping stones for progress.

REFERENCES

Joint Commission on Mental Health of Children. *Crisis in Child Mental Health: Challenge for the 1970s*. New York: Harper & Row, 1970.

Lambert, N., editor. *The Protection and Promotion of Mental Health in Schools*. Bethesda, Maryland: U.S. Department of Health, Education, and Welfare, Mental Health Monograph Number 5, 1965.

Lawrence, M. *The Mental Health Team in the Schools*. New York: Behavioral Publications, 1971.

Long, N. Affadavit to Civil Action Number 1939–71, Peter Mills et al. v. D.C. Board of Education et al., 1972.

Sarason, S.; Levine, M.; Goldenberg, I.; Cherlin, D.; and Bennett, E. *Psychology in Community Settings: Clinical, Educational, Vocational, Social Aspects*. New York: Wiley, 1966.

Index